Discipleship and Unity

Discipleship and Unity

Bonhoeffer's Ecumenical Theology

Cole Jodon

LEXINGTON BOOKS/FORTRESS ACADEMIC
Lanham • Boulder • New York • London

Published by Lexington Books/Fortress Academic
Lexington Books is an imprint of The Rowman & Littlefield Publishing Group, Inc.
4501 Forbes Boulevard, Suite 200, Lanham, Maryland 20706
www.rowman.com

86-90 Paul Street, London EC2A 4NE, United Kingdom

British Library Cataloguing in Publication Information Available

Library of Congress Cataloging-in-Publication Data

Names: Jodon, Cole, 1991– author.
Title: Discipleship and unity : Bonhoeffer's ecumenical theology / Cole Jodon.
Description: Lanham : Lexington Books/Fortress Academic, [2022] | Includes
    bibliographical references and index. | Summary: "In Discipleship and Unity:
    Bonhoeffer's Ecumenical Theology, Cole Jodon presents Bonhoeffer's ecumenical
    theology—a theology grounded in an understanding of the church as the person of
    Christ, and practiced in active obedient discipleship"—Provided by publisher.
Identifiers: LCCN 2022011960 (print) | LCCN 2022011961 (ebook) | ISBN
    9781978711945 (cloth) | ISBN 9781978711952 (epub)
Subjects: LCSH: Bonhoeffer, Dietrich, 1906–1945. | Church—Unity.
Classification: LCC BX4827.B57 J63 2022 (print) | LCC BX4827.B57 (ebook) |
    DDC 230/.04—dc23/eng/20220411
LC record available at https://lccn.loc.gov/2022011960
LC ebook record available at https://lccn.loc.gov/2022011961

For Mum and Pap

Contents

Acknowledgments

Writing this book has been a journey. Many people have contributed to the book that you hold in your hands, and I would like to take this opportunity to thank them. This book is better because of their work.

I am particularly grateful for all of the work Tom Greggs and Michael Mawson put into both shaping this book and shaping me, as my mentors and friends. Additionally, Philip Ziegler and Keith Clements contributed significantly through their insights regarding the ideas you will find in the following pages.

Throughout the entire journey of writing this book, I have been blessed to have friends and colleagues who encourage, challenge, and sharpen my thought, including Joy Allen, Amy Erickson, Brandin Francabandera, Kevin O'Farrell, Marty Phillips, Garrett Reinhardt, Jake Rollison, and Carlos Thompson among others.

I am grateful for the work of Neil Elliott and Gayla Freeman at Lexington Books/Fortress Academic, guiding this book through the various stages of publication. I am likewise grateful for the careful and insightful comments of the anonymous reviewer for Lexington Books, whose work helped me in clarifying and strengthening my writing.

Finally, this work has only been made possible through the constant love and support of my family. My parents, to whom this book is dedicated, have supported me in a great many ways throughout this work and throughout my life. God has blessed me more through you than I will ever know or be able to express. I love you. This love and thankfulness extend also to my wife, Alexandra, who has believed in me since the day we met. I love you.

Abbreviations

WORKS BY BONHOEFFER

DBWE 1   *Sanctorum Communio: A Theological Study
         of the Sociology of the Church.* Dietrich
         Bonhoeffer Works, Volume 1. Edited by
         Clifford J. Green. Trans. Reinhard Krauss and
         Nancy Lukens. Minneapolis: Fortress Press, 1998.
DBWE 2   *Act and Being: Transcendental Philosophy
         and Ontology in Systematic Theology.* Dietrich
         Bonhoeffer Works, Volume 2. Edited by
         Wayne Whitson Floyd, Jr. Trans. H. Martin
         Rumscheidt. Minneapolis: Fortress Press, 1996.
DBWE 3   *Creation and Fall.* Dietrich Bonhoeffer Works,
         Volume 3. Edited by John W. de Gruchy.
         Trans. Douglas Stephen Bax. Minneapolis:
         Fortress Press, 1997.
DBWE 4   *Discipleship.* Dietrich Bonhoeffer Works,
         Volume 4. Trans. Barbara Green and Reinhard
         Krauss. Minneapolis: Fortress Press, 2001.
DBWE 5   *Life Together. The Prayerbook of the Bible.*
         Dietrich Bonhoeffer Works, Volume 5. Edited
         by Geffrey B. Kelly. Trans. Daniel W. Bloesch
         and James H. Burtness. Minneapolis: Fortress
         Press, 1996.

DBWE 6	*Ethics.* Dietrich Bonhoeffer Works, Volume 6. Edited by Clifford J. Green. Trans. Reinhard Krauss, Charles C. West, and Douglas W. Stott. Minneapolis: Fortress Press, 2005.
DBWE 7	*Fiction from Tegel Prison.* Dietrich Bonhoeffer Works, Volume 7. Edited by Clifford J. Green. Trans. Nancy Lukens. Minneapolis: Fortress Press, 1999.
DBWE 8	*Letters and Papers from Prison.* Dietrich Bonhoeffer Works, Volume 8. Edited by John W. de Gruchy. Trans. Isabel Best, Lisa E. Dahill, Reinhard Krauss, and Nancy Lukens. Minneapolis: Fortress Press, 2009.
DBWE 9	*The Young Bonhoeffer: 1918-1927.* Dietrich Bonhoeffer Works, Volume 9. Edited by Paul Duane Mathey, Clifford J. Green, and Marshall D. Johnson. Trans. Mary C. Nebelsick with Douglas W. Stott. Minneapolis: Fortress Press, 2003.
DBWE 10	*Barcelona, Berlin, New York: 1928-1931.* Dietrich Bonhoeffer Works, Volume 10. Edited by Clifford J. Green. Trans. Douglass W. Stott. Minneapolis: Fortress Press, 2008.
DBWE 11	*Ecumenical, Academic, and Pastoral Work: 1931-1932.* Dietrich Bonhoeffer Works, Volume 11. Edited by Victoria J. Barnett, Mark S. Brocker, and Michael B. Lukens. Trans. Anne Schmidt-Lange, with Isabel Best, Nicolas Humphrey, and Marion Pauck. Minneapolis: Fortress Press, 2012.
DBWE 12	*Berlin: 1932-1933.* Dietrich Bonhoeffer Works, Volume 12. Edited by Larry L. Rasmussen. Tran. Isabel Best and David Higgins. Minneapolis: Fortress Press, 2009.
DBWE 13	*London: 1933-1935.* Dietrich Bonhoeffer Works, Volume 13. Edited by Keith Clements. Trans. Isabel Best. Minneapolis: Fortress Press, 2007.
DBWE 14	*Theological Education at Finkenwalde: 1935-1937.* Dietrich Bonhoeffer Works, Volume 14. Edited by H. Gaylon Barker and Mark S. Brocker. Trans. Douglas W. Stott. Minneapolis: Fortress Press, 2013.

DBWE 15	*Theological Education Underground: 1937-1940*. Dietrich Bonhoeffer Works, Volume 15. Edited by Victoria J. Barnett. Trans. Victoria J. Barnett, Claudia D. Bergmann, and Peter Frick, with Scott A. Moore. Minneapolis: Fortress Press, 2012.
DBWE 16	*Conspiracy and Imprisonment: 1940-1945*. Dietrich Bonhoeffer Works, Volume 16. Edited by Mark S. Brocker. Trans. Lisa E. Dahill. Minneapolis: Fortress Press, 2006.

WORLD COUNCIL OF CHURCHES

WCC	World Council of Churches
TS	World Council of Churches Central Committee. "The Church, the Churches, and the World Council of Churches." Geneva: WCC, 1950.
BEM	World Council of Churches, Commission on Faith and Order. "Baptism, Eucharist and Ministry." Faith and Order Paper No. 111. Geneva: WCC Publications, 1982.
CUV	World Council of Churches Central Committee. "Common Understanding and Vision of the WCC." Geneva: WCC, 1997.
TCV	World Council of Churches, Commission on Faith and Order. "The Church: Towards a Common Vision." Faith and Order Paper No. 214. Geneva: WCC Publications, 2013.
Constitution	"Constitution and Rules of the World Council of Churches." As amended by the Central committee of the WCC in Geneva, Switzerland, 2018.
"Come and See"	World Council of Churches, Commission on Faith and Order. "Come and See: A Theological Invitation to the Pilgrimage of Justice and Peace." Faith and Order Paper No. 224. Geneva: WCC Publications, 2019.

Introduction

The unity of the church has long been a subject of debate. On the one hand, Jesus' prayer for the unity of his followers in John 17 and the Nicene Creed's affirmation of "one, holy, catholic church" have taught Christians to believe that the church is one. On the other hand, events such as the Great Schism and the Reformation, paired with the plurality of church denominations found today, have challenged that belief and forced Christians and theologians alike to continue grappling with the topic of church unity.

For the last century, the ecumenical movement has emerged and evolved to become a movement rife with those interested in the unity of the church. Through the years, the ecumenical movement has fostered dialogue and unified service on a scale larger than the world has seen. Over the last couple of decades, however, there has been a rising concern within ecumenical circles about a declining interest in traditional ecumenism.[1]

---

[1] Works that have addressed this situation include Clements, Keith. *Ecumenical Dynamic: Living in More than One Place at Once.* Geneva: WCC Publications, 2013; Raiser, Konrad. *Ecumenism in Transition: A Paradigm Shift in the Ecumenical Movement?* Geneva: WCC Publications, 1991; Kinnamon, Michael. *Can a Renewal Movement be Renewed? Questions for the Future of Ecumenism.* Grand Rapids: Eerdmans, 2014; Avis, Paul. *Reshaping Ecumenical Theology.* London: T&T Clark International, 2010; Pottmeyer, Hermann J. "The Reception Process: The Challenge at the Threshold of a New Phase of the Ecumenical Movement." In *Ecumenism: Present Realities and Future Prospects,* edited by Lawrence S. Cunningham, 149–169. Notre Dame, IN: University of Notre Dame Press, 1998; World Council of Churches Program on Ecumenical Theological Education. "Ecumenical Formation in Theological Education: Ten Key Convictions." *Ministerial Formation* 110 (April 2008): 82–88; Harmon, Steven R. *Ecumenism Means You, Too: Ordinary Christians and the Quest for Christian Unity.* Eugene, OR: Cascade Books, 2010.

Works from a Roman Catholic perspective that touch on this subject include Kasper, Walter. "May They All Be One: But How? A Vision of Christian Unity for the Next Generation." *Ecumenical Trends* 40, (2011): 1–15. O'Gara, Margaret. "Ecumenical Dialogue: The Next Generation." In *CTSA Proceedings,* 63, 94–103, 2008; Kasper, Walter Cardinal *That They May All Be One: The Call to Unity Today.* New York: Burns & Oates, 2004.

Many factors contribute to this decline. Some, but not all, of these factors include the decline of mainline denominations, the rise of Pentecostal
and non-denominational churches, globalization, secularization, and the
southward shift of the center of Christianity globally. Not all of these factors
are bad things. Globalization and the changing ethnic center of Christianity
present marvelous possibilities for following Christ together in the world.
Moreover, there is much to be learned from Pentecostal and non-denominational churches, which have seen a recent rise in numbers. None of this is to
say that the current ecumenical movement has been inactive or impotent in
the world. Ecumenical discourse continues along theological lines in a wide
variety of forums, and ecumenical organizations continue to have real, practical impact through unified service and mission throughout the globe. That
said, the consternation over the future of organized ecumenism is warranted
and has become an ongoing topic of interest for ecumenists.

When Dietrich Bonhoeffer attended his first ecumenical conference in
1931—The Cambridge Conference—he emerged not only with his first
official position in the ecumenical movement as a youth secretary but also
with a nagging question: What does it mean to be church?[2] The topic of the
church had been a central interest of Bonhoeffer's since his doctoral work,
but now he was considering the topic from an ecumenical viewpoint. In 1932,
he explored this question in detail in his ecumenical lecture in Ciernehorske
Kupele, Czechoslovakia, writing, "The work of our World Alliance—con-
sciously or unconsciously—is grounded in a very distinct conception of
church. . . . The church is the presence of Christ on earth; the church is
Christus Praesens."[3] In this lecture, Bonhoeffer articulates an ecumenical
theology built upon an understanding of the ecumenical movement *as church*,
with the purpose of hearing and proclaiming Christ's commands in the world.
This is the core of his ecumenical theology—an ecumenical movement built
upon a self-understanding as church as the present person of Christ, defining
ecumenical action as obedience to Christ, or, what is the same, discipleship. In other words, Bonhoeffer's ecumenical theology is founded upon his
account of ecclesiology and posits discipleship as its operative theological
content. The result is a protean ecumenical theology capable of taking many
different forms while both preserving the diversity of theological heritages
of denominations and emphasizing unified action. The result is an ecumenism of discipleship. Such an ecumenical theology offers valuable insights
for the contemporary ecumenical landscape. This book, therefore, is a close
study of Bonhoeffer's thought in his ecumenical works with the purpose of

---

[2] Clements, Keith. *Dietrich Bonhoeffer's Ecumenical Quest.* World Council of Church Publications,
   2015.
[3] DBWE 11:358–359.

providing a constructive account of his ecumenical theology. Undergirding this book is the conviction that Bonhoeffer's ecumenical theology makes a valuable contribution to ongoing efforts to reflect on the nature and work of the ecumenical movement.[4]

Another conviction driving this book is that Bonhoeffer's ecumenical theology as presented in his ecumenical works has not been given the hearing it deserves. Few theologians are as universally beloved as Bonhoeffer. Even so, Bonhoeffer's consistent involvement in the ecumenical movement and his own articulation of his ecumenical theology have received relatively little attention. Prior to this book, only two books have been written focusing on Bonhoeffer's ecumenical theology: Keith Clements' *Dietrich Bonhoeffer's Ecumenical Quest* and Javier Garcia's *Recovering the Ecumenical Bonhoeffer: Thinking after the Tradition.*[5] Apart from these books, only a smattering of articles attend to Bonhoeffer's ecumenical involvement, with even fewer focusing on the *theological content* of his ecumenical works.[6]

But what *has* been said of Bonhoeffer's ecumenical theology? Clements' book essentially provides an ecumenical biography of Bonhoeffer's life, arguing that ecumenism is a continuous thread in Bonhoeffer's life and works. Clements draws out Bonhoeffer's ecumenical thought along the way of his diachronic, biographical study and finishes his text with a chapter on the influence of Bonhoeffer's thought upon ecumenism since his death,

---

[4] The book's primary objective is to clarify and articulate Bonhoeffer's ecumenical theology. The Conclusion chapter places this theology in conversation with some of the contemporary discourse. Rather than inserting Bonhoeffer's thought within ecumenism writ large (which would be much too wide a conversation partner) or within a specific ecumenical dialogue (which would be narrower than the first constructive account of Bonhoeffer's ecumenical theology deserves), the book's main body text simply presents Bonhoeffer's ecumenical theology on its own terms and allows related ecumenical sources to have their say in the footnotes.

[5] Clements, *Dietrich Bonhoeffer's Ecumenical Quest*; Garcia, Javier A. *Recovering the Ecumenical Bonhoeffer: Thinking after the Tradition.* Lanham: Lexington Books/Fortress Academic, 2019.

[6] There are been several salutary articles written on the *historical context* of Bonhoeffer's ecumenical thought, though these provide only brief engagement with the *theological content* of that thought. See Raiser, Konrad. "Bonhoeffer and the Ecumenical Movement." In *Bonhoeffer for a New Day: Theology in a Time of Transition,* edited by John de Gruchy. Grand Rapids: Eerdmans, 1997; Visser't Hooft, W.A. "Dietrich Bonhoeffer and the Self-Understanding of the Ecumenical Movement." *Ecumenical Review* 28 (1976); Duchrow, Ulrich. *Conflict Over the Ecumenical Movement: Confessing Christ Today in the Universal Church.* Trans. David Lewis. Geneva: WCC, 1981; idem, "The Confessing Church and the Ecumenical Movement." *Ecumenical Review* 33 (1981): 212–231; Barnett, Victoria. "Dietrich Bonhoeffer's Ecumenical Vision." *The Christian Century* 112, no. 14 (April 26, 1995): 454–457; Barnett, Victoria. "The Ecumenical and Interfaith Landscape in Bonhoeffer's Times." *The Ecumenical Review* 67, no. 2 (July 2015): 302–307; Moses, John A. "Dietrich Bonhoeffer's Prioritization of Church Unity (*Oekumene*)," *Journal or Religious History* 24, no. 2 (June 2000): 196–212; Moses, John A. "Dietrich Bonhoeffer's Concept of the 'True' Church." *St Mark's Review* 169 (Aut 1997): 16–22.

Part of this lack of attention is due to the fact that the English publications of Bonhoeffer's ecumenical works are relatively recent (DBWE 13 was published in 2007, Clements' book in 2015, and DBWE 11, 12, and 14 between those years).

and the ways in which Bonhoeffer's ecumenical thought continues to present challenges to the current ecumenical landscape. Clements' book is an invaluable resource for anyone interested in the biographical account of Bonhoeffer's ecumenical involvement. Garcia's book considers Bonhoeffer's theology from his broader corpus in relation to Luther and Calvin in order to insert Bonhoeffer's thought into the contemporary Lutheran-Reformed Dialogue. As such, Garcia's book does not closely attend to Bonhoeffer's ecumenical works. Garcia himself writes, "I do not focus on Bonhoeffer's articulation of his ecumenical theology."[7] Between these two books, then, is a thorough account of Bonhoeffer's ecumenical involvement, which draws out his ecumenical theology along the way, and a rich account of the locus of Bonhoeffer's thought between Luther and Calvin, which makes a nice contribution to contemporary Lutheran-Reformed Dialogue.

While Clements' and Garcia's books are both valuable to Bonhoeffer scholarship and contemporary ecumenical discourse, there remains a need to address Bonhoeffer's ecumenical theology further. This book contends that Bonhoeffer's ecumenical theology as expressed in his ecumenical works ought to be considered and taken seriously on its own terms. Only in this way can Bonhoeffer's continuing value to ecumenical discourse be fully recognized. The aim of this book, therefore, is to examine Bonhoeffer's ecumenical works and provide a systematic constructive account of the theology presented therein. To this end, the book develops the "very distinct conception of church" in which Bonhoeffer grounds his ecumenical theology, along with the understanding of church unity and church visibility inherent to that conception, in order to provide the foundation of Bonhoeffer's ecumenical theology before moving to highlight discipleship as the operative theological content of Bonhoeffer's ecumenical works and present the distinctive ecumenical theology that emerges from that foundation—Bonhoeffer's ecumenism of discipleship.

In doing so, this book makes several significant claims that bear importance not just to ecumenists and Bonhoeffer scholars but to those within the church writ large. These claims include (but are not limited to) the following: the church is created and sustained by the work of God, and the church is the revelatory person of Christ (chapter 1); church unity is also created and sustained by God, and church unity is an inherent reality of the church (chapter 2); the unity of the church is not merely a mystical reality but a concrete and practical reality even now before the eschaton (chapter 2); church visibility is not a *goal* of ecumenical work (the goal of which is discipleship) but an inevitable *by-product* of obedient discipleship to Christ (chapter 3);

---

[7] Garcia, *Recovering the Ecumenical Bonhoeffer*, 17.

discipleship is the practical content (the operative theological content) of the human agent within ecumenical work (chapter 4); and ecumenism as discipleship includes *everyone* within the church—not just those involved in official ecumenical organizations (chapter 5).

Before the book moves to make these claims and provide this constructive account of Bonhoeffer's ecumenical theology, a brief introduction to both Bonhoeffer's ecumenical works and his concept of discipleship is helpful for grasping the book's ongoing argument. It should be said from the start that Bonhoeffer was not a significant or prominent figure in the ecumenical movement during his lifetime.[8] He became involved in the ecumenical movement when he attended a conference of the World Alliance in Cambridge in August 1931, where he was given the role of international youth secretary.[9] He would never rise above this position. Most of what Bonhoeffer did in this position was coordinate with various ecumenists regarding upcoming conferences, write up reports on conferences, and—every so often—he was given the opportunity to present or to give an address. That said, Willem Visser't Hooft has noted that Bonhoeffer was not in attendance at many of the most significant ecumenical conferences of his day.[10] When Bonhoeffer was given the opportunity to speak at ecumenical gatherings, however, he spoke his mind. For this reason, it is possible to attend to Bonhoeffer's ecumenical works and glean from them all that is needed to provide a constructive account of his ecumenical theology.

When the book refers to Bonhoeffer's "ecumenical works," it is referring to four works in particular: (1) "On the Theological Foundation of the Work of the World Alliance"; (2) "Address in Gland"; (3) "Address to the Fano Conference"; and (4) "The Confessing Church and the Ecumenical Movement." The first three of these works are addresses delivered by Bonhoeffer at ecumenical conferences, while the fourth is an essay he wrote directly concerning the ecumenical movement of his day. A brief introduction to the context and content of these addresses and essays is helpful for reference when the book attends to them later.[11]

---

[8] Barnett, "The Ecumenical and Interfaith Landscape in Bonhoeffer's Times," 307.

[9] Clements, *Dietrich Bonhoeffer's Ecumenical Quest*, 58.

[10] Visser't Hooft, "Dietrich Bonhoeffer and the Self-Understanding of the Ecumenical Movement," 198. In spite of this fact, Bonhoeffer made an impact upon prominent ecumenical figures such as Willem Visser't Hooft and George Bell, who are responsible for introducing strains of Bonhoeffer's ecumenical thought into the World Council of Churches and in so doing are also responsible for making Bonhoeffer a larger name ecumenically than it was during his lifetime. For more on Bonhoeffer's relationship with—and reception by—Visser't Hooft and Bell, see Clements, *Dietrich Bonhoeffer's Ecumenical Quest*, 117–126; 271–282.

[11] A brief word concerning the omission of the Barmen Declaration from this list is warranted. Given Bonhoeffer's enthusiastic support of—and commitment to—both the Barmen Declaration and the Confessing Church, it would be argued that the Barmen Declaration deserved to be counted among these ecumenical works. The reason for not counting the Barmen Declaration among these texts is

Bonhoeffer delivered his lecture "On the Theological Foundation of the Work of the World Alliance" at the International Youth Peace Conference in Ciernehorske Kupele, Czechoslovakia—a conference that was held between July 20 and 30, 1932. The conference itself was not a momentous occasion; indeed, Clements describes the conference as a "gathering, more in the nature of a retreat than a formal conference."[12] Bonhoeffer's address, however, is a landmark text among his ecumenical works, because it contains within it all of his ecumenical theology.[13]

Much of the ecumenical landscape at the time was focused on the topic of armament and peace amid the rising tensions of the early 1930s. Thus, the topic of peace was also part of the discussion of the International Youth Peace Conference in Czechoslovakia. In addition to the topic of peace, papers given by Wilhelm Stahlin and Wilhelm Zoellner at a conference in Berlin four months prior to these events played heavily on Bonhoeffer's mind.[14] Stahlin and Zoellner both advocated for a theology of the orders of creation—a theology which claims that that which exists must be what is willed by God—which Bonhoeffer saw as dangerous, given the social climate of the day (indeed, this theology of orders of creation at times played into the advancement of anti-Semitic thought).[15] It was on these two issues—peace and the orders of creation—that Bonhoeffer wanted to speak.[16] He was adamant, however, that in order to speak on such issues, the ecumenical movement must first have a theology of its own.[17] The primary contribution of his address was to provide this ecumenical theology. Bonhoeffer suggested that the ecumenical movement should understand itself as church—specifically the church as *Christus Praesens*—and that it should understand its role in the world as proclaiming the commands of Christ to the world.[18] This is the theological foundation of ecumenism referred to in the title of the address, and it

---

that Bonhoeffer was not an author of this document, and therefore the document is not really one of *his* ecumenical works, regardless of his support of it. The Barmen Declaration could be helpful as a depiction of how Bonhoeffer envisioned ecumenical engagement within his context. That said, this depiction of the Barmen Declaration as an example of what Bonhoeffer intends ecumenically can only be considered as *an* example and not *the* example. Bonhoeffer's emphasis on Christ's freedom to command determines that no single ecumenical model can be taken to be *the* ecumenical model universally for all time.

[12] Clements, *Dietrich Bonhoeffer's Ecumenical Quest*, 72.

[13] The lecture is found in DBWE 11:356–369.

[14] Clements, *Dietrich Bonhoeffer's Ecumenical Quest*, 71.

[15] Bonhoeffer wrote both a preliminary report and a primary report—both of which provided the details of the conference. DBWE 11:345–355.

[16] For more on Bonhoeffer's approach to the orders of creation and the topic of peace, see Clements, *Dietrich Bonhoeffer's Ecumenical Quest*, 74–78.

[17] DBWE 11:356.

[18] DBWE 11:358–359.

is from this theology that Bonhoeffer's responses to the orders of creation and to the topic of peace emerge.[19]

"On the Theological Foundation of the Work of the World Alliance" is integral to this book because it presents the whole of Bonhoeffer's ecumenical vision. Although Bonhoeffer does not detail the ecclesiology denoted by an understanding of the ecumenical movement as the church as *Christus Praesens*, he does identify this ecclesial understanding as the theology from which ecumenical work emerges.[20] It is the primary task of this book to provide a full account of the ecumenical theology that is completely present in germ within this address.

Bonhoeffer gave his "Address in Gland" at the *Youth Conference of World Alliance and Life and Work*, in Gland, which was held from August 25 to 31, 1932. This conference was a more notable event than the conference held in Ciernehorske Kupele a few weeks prior.[21] The content of Bonhoeffer's address was more or less the same as in Czechoslovakia. Clements lists the repeated content as follows:

> The church, and therefore the World Alliance, as the community of those who hear the word of Christ in and for the world; the distinction between war and struggle; the requirements of truth and justice not subordinate to peace; Christ as presence in the church.[22]

It is no surprise that the content is so consistent between these two ecumenical works, given their close proximity to one another chronologically.

The third of Bonhoeffer's ecumenical works is his "Address to the Fano Conference."[23] By the time of the conference in Fano (August 22–30, 1934), Hitler was in power in Germany and the church struggle was in full swing, with the Confessing Church having already produced the Barmen Declaration. The effect these developments had on Bonhoeffer's ecumenical theology was not to change it, but only to make it more urgent and more immediately practicable. Bonhoeffer's address in Fano has come to be known as his "Peace Sermon," because of his adamant and impassioned claim that peace was Christ's command for the day—the command Bonhoeffer exhorted the ecumenical movement to proclaim unequivocally. In this address, he does not speak of the orders of creation but focuses on the issue of peace. In this

---

[19] DBWE 11:363–369.
   Ryan Tafilowski attends to Bonhoeffer's approach to the orders of creation. Tafilowski, Ryan. "A Reappraisal of the Orders of Creation." *Lutheran Quarterly* 31, no. 3 (Fall 2017): 288–309.
[20] DBWE 11:358–359.
[21] Clements, *Dietrich Bonhoeffer's Ecumenical Quest*, 72–73.
[22] Clements, Ibid., 82.
[23] DBWE 13:307–310.

context, Bonhoeffer's ecumenical theology evinces its concrete nature. He urges the ecumenical movement—as the church—to proclaim Christ's command of peace in the world.[24] The ecumenical theology he promotes—in its simplest explanation—is that the ecumenical movement is the church and has the task of proclaiming Christ's commands, or, as Bonhoeffer puts it in his address, "The ecumenical church . . . [concerns itself] with the commandments of God, and regardless of consequence transmits these commandments to the world."[25] Put otherwise, he promotes an ecumenism of discipleship.

Bonhoeffer's words did not go unheard in Fano; a resolution was drawn up in which the World Alliance offered statements in support of the stance of the Confessing Church without reference to some of the specific issues (like the Aryan paragraph) opposed by the Confessing Church.[26] That said, Clements is careful to articulate Bonhoeffer's relatively minor role in the conference and the fact that the German situation at large—more than Bonhoeffer's stance itself—garnered much of the attention of those who attended.[27]

Bonhoeffer's final ecumenical work was his 1935 essay, "The Confessing Church and the Ecumenical Movement." Clements refers to this essay as "the great *summa* of Bonhoeffer's contribution to ecumenical thought" and notes that the essay "includes but goes beyond the challenges he had issued before" in his previous ecumenical works.[28]

Bonhoeffer penned the essay shortly after he began his time at the underground seminary at Finkenwalde. Soon before he did so—likely the catalyst of Bonhoeffer's decision to write the essay itself—Bonhoeffer declined an invitation by Leonard Hodgson to an ecumenical conference held by the Faith and Order commission. The reason for his refusal to attend is that the conference would be attended by representatives of the Reich Church, and Bonhoeffer told Hodgson in a letter, "Being a minister of the Confessional Church I cannot attend an oecumenical conference unless it either excludes the Reich Church or ventures openly to charge both the Reich Church and the Confessional Church with responsibility."[29] The essay was published in

---

[24] DBWE 13:309.

[25] DBWE 13:307.

[26] Clements, *Dietrich Bonhoeffer's Ecumenical Quests*, 139–140. For a more detailed account of the historical setting of the Fano conference, its resolution, and Bonhoeffer's involvement, see Clements' chapter "'The Hour is Late:' Fano 1934 in Context," in *Dietrich Bonhoeffer's Ecumenical Quest*, 127–157.

[27] Clements, *Dietrich Bonhoeffer's Ecumenical Quest*, 144.

[28] Clements, Ibid., 168.

[29] DBWE 14:72.
  For a full account of the historical and biographical material surrounding Bonhoeffer's refusal to attend the Faith and Order conference, and this essay, see Clements, *Dietrich Bonhoeffer's Ecumenical Quest*, 165–174.
  Clements, *Dietrich Bonhoeffer's Ecumenical Quest*, 172–173.

Evangelische Theologie in August of 1935 but received little attention at the time.[30]

The central claim of the article is that the Confessing Church and the ecumenical movement pose questions of one another.[31] The question posed to the ecumenical movement is whether or not it is church.[32] The question posed to the Confessing Church is whether or not their understanding of the church is too exclusive.[33] Bonhoeffer's stance on these questions is that the ecumenical movement *ought* to self-identify as church, and that the Confessing Church is not too exclusive but must be ever wary of becoming so.[34] The essay is consistent with his earlier ecumenical works, becoming even more urgent and concrete. Taken together, these essays and lectures form Bonhoeffer's ecumenical works.

Having introduced what is meant by Bonhoeffer's ecumenical works, his concept of discipleship should likewise be introduced here, since this book continually identifies it as the practical content of ecumenical work. Bonhoeffer's concept of discipleship is detailed at length in chapter 4, but the salient points of this concept are helpful here.[35] Before providing these points, however, it is helpful to detail what Bonhoeffer does *not* mean when he speaks of discipleship.

Michael Mawson adroitly situates Bonhoeffer's concept of discipleship in contrast to three prevailing contemporary understandings of the term.[36] A common thread in these three approaches to discipleship is the idea that discipleship is primarily at the disposal of the human agent. Put differently, these approaches consider discipleship to be *principally* about what we (humans) do. The first approach—a biblical studies approach—posits discipleship as a recipe provided in scripture—available to the human agent if only they would

---

[30] Clements, *Dietrich Bonhoeffer's Ecumenical Quest*, 172–173.

[31] DBWE 14:397.

[32] DBWE 14:399.

[33] DBWE 14:409.

[34] DBWE 14:411–412.

[35] Albert van der Ziel and Joseph S. Harvard both have written articles on Bonhoeffer's concept of discipleship, which are more biographical in their content than theological. Van der Ziel, Albert. "Following Jesus: The Continuing Challenge of Dietrich Bonhoeffer." *Reformed Journal* 27, no. 11 (November 1977): 22–25; Harvard, Joseph S. "The Continuing Cost of Discipleship." *Journal for Preachers* 7, no. 4 (Pentecost 1984): 2–7.

Andrew Root has considered Bonhoeffer's concept of discipleship and its implications for youth ministry. Root, Andrew. *Bonhoeffer as a Youth Worker: A Theological Vision for Discipleship and Life Together.* Grand Rapids: Baker Academic, 2015.

[36] Mawson, Michael G. "Suffering Christ's Call: Discipleship and the Cross." *The Bonhoeffer Legacy* 3, no. 2 (2015): 1–18.

Philip Ziegler also provides a thorough survey of various approaches to discipleship, Ziegler, Philip G. *Militant Grace: The Apocalyptic Turn and the Future of Christian Theology.* Grand Rapids: Baker Academic, 2018; especially 187–200.

interpret it correctly;[37] the second approach—an Anabaptist approach—posits discipleship as a political social agenda to be chosen and employed by Christians—the model for which is the life and actions of Jesus;[38] the third approach—an evangelical and Protestant approach—posits discipleship as a set of "practices and disciplines that might sustain and deepen faith post conversion."[39] In each of these approaches, the need for a divine agent (God) to play an active role in discipleship is either unnecessary or made subsidiary to the working of the human agent. Stated differently, the cart is put before the horse, or the horse is altogether forgotten. Against these approaches, for Bonhoeffer, discipleship "is about receiving Christ or being formed by Christ."[40] For Bonhoeffer, the action of divine agency (the action of God) is the catalyst and continuing guide of the action of human agency within discipleship. This is not to say that there is no action done by the human agent. Discipleship still requires action on the part of the human agent, but that action is a *response* to Christ's action. Discipleship is purely about encountering Christ, being formed by Christ, and responding to that encounter by being obedient to Christ's commands. As Bonhoeffer puts it in *Discipleship*, "Jesus Christ is the only content" of discipleship.[41]

This book avers that Bonhoeffer's concept of discipleship is comprised of four key components: (1) a Christological orientation;[42] (2) Christ's concrete commands and the disciples' simple obedience;[43] (3) discipleship is inherently ecclesiological and communal;[44] and (4) disciples remain vulnerable to sin and must repent when they find themselves to be in sin.[45] Put otherwise, Christ encounters the human agent and calls them to discipleship; the human agent's response is to look only to Christ and to obey his commands. These first two components provide the essential content of discipleship—hearing and obeying the command of Christ. That content is ecclesial and communal as the disciple is called and drawn into the church;[46] and the disciple—who remains vulnerable to sin—must repent when they find themselves to be in sin.[47] When the book refers to Bonhoeffer's concept of discipleship, therefore,

---

[37] Mawson indicates N. T. Wright as emblematic of this approach. Mawson, "Suffering Christ's Call," 8–9.

[38] John Howard Yoder is emblematic of this approach. Yoder, John Howard. *The Politics of Jesus: Vicit Agnus Noster*. Grand Rapids: Eerdmans, 1972.

[39] Mawson, "Suffering Christ's Call," 2.

[40] Mawson, Ibid., 10.

[41] DBWE 4:59.

[42] DBWE 4:57–59; 74; 287–288.

[43] DBWE 4:57.

[44] DBWE 4:202.

[45] DBWE 4:241; 279.

[46] DBWE 4:219.

[47] DBWE 4:241; 279.

it intends a hearing and doing of Christ's commands that is ecclesial by nature and marked with repentance.

In providing these components of Bonhoeffer's concept of discipleship, a glaring question remains: How do disciples discern the command of Christ? If discipleship is the operative theological content of Bonhoeffer's ecumenical theology and discipleship is characterized by hearing and doing Christ's commands, an understanding of *how* those commands are heard is critical to an account of an ecumenism of discipleship.[48]

Bonhoeffer asserts in *Discipleship* that if the disciple wants to hear the command they need to go where Christ is present—the church.[49] Bonhoeffer's account of the church as *Christus Praesens* denotes three ways in which Christ is present in the church: Word, sacrament, and church-community.[50] By narrating these places as there where Christ is present and where the command of Christ can be heard, Bonhoeffer grounds his understanding of discernment ecclesiologically via Christology. This is significant because it means that Bonhoeffer's claim that the practical content of ecumenical action is to hear and proclaim Christ's commands is not overly subjective or individualized. In other words, Bonhoeffer's concept guards against the idea of someone simply saying that they *feel* like something is the command of God and, therefore, it must be so without any accountability for that claim. Instead, the command is heard *together in the church* where Christ is present.

---

[48] Lisa Dahill and Laurel Schneider have both written articles on Bonhoeffer and discernment. Dahill, Lisa E. "Probing the Will of God: Bonhoeffer and Discernment." *Dialog* 41, no. 1 (2002): 42–49; Schneider, Laurel C. "'The Call Was Not Meant for You Alone:' Dietrich Bonhoeffer on Discerning the Call." *Chicago Theological Seminary Register* 94, no. 2–3 (2007): 17–22.

[49] DBWE 4:202.

[50] DBWE 12:314.

In *Ethics*, Bonhoeffer locates the divine command in his account of the mandates—of which the church is but one of four. That said, Bonhoeffer is not deviating from his earlier articulations of hearing the command. In discussing the mandates in this way, Bonhoeffer is not establishing four principles that are in and of themselves the locus of the command. Rather, the mandates remain indexed to obedience to Christ. Brian Brock puts it thus: "The mandates are thus not properly understood as metaphysical axioms, ethical blueprints, or programs; they are Christologically keyed signposts indicating the features of reality that allow us to encounter Christ. . . . The mandates have no salvific value, or even penultimate conceptual worth. . . . In themselves [the mandates] are inconsequential; what matters is the 'obedience of faith rendered within them'" (Brock, *Singing the Ethos of God*, 90–92). Brock rightly asserts that it is in encountering Christ's command in Scripture (one of the ways in which Christ is present in the church as Word) that the mandates are identified, and it is only in obedience to Christ's commands that the mandates hold any value. Thus, the mandates are actually indexed under discipleship, rather than discipleship being indexed under the mandates. All of this said—given the position of the mandates within discipleship; the consistency with which Bonhoeffer refers to Christ's presence in the church as Word, sacrament, and church-community; and the inconsistency of Bonhoeffer's own list of the mandates—the book understands Christ's presence in the church as the locus of Christ's command and henceforth does not engage with Bonhoeffer's account of the mandates. For more on Bonhoeffer and the mandates, see, DBWE 6:388–408, Brock, Brian. *Singing the Ethos of God. On the Place of Christian Ethics in Scripture*. Grand Rapids: Eerdmans, 2007, 71–95.

There is a final clarifying point to be made before moving to chapter 1. A cursory glance at the chronology of Bonhoeffer's publications indicates that his ecumenical works predate his 1937 publication of *Discipleship*. This fact does not undermine the book's argument that Bonhoeffer's ecumenical works share the key components of his concept of discipleship, thus evincing an ecumenism of discipleship. That these works are consistent with Bonhoeffer's concept of discipleship demonstrates that Bonhoeffer was a consistent and coherent thinker. Indeed, Bonhoeffer himself acknowledged the consistency of his thought.[51] Some form of Bonhoeffer's concept of discipleship is clear throughout his corpus, under different names. In his early dissertation *Sanctorum Communio*, Bonhoeffer describes a "community of love" which largely accomplishes what his concept of discipleship accomplishes.[52] In his later work *Ethics*, these themes emerge in his discussion of responsibility.[53] The stance of this book is that Bonhoeffer's *clearest expression* of

---

[51] DBWE 8:357–359.

[52] DBWE 1:170–192. The ideas undergirding discipleship are particularly prevalent here: "*Love for our neighbor is our will to embrace God's will for the other person.* . . . In Christ God loves human beings and opens the divine heart; and in giving God's own self to sinful human beings God renews them at the same time and makes the new community possible and real; but this means that *God's love wills community.* . . . We thus come to the fundamentally important conclusion that *community with God for us exists only in faith.* . . . It is an article of faith that God through Christ has entered into a community of love with us . . . my community of love with my neighbor can also exist only by having faith in God, who in Christ has fulfilled the law for me and loved my neighbor, who draws me into the church-community, which means into the love of Christ, and creates a bond between myself and my neighbor . . . Christian community of love between human beings means unrestrictedly surrendering to the other out of obedience to God's will . . . community (in the broader sense) is actually organized for a single purpose, namely to accomplish God's will. . . . In order to come to a full understanding we will have to consider that the community of saints knows that its structure is organized according to the principle of authority. It is community only because of the divine will ruling in it. This association of authentic rule between God and us in revelation is paradoxical because God rules by serving; this is what the concept of the love of God entails. God commands, and, in command, God's very own self . . . puts the will to obey and the understanding of what is commanded into our hearts; but this means that God establishes community among human beings and between them and God." DBWE 1:171–177, italics original.

[53] Many instances throughout *Ethics* demonstrate a consistency between Bonhoeffer's concepts of discipleship and responsibility. For example, Bonhoeffer writes: "The message of the church to the world can be none other than the word of God to the world. This word is: Jesus Christ, and salvation in this name. It is in Jesus Christ that God's relationship to the world is determined. We do not know any other relationship of God to the world apart from Jesus Christ. Therefore the church, too, has no relationship to the world other than through Jesus Christ. This means that the proper relationship of the church to the world does not derive from some natural law, or law of reason, or universal human rights, but *solely* from the gospel of Jesus Christ. . . . The message of God's love for the world places the church community into a relationship of *responsibility* for the world. In both word and deed, the church-community has to witness to the world concerning its faith in Christ, to work on removing any offense, and to make room for the gospel in the world. Wherever this responsibility is denied, Christ is denied; for it is the responsibility that corresponds to God's love of the world." Bonhoeffer's entire approach to the external ordering of the church to the world here mirrors his understanding of discipleship. There is a Christological orientation to hear the commandment of Christ, a responsibility to obediently do that commandment, and to do so as church. DBWE 6:357–358.

these ideas is his concept of discipleship.[54] If there is a precursor to point to regarding the theology presented in his ecumenical works, it is most certainly his account of the church as *Christus Praesens*, which can be seen as early as his doctoral dissertation, *Sanctorum Communio*.

In describing Bonhoeffer's ecumenical theology as an ecumenism of discipleship, the book does not intend to claim that his work in *Discipleship* founded his ecumenical theology (which would be a chronological fallacy) or that his ecumenical work was a precursor to his concept of discipleship (which could perhaps be argued). Instead, in describing Bonhoeffer's ecumenical theology as an ecumenism of discipleship, the book is indicating *the substance of the human agent's work within ecumenical work*. A key argument of the book is that, for Bonhoeffer, all ecumenical work is grounded in his conception of the church as *Christus Praesens*, which means that the church, its unity, and its visibility are chiefly works of divine agency. To describe Bonhoeffer's ecumenical theology as an ecumenism of discipleship, therefore, denotes and emphasizes the work of the human agent in ecumenical work.

In the pages that follow, Bonhoeffer's ecumenical vision is presented. Grounded in a particular understanding of the church, and practiced in active obedient discipleship to Christ, this ecumenical vision provides a distinctive and vibrant approach to ecumenism that deserves to be understood on its own terms. The hope of this book is that, by enumerating Bonhoeffer's ecumenical theology as articulated in his ecumenical works, its constructive account of Bonhoeffer's ecumenism of discipleship can serve as a fresh ecumenical approach from a familiar and beloved voice. At its heart, this book serves to advance an ecumenical theology enlivened by the living and present Christ who calls his church to follow after him together.

---

[54] DeJonge notes, in *Discipleship* "Bonhoeffer has in place an account of discipleship that formally mirrors his account of 'being in Christ' in *Act and Being*. There Bonhoeffer describes being in Christ as the coordination of being in the church and the act of faith; faith is the precondition of being in the church, and being in the church is the precondition of faith. But the possibility of this coordination depends on something outside it: revelation. Therefore, the structure of being in Christ is a coordination of act and being that depends on being acted upon. Similarly, in *Discipleship*, Jesus' call (being acted upon) produces a coordination of act and being, namely a situation (being) that makes faith (act) possible, which is simultaneously a situation made possible by faith," DeJonge, Michael P. *Bonhoeffer's Theological Formation: Berlin, Barth, and Protestant Theology*. Oxford: Oxford University Press, 2012, 133.

Chapter 1

The Church

In July of 1932, Dietrich Bonhoeffer attended and presented at an ecumenical conference in Ciernehorske Kupele, Czechoslovakia—a conference he would leave early in order to vote against Hitler. Bonhoeffer participated in this conference as a substitute for his friend Max Diestel, who had fallen ill. Bonhoeffer himself called the conference "rather mediocre," but the lecture he gave is his most significant ecumenical work—in content, if not in immediate impact. Indeed, the lecture ought to be considered the Rosetta Stone of Bonhoeffer's ecumenical theology. In the lecture, he seeks to provide a "theology of the ecumenical movement."[1] The core of both the lecture and Bonhoeffer's ecumenical theology as a whole is contained within these words:

> The work of our World Alliance—consciously or unconsciously—is grounded in a very distinct conception of church. The church as the one church-community of the Lord Jesus Christ, who is the Lord of the world, has the task of speaking his word to the entire world . . . under which authority does the church speak, when it proclaims this claim of Christ on the world? Under the only authority in which the church is in a position to speak, in the authority of the Christ who is present and living in it. The church is the presence of Christ on earth; the church is *Christus Praesens*.[2]

These words are decisive for Bonhoeffer's ecumenical theology. With these words, Bonhoeffer provides that theology's foundation and task. The

---

[1] Schlingensiepen, Ferdinand. *Dietrich Bonhoeffer 1906-1945: Martyr, Thinker, Man of Resistance.* Translated by Isabel Best, London: T&T Clark, 2010, 00.
[2] DBWE 11:358–359.

15

foundation of this ecumenical theology is his understanding of the church. The task of this theology is to speak Christ's commands to the world, or, what is the same, to concretely follow Christ's commands in the world. This is the whole of Bonhoeffer's ecumenical theology. This is the ecumenical theology this book endeavors to articulate—an ecumenical theology that claims the church is one as the person of Christ and that disciples of Christ participate in that unity through their active discipleship to Christ. In order to unpack all of the contours of this ecumenical theology, however, it is necessary to begin with its foundation—the church. This first chapter, therefore, attends to the "very distinct conception of church" in which Bonhoeffer grounds his ecumenical theology. He sums up this conception when he states: "The church is the presence of Christ on earth; the church is *Christus Praesens*."[3]

To provide Bonhoeffer's account of ecclesiology, the chapter attends to what the church *is* as Christ's presence and the ways in which Christ is present in the church. First, the chapter must clarify that defining Bonhoeffer's account of ecclesiology as *Christus Praesens* is faithful to his understanding of ecclesiology throughout his life, and not simply in this one ecumenical lecture. Second, the chapter unpacks what Bonhoeffer understands the church to be—the revelatory person of Christ—by drawing out his concepts of person and revelation and the relation of these concepts to his understanding of the church as the presence of Christ. Third, the chapter details the three ways in which Bonhoeffer understands Christ to be present in the church: as Word, sacrament, and church-community. In doing so, the chapter reveals an ecclesiology in which the church is created by God and structured by Christ's presence within it; this church is understood as person rather than as institution; and, the activity of those within this person that is the church is active discipleship.[4] The chapter closes by addressing and dismissing two

---

[3] DBWE 11:358–359.

[4] When Bonhoeffer identifies the church as the person of Christ, he is not making a claim that the church in its *institutional* forms—in its offices, buildings, practices, or even doctrines—is Christ's presence on earth, rather, he intends that the church is the presence of the *person* of Christ on earth today. This is critical. For Bonhoeffer, the church is not understood to be an institution but a person—the revelatory person of Christ. This claim pushes attention away from describing the church in terms of institutional forms and toward understanding the church in a primarily *theological* way. In terms of the topography of doctrines, this means that ecclesiology is indexed to the doctrine of God. The church is a work of divine agency (meaning it is created and sustained by God). Humans do not create the church. God's work to create the church creates space within it for humans to work in active discipleship.

Tom Greggs discusses the topography of doctrines in like fashion, arguing that in systematic theology, doctrines have an immediate *res* and an ultimate *res*, and that what a theologian identifies as the ultimate *res* of a particular doctrine significantly affects the way in which that doctrine is presented and understood by that theologian. To use Greggs' terminology, the book is arguing, here, that the ultimate *res* of Bonhoeffer's account of ecclesiology is the doctrine of God. So, Bonhoeffer's ecumenical theology and concept of discipleship stem from his account of ecclesiology, and his ecclesiology stems from its ultimate *res* in the doctrine of God. Greggs, Tom. "Bearing Sin

concerns: whether Bonhoeffer's ecclesiology collapses into Christology and whether Bonhoeffer's ecclesiology undermines ecumenism. By providing Bonhoeffer's account of ecclesiology, the chapter provides the foundation of his ecumenical theology.

CHRISTUS PRAESENS AS AN IDENTIFIER OF BONHOEFFER'S ECCLESIOLOGY

Those who are unfamiliar with Bonhoeffer's ecumenical works, but have read his other works may be curious as to the reasoning behind this book's consistent use of the term *Christus Praesens* to identify his account of ecclesiology. After all, Bonhoeffer frequently details his ecclesiology outside of his ecumenical works and rarely utilizes this terminology. Indeed, works in which Bonhoeffer attends to the church either directly or tangentially include his dissertations (*Sanctorum Communio* and *Act and Being*); class lectures such as "The Nature of the Church," "The Visible Church in the New Testament," and "Lectures on Christology"; and his essay "What Is Church?" as well as *Discipleship* and *Ethics*.

Bearing in mind the consistent and thorough attention Bonhoeffer gives to the church, it is no surprise that his account of ecclesiology is robust and complex. Given this complexity, is there a shorthand name that appropriately identifies this account? Bonhoeffer scholars have rightly highlighted the significance of sociality and personhood to his account of ecclesiology, alongside the sociological contours of that account. Indeed, the sociality of how Christ relates to humanity and mediates relations between and among humans is a defining trait of this account of ecclesiology (as will be detailed in this chapter). That said, while sociality and personhood are certainly integral to Bonhoeffer's ecclesiology, Bonhoeffer himself identifies *Christus Praesens* as a shorthand for his account of ecclesiology. Such an identifier does not dismiss the sociological, social, and person-based dimensions of Bonhoeffer's ecclesiology but rather holds these together under the understanding of the church as the present Christ; realized in Christ's life, death, and resurrection; and actualized through the work of the Holy Spirit.

Bonhoeffer provides the term *Christus Praesens* as the shorthand descriptor of his ecclesiology in his ecumenical lecture in Czechoslovakia, stating, "The church is the presence of Christ on earth; the church is *Christus*

---

in the Church: The Ecclesial Hamartiology of Bonhoeffer." In *Christ, Church, and World: New Studies in Bonhoeffer's Theology and Ethics,* edited by Michael Mawson and Philip G. Ziegler, 77–100. London, UK: Bloomsbury T&T Clark, 2016; especially 77–79.

Praesens."[5] This is the account of ecclesiology that Bonhoeffer identifies as the foundation of his ecumenical theology. When one analyzes Bonhoeffer's ecclesiological thought beyond this lecture, it becomes clear that this term is an apt descriptor of the ecclesiology he intends. Thus, despite the sparse explicit usage of the term *Christus Praesens*, the *content* of that term ubiquitously determines his ecclesiology throughout his corpus. A quick survey of the previously mentioned works bears this out, evincing *Christus Praesens* as an appropriate identifier for his account of ecclesiology.

In *Sanctorum Communio*, Bonhoeffer writes, "[the church-community] is not merely *a means to an end but also an end in itself. It is the present Christ himself, and this is why 'being in Christ' and 'being in the church-community' is the same thing.*"[6] Furthermore, when detailing the New Testament vision of the church, he writes,

> Christ is also at all times *a real presence for the church,* for it is Christ's body, and the people are members of this body, or members of Christ himself. . . . *The church is the presence of Christ in the same way that Christ is the presence of God.*[7]

In both of these quotations, Bonhoeffer explicitly identifies Christ's presence as the church (the literal meaning of *Christus Praesens*) as definitive of the church as a whole.

In *Act and Being*, Bonhoeffer writes, "[Revelation], must . . . be thought in the church, *for the church is the present Christ, 'Christ existing as community'* . . . Christ is the corporate person of the Christian community of faith."[8] Here, again, Bonhoeffer is clear that Christ's presence as church is a defining trait of how he understands the church.

In *Discipleship*, Bonhoeffer writes,

> If we want to hear [Christ's] call to discipleship, we need to hear it *where Christ himself is present. It is within the church.* . . . Here he is, the whole Christ, the very same who encountered the disciples. Indeed, here he *is already present* as the glorified, the victorious, the living Christ.[9]

The reason Bonhoeffer identifies the church as the place where Christ's command can be heard is because *the church is Christ's presence.* Also in

---

[5] DBWE 11:359.
[6] DBWE 1:190. Italics original.
[7] DBWE 1:139–141. Italics added for emphasis.
[8] DBWE 2:110 111. Italics added for emphasis.
[9] DBWE 4:202. Italics added for emphasis.

Discipleship, Bonhoeffer states, "Since Pentecost Jesus Christ lives here on earth in the form of his body, the church-community. . . . Since the ascension, Jesus Christ's place on earth has been taken by his body, the church. *The church is the present Christ himself.*"[10] Here, Bonhoeffer unambiguously states that he understands the church in terms of Christ's presence—or, what is the same, that he understands it as *Christus Praesens.*

In his lecture "The Nature of the Church," Bonhoeffer declares, "[The church] is the place of the *present Christ.*"[11] In this same lecture series, he also states,

> The church-community is Christ; *Christ is the church-community.* . . . The form of revelation as person is Christ and Spirit. . . . *The church itself is the present Christ! The presence of God on earth is Christ; the presence of Christ on earth is the church. Person is the church, is the form of the presence of the Second Person of the Trinity.*[12]

And, "*The church of today is the presence of Christ on earth.* This presence is to be understood as follows, that the church-community is Christ."[13] Over and over again in these quotations, Bonhoeffer highlights Christ's presence as the defining trait of the church.

In his essay, "What is Church?" Bonhoeffer writes,

> *Church is the presence of God in the world;* truly in the world, truly a *present God* . . . Church is the awakening of the world through a miracle, through the *presence* of the life-creating God calling from death into life.[14]

Though he utilizes language of God rather than Christ in this excerpt, it is nevertheless clear that the church is defined by God's presence.

In "Lectures on Christology," Bonhoeffer writes,

> As the Crucified and Risen One, Jesus is at the same time the Christ who is *present now.* . . . He is to be understood as *present* in time and space. *Nunc et hic, the two flow together in the concept of the church. Christ in his person is indeed present in the church as person. Thus the presence of Christ is there in the church.*[15]

---

[10] DBWE 4:218. Italics added for emphasis.
[11] DBWE 11:278. Italics added for emphasis.
[12] DBWE 11:301. Italics added for emphasis.
[13] DBWE 11:304. Italics original.
[14] DBWE 12:263. Italics added for emphasis.
[15] DBWE 12:310. Italics added for emphasis.

Thus, in "Lectures on Christology," Bonhoeffer again views the church in terms of Christ's presence.

In his lecture series "The Visible Church in the New Testament," Bonhoeffer states, "The space of Christ in the world is occupied by the *church; it is the present Christ*. It is to be understood as a person, as a human being, not as a multiplicity, but as a unity."[16] In this same lecture series, Bonhoeffer claims, "The church-community of Christ *is the present Christ* in the Holy Spirit."[17] Clearly, in this lecture, Bonhoeffer maintains his understanding that the church is defined in terms of Christ's presence.

Finally, in *Ethics*, Bonhoeffer writes,

> [The church] follows in discipleship the one who was the Christ precisely in being there completely for the world and not for himself. The church as a distinct corporate entity is thus subject to a double divine purpose . . . namely, being oriented to the world, and, in this very act, simultaneously being oriented toward itself *as the place where Jesus Christ is present.*[18]

Even in a work as late in Bonhoeffer's life as *Ethics*, he forwards an account of the church defined by Christ's presence.

These quotations evince a consistent thread running through Bonhoeffer's ecclesiological thought throughout the course of his life and written works. Each time Bonhoeffer details the church, he pinpoints the presence of Christ as definitive of the church. In light of this exhaustive consistency across Bonhoeffer's articulations of the church (and his own identification of his ecclesiology with this term), the shorthand phrase *Christus Praesens* is an undeniably appropriate shorthand name for his account of ecclesiology. This book will, therefore, consistently use this identifier in reference to Bonhoeffer's understanding of the church.

BONHOEFFER'S ACCOUNT OF ECCLESIOLOGY

Bonhoeffer's Concept of Person

Bonhoeffer's account of the church is built upon an understanding of the church as the person of Christ. To discuss the church as the person of Christ, it is important to grasp what a person is in general.[19] This concept

---

[16] DBWE 14:446. Italics original.
[17] DBWE 14:449. Italics added for emphasis.
[18] DBWE 6:405. Italics added for emphasis.
[19] Bonhoeffer's concept of person is something of a contentious subject. Clifford Green and Michael DeJonge are largely in agreement with one another, both identifying the concept of person as the

of person does more than just explain the form of the church; it also provides Bonhoeffer's understanding of how persons relate to one another—individually and communally. Studying Bonhoeffer's concept of person, therefore, is crucial for understanding his account of what the church is and what it means to be within that church. This concept is attended to in great detail in Bonhoeffer's dissertation *Sanctorum Communio*.[20] A study of this work reveals a concept of person that operates at both the individual and collective levels, which ultimately yields an understanding of the church as the person of Christ. [21]

---

central category of Bonhoeffer's early works and his theology at large, with Green arguing that Bonhoeffer has a theology of sociality, and DeJonge arguing that Bonhoeffer has a "person theology." Both Green and DeJonge see the concept of person as more or less static and consistent throughout Bonhoeffer's theology. In contrast to these two is Michael Mawson, who argues that the concept of person is not the central category of *Sanctorum Communio*, but rather that Bonhoeffer's concept of person is in service to his account of ecclesiology, which Mawson sees as the central focus of *Sanctorum Communio*. Moreover, Mawson asserts that Bonhoeffer provides three distinct concepts of person in *Sanctorum Communio* alone, along a dialectic of humanity in the primal state, after the fall, and humanity in Christ. This book follows Mawson insofar as it views Bonhoeffer's concept of person as a concept in service to his ecclesiology. This book does not investigate the dialectic that Mawson proposes but would not refute it. Green, Clifford J. *Bonhoeffer: A Theology of Sociality*. Cambridge University Press; Eerdmans, 1999, 28–29 and 63–65; DeJonge, Michael P. *Bonhoeffer's Theological Formation: Berlin, Barth, and Protestant Theology*. Oxford: Oxford University Press, 2012, 7–14; Mawson, Michael G. *Christ Existing as Community: Bonhoeffer's Ecclesiology*. Oxford: Oxford University Press, 2018, 5. For a further account of Bonhoeffer and sociality, see Harvey, Barry. "The Narrow Path: Sociality, Ecclesiology, and the Polyphony of Life in the Thought of Dietrich Bonhoeffer." In *Being Human, Becoming Human: Dietrich Bonhoeffer and Social Thought*, edited by Jens Zimmermann and Brian Gregor, 102–126. Cambridge: James Clarke & Co., 2010.

This book does not address the significance of Bonhoeffer's concept of person for discussions on disability. For such a discussion, see Mawson, Michael. "Creatures Before God: Bonhoeffer, Disability and Theological Anthropology." In *Christ, Church and World: New Studies in Bonhoeffer's Theology and Ethics*, edited by Michael Mawson and Philip G. Ziegler, 119–140. London: Bloomsbury T&T Clark, 2016.

This book, likewise, does not attend to the concept of embodiment as such. For literature on this subject, see Dahill, Lisa E. "Con-Formation with Jesus Christ: Bonhoeffer, Social Location, and Embodiment." In *Being Human, Becoming Human: Dietrich Bonhoeffer and Social Thought*, edited by Jens Zimmermann and Brian Gregor, 176–190. Cambridge: James Clarke & Co., 2010.

[20] The concept of person also features prominently in Bonhoeffer's work in *Act and Being* and "Lectures on Christology." In *Act and Being*, Bonhoeffer discusses the concept of person in light of the concept of revelation. In "Lectures on Christology," he discusses the concept of person with a focus upon the person of Christ. DBWE 2:117–118; DBWE 2:144–146; DBWE 2:151–161; DBWE 12:304–315.

[21] For more on Bonhoeffer's account of humanity and his concept of person, see Marsh, Charles. *Reclaiming Bonhoeffer: The Promise of His Theology*. Cambridge, MA: Oxford University Press, 1994; Busch Nielsen, Kirsten. "Community Turned Inside Out: Dietrich Bonhoeffer's Concept of the Church and Humanity Reconsidered." In *Being Human, Becoming Human: Dietrich Bonhoeffer and Social Thought*, 91–101, 2010. Zimmermann, Jens. "Dietrich Bonhoeffer and Martin Heidegger: Two Different Visions of Humanity." In *Bonhoeffer and Continental Thought: Cruciform Philosophy*, edited by Brian Gregor and Jens Zimmermann, 102–133. Bloomington, IN: Indiana University Press, 2009. Northcott, Michael S. "'Who am I?': Human Identity and the Spiritual Disciplines in the Wisdom of Dietrich Bonhoeffer." In *Who Am I?: Bonhoeffer's Theology Through His Poetry*, edited by Bernd Wannenwetsch, 12–29. London: Bloomsbury, 2009. Peck, William

The Concept of Person at the Individual Level

Sanctorum Communio is a theological study of Christian social philosophy and sociology, which Bonhoeffer posits can truly only be found in an understanding of the church.[22] However, Bonhoeffer brings the concept of person to the forefront of the discussion as the starting point and foundation to the ecclesiology he draws out in the final chapter. He claims that since communities are always related to persons, a study of the community of the church requires a study of "the Christian concept of person."[23]

Bonhoeffer views the concepts of person, community, and God as deeply interrelated.[24] For him, any account of one of these subjects will require an account of the other two. He writes,

> A concept of God is always conceived in relation to a concept of person and a concept of a community of persons . . . [I]n order to arrive at the essence of the Christian concept of community, we could just as well begin with the concept of God as with that of person. [25]

As such, he develops a concept of person which is crucially related to his understanding of community and God. The three concepts are held together. For Bonhoeffer, this ultimately is found in an understanding of the church as the person of Christ.

Jay. "Proposal Concerning Bonhoeffer's Concept of the Person." *Anglican Theological Review* 50, no. 4: 311–329.

    Several thinkers have taken Bonhoeffer's approach to the concept of person—particularly his account of the new humanity and being in Christ—and posited that Bonhoeffer is a Christian humanist. Foremost among these thinkers is Jens Zimmermann. Although this book is in harmony with the work of these thinkers regarding their presentation of the theological construction of Bonhoeffer's account of the new humanity, the book would contend that such an account funds Bonhoeffer's account of discipleship—rather than Christian humanism—as its practical theological content, though the two positions undoubtedly have much in common. De Gruchy, John W. "Dietrich Bonhoeffer as Christian Humanist." In *Being Human, Becoming Human: Dietrich Bonhoeffer and Social Thought,* edited by Jens Zimmermann and Brian Gregor, 3–24. Cambridge: James Clarke & Co., 2010; Zimmermann, Jens. "Being Human Becoming Human: Dietrich Bonhoeffer's Christological Humanism." In *Being Human, Becoming Human: Dietrich Bonhoeffer and Social Thought,* edited by Jens Zimmermann and Brian Gregor, 25–48. Cambridge: James Clarke & Co., 2010; Frick, Peter. "Bonhoeffer's Theology and Economic Humanism: An Exploration in Interdisciplinary Sociality." In *Being Human, Becoming Human: Dietrich Bonhoeffer and Social Thought,* edited by Jens Zimmermann and Brian Gregor, 49–70. Cambridge: James Clarke & Co., 2010; Green, Clifford J. "Sociality, Discipleship, and Worldly Theology in Bonhoeffer's Christian Humanism." In *Being Human, Becoming Human: Dietrich Bonhoeffer and Social Thought,* edited by Jens Zimmermann and Brian Gregor, 71–90. Cambridge: James Clarke & Co., 2010.

[22] DBWE 1:23.
[23] DBWE 1:34.
[24] DBWE 1:34.
[25] DBWE 1:34.

Before he articulates his own concept of person, Bonhoeffer identifies and dispatches four philosophical approaches to the concept of person: an Aristotelian approach, Stoicism, Epicureanism, and an epistemological approach.[26] Bonhoeffer's own approach to the concept of person is largely contrasted with that of the epistemological approach.

Bonhoeffer identifies an epistemological approach with figures such as Kant and Descartes. Kant developed the concept of the reasoning subject as the starting point for an understanding of human existence, and Descartes developed this further ("I think therefore I am"). For Kant, actions are moral or immoral according to what he called the Categorical Imperative, by which he meant actions and principles which can be universalized (meaning they will always be good). Bonhoeffer identifies this epistemological approach to personhood as one in which personhood is found in the pursuit of a universal principle. He rejects this approach to personhood for two reasons. First, such an approach engenders a subject-object account of relationships (meaning that by placing such gravity on the reasoning subject, others are related to simply as objects—things or entities to be known—rather than as persons). Second, Bonhoeffer rejects this approach because by defining personhood in the pursuit of a universal principle, the individuals lose their individuality, becoming only many like beings; furthermore, he rejects this approach because such like beings never experience community, only sameness.[27]

Bonhoeffer explicates his own concept of person following the argumentation of his rejection of an epistemological concept of person. His stance that an epistemological view negates community is due to his claim that social connections cannot be formed simply through the pursuit of a universal principle. Such a pursuit does not require humans to relate to one another. For Bonhoeffer, *personhood can only take place within sociality*, because personhood can only arise in response to someone other than oneself. Bonhoeffer puts it this way: "I enter [the social] sphere *only when my intellect is confronted by some fundamental barrier*."[28] This relationship is what Bonhoeffer calls an "I-You relation," which he uses to replace the epistemological subject-object relation.[29] So, an epistemological approach to personhood presents a reasoning subject that has and maintains its personhood by way of being a reasoning subject, and which comes to know other things (objects, which in this case can mean other people) through its capability to understand

---

[26] Bonhoeffer's stance on these four approaches may or may not depict the viewpoints accurately. This section is only concerned with how Bonhoeffer understands them, rather than a faithful depiction of the viewpoints themselves. DBWE 1:36–43.

[27] Bonhoeffer's account to all four of these approaches can be found in DBWE 1:36–43.

[28] DBWE 1:45.

[29] DBWE 1:52.

those things. From this standpoint, the individual person defines themselves and others around them.

Over against this, Bonhoeffer posits an "I," which is incapable of personhood within itself but becomes a person by being transcended—by encountering another person. Personhood arises "at the moment of being addressed," when "the person enters a state of *responsibility* or, in other words, of decision."[30] The "I" arises when it is addressed by a "You." Such a distinction means that personhood is always tied to a specific concrete situation of *encounter*.[31] Bonhoeffer's concept of person comes from the claim of an other and the moment of having to respond (being responsible).[32] As such, the concept of person is always connected to the concept of community, because personhood requires sociality—it requires an encounter with one other than oneself.

However, to locate the person in the moment of responsibility is not yet to have a *Christian* concept of person. This concept of person is Christian because, for Bonhoeffer, the person "originates only in relation to the divine . . . only in the absolute duality of God and humanity; only in experiencing the barrier does the awareness of oneself as ethical person arise."[33] Basically, a Christian concept of personhood emerges from relation to God. What does this mean? As stated earlier, the person does not arise from within itself but rather must be encountered by one other than oneself. The problem is, according to Bonhoeffer, that because of sin, humans are incapable of encountering each other. In *Act and Being*, Bonhoeffer describes this as *cor curvum in se*—the heart turned in upon itself.[34] Through sin, humans are directed only to themselves, directed only inwardly, and are incapable of encountering or being encountered by another whose heart is also turned in upon itself. Because humans are incapable of breaking free from this self-direction, God must encounter the human and open them back up to the other.

As such, human beings are, from the start, determined by a relationship to God. Michael Mawson draws this out eloquently, writing,

---

[30] DBWE 1:48.
[31] Ulrik Becker Nissen attends to Bonhoeffer's understanding of personhood through encounter. Furthermore, Wayne Floyd has illumined Kant and Hegel as interlocutors for Bonhoeffer's concept of encounter. Nissen, Ulrik Becker. "Responding to Human Reality: Responsibility and Responsiveness in Bonhoeffer's Ethics." In *Being Human, Becoming Human: Dietrich Bonhoeffer and Social Thought,* edited by Jens Zimmermann and Brian Gregor, 191–214. Cambridge: James Clark & Co., 2010; Floyd, Wayne. "Encounter with an Other: Immanuel Kant and G.W.F. Hegel in the Theology of Dietrich Bonhoeffer." In *Bonhoeffer's Intellectual Formation,* edited by Peter Frick, 83–119. Tubingen: Mohr Siebeck, 2008.
[32] DBWE 1:49.
[33] DBWE 1:49.
[34] DBWE 2:137. His use of this phrase draws from Luther.

Bonhoeffer claims that the human being is a person only in its situation or standing before God. God constitutes and affirms the human being as person through a personal address and encounter. More specifically, God addresses and encounters the human being as its transcendent other.[35]

In describing the way in which God encounters the human being, Mawson states, "God addresses and constitutes the human being as person *through a concrete human other* . . . God's claim is mediated for us, essentially and primarily, by other people, and is bound to sociality."[36] Thus, God encounters the human—principally through other people—and opens them up to others. In this way, Bonhoeffer holds together the concepts of person, community, and God.

By locating personhood in the moment of responsibility, it would be possible to mistake Bonhoeffer for attributing personhood to the act or work of another human being. After all, if the claim to responsibility comes from the You, then the I is dependent upon the You. Bonhoeffer is clear, however, that the You does not make someone into an I by their own willing, but rather *"God or the Holy Spirit joins the concrete You; only through God's active working does the other become a You to me from whom my I arises."*[37] At stake in this statement is that it is God who mediates becoming a person rather than other humans.[38] This is how God mediates personhood through the encounter with another person. In his concept of personhood, Bonhoeffer emphasizes the centrality of the work of God. The person originates in relationship with God.[39] It is this relationship of God entering the person as I that

---

[35] Mawson, *Christ Existing as Community*, 62.

[36] Ibid, 64.

[37] DBWE 1:54–55.

[38] DBWE 1:54–56. In other words, even though Bonhoeffer posits personhood in encounter with an other, he does not mean that someone can make an other into a person in a malicious way. It is not that people have the power to abusively install selfhood on someone else; it is an encounter with Christ who calls and shapes the person into Christ's own person.

[39] DBWE 1:54–56.

Ernst Feil argues that in *Sanctorum Communio* Bonhoeffer's concept of person differs from that of *Act and Being* and his later works because, in *Sanctorum Communio*, Bonhoeffer understands the person as encountered by God or the Holy Spirit, with no explicit mention of Christ. Feil further argues, regarding Bonhoeffer's term "Christ existing as church-community" that "neither the use nor the meaning of the phrase manifests an explicitly christological intention. . . . The phrase is meant to show . . . that the church is a collective person." Although this book agrees with Feil's understanding of the Christological emphasis of Bonhoeffer's concept of collective persons, this book would disagree with Feil that Christ has been left out of the encounter in *Sanctorum Communio*. Feil acknowledges that Bonhoeffer argues in *Sanctorum Communio* that "Christ is the sole foundation upon which the edifice of the church rests" and "Communion with God exists only through Christ, but Christ is present only in his church, hence there is communion with God only in the church." Even in light of these quotations, Feil maintains his stance. This book would argue that, even though Bonhoeffer's approach to this encounter is more *explicitly* Christological in *Act and Being and beyond*, the concept of person in *Sanctorum Communio* is still critically Christological as it is Christ's vicarious representative action which creates the new humanity, and leads this concept of person to be constitutive of Bonhoeffer's understanding of the church as it is through this concept that Bonhoeffer is able to connect individuals and communities.

The Concept of Person at the Collective Level

Significant to Bonhoeffer's account of ecclesiology is that his concept of person includes collectives in addition to individual persons. Bonhoeffer's concept of person is not reduced simply to the individual—even the individual in a social sphere of other individuals—rather, it accounts for what he calls "collective persons." [40]

Bonhoeffer develops this concept of collective persons in *Sanctorum Communio* in a discussion on original sin.[41] Classically, the doctrine of original sin has been presented as the following: Adam sinned in the Garden of Eden, and all of humanity itself fell with Adam in that sin, meaning that human nature has been ontologically disfigured and fallen as a result of Adam's action. Bonhoeffer does not follow this account of original sin but instead re-narrates it. Bonhoeffer identifies the purpose of the doctrine of original sin as *"finding the act of the whole in the sinful individual act*, without making the one the reason for the other."[42] In other words, Bonhoeffer wants to narrate original sin in a way that depicts sin as an act that is individual and at the same time the act of all of humanity, without claiming that the sinfulness of the whole of humanity (or, in the classical sense, Adam's sin) is the reason for the sinful individual act. This re-narration shifts the focus away from the idea that the individual sinful acts that have taken place since Adam's sin are due to Adam's sin. For Bonhoeffer, it is not the case that one can simply blame Adam's act for their own sinfulness.

Instead of positing Adam's sin as the reason for all subsequent sins, Bonhoeffer argues that in each individual sin, all of humanity falls. Or, as Bonhoeffer puts it: "All humanity falls with each sin, and not one of us is in principle different from Adam; that is, everyone is also the 'first' sinner."[43] This move holds every person accountable for their sin while attributing it to the sinfulness of the whole. In this way, all of humanity is culpable for each individual sin and each sinner represents all of humanity in their sinful act.[44] Thus, in each individual sinful act, all of humanity falls with that sin.

---

it is the person of Christ who is the new humanity. Feil, Ernst. *The Theology of Dietrich Bonhoeffer*. Minneapolis: Fortress Press, 1985, 61–64.

[40] DBWE 1:121.
[41] DBWE 1:109–121.
[42] DBWE 1:115.
[43] DBWE 1. 115.
[44] DBWE 1:115.

It is precisely in this relation of the individual to the whole that Bonhoeffer's concept of person develops its collective level—collective persons. The collective fall of humanity in each individual sinful act evinces a collective person. This is what Bonhoeffer calls the collective person of Adam. The collective person of Adam is the collective person that takes shape around each and every individual sin as humanity falls with each act. It is a collective person, but it is not one that experiences community. Because this collective person is determined by the collection of the sinful and self-directed individuals, the collective person of Adam is characterized by isolation and self-will—closed in upon itself. Bonhoeffer writes, "The structure of humanity-in-Adam is unique because it is both composed of many isolated individuals and yet is one, as the humanity that has sinned as a whole."[45] Thus, the collective person of Adam is the collective person that is formed in each sinful act—it is a collective person of isolated individuals who are turned in upon themselves.

In contrast to the collective person of Adam, Bonhoeffer describes the collective person of Christ.[46] Humanity falls in the collective person of Adam; humanity rises in the collective person of Christ. In order to draw out the structure of this collective person, it is necessary first to detail an important concept in Bonhoeffer's works—vicarious representative action (*Stellvertretung*). Clifford Green, in his editor's commentary to the English edition of *Sanctorum Communio*, describes what is meant in the German word *Stellvertretung*, writing, "Literally the word means to represent in place of another—to act, advocate, intercede on behalf of another."[47] As such, vicarious representative action means to act in place of another. It is a deliberate act of representation. For Bonhoeffer, vicarious representative action is principally Christological—it is something Christ does before it can even be imagined that another human being might do it.

Specifically, Christ acts as vicarious representative for all of humanity. Jesus' vicarious representative actions is found in the entirety of his incarnate life. The very act of becoming human was an act on behalf of humanity. All of Christ's sinless, human life, his death, his resurrection, his ascension, and his ongoing intercession are included in the vicarious representative action he does on behalf of humanity. It is through this vicarious representative action that Christ re-creates humanity into the new humanity, which is the collective person of Christ. Just as humanity falls in each individual sinful act as the collective person of Adam, humanity is re-created into the collective person

---

[45] DBWE 1:121.

[46] DBWE 1:121.

[47] DBWE 1:120.

of Christ, the new humanity, through the vicarious representative action of Christ. In this collective person of Christ, community with God is restored.[48]

The question could be raised as to why Adam's action does not qualify as vicarious representative action. Bonhoeffer identifies two distinct differences between Adam's (and our) action and Christ's action. The first is that Adam's (and our) action is only *incidentally* representative, while Christ's is *deliberately* so. Bonhoeffer clarifies, "Adam does not intentionally act as a vicarious representative; on the contrary, Adam's action is extremely egocentric. That its effect closely resembles a deliberately vicarious representative action must not obscure the *entirely different basic premise*."[49] Although Adam's action is representative, it is not action deliberately done for others, but specifically done selfishly, seeking only gain for oneself.

The second difference is that Christ's action is permanent. It is done once and for all. It is finished. Bonhoeffer states, "In the old humanity the whole of humanity falls anew . . . with every person who sins; in Christ, however, humanity has been brought once and for all—this is essential to *real* vicarious representative action—into community with God."[50] There is finality to the collective person of Christ. The collective person of Christ is not one that will fall and need re-creation. The collective person of Christ is established and will have no end. The collective person of Christ is forever.

More must be said of the collective person of Christ. In his life, death, and resurrection, Christ acts as vicarious representative for humanity, thereby creating the new humanity. But what does any of this have to do with the church? This collective person of Christ *is* the church. Bonhoeffer writes,

> The church-community exists through Christ's action. . . . The relation of Christ to the church is twofold. Christ is the foundation. . . . But Christ is also at all times a real presence for the church, for it is Christ's body, and the people are members of his body.[51]

The church is to be understood as the person of Christ.[52] Christ encounters those who are turned in upon themselves and breaks them open to encounter

---

[48] DBWE 1:146; DBWE 1:155–157.

[49] DBWE 1:146.

[50] DBWE 1:146.

[51] DBWE 1:137–139.

[52] DBWE 1:158. Bonhoeffer discusses the person of Christ at greater length in his "Lectures on Christology." DBWE 12:300–360.

     For more on Bonhoeffer's account of Christology, see Hooton, Peter. "Community and Christology in the Theology of Dietrich Bonhoeffer." *St Mark's Review* 233 (October 2015): 26–41. Aveling, Harry G. "Dietrich Bonhoeffer's Christology." *Colloquium* 16, no. 1 (October 1983): 23–30.

Christ and other people. In doing so, Christ creates the new humanity within himself—a collective person characterized by community rather than isolation. This community will be discussed in greater detail in the chapter's later discussion of Christ's presence in the church as church-community. Important for the present topic is that Bonhoeffer understands the church as a person—specifically, the new humanity, the collective person of Christ, created through Christ's vicarious representative action. What Bonhoeffer intends in his understanding of the church, therefore, is an understanding that the church itself is the present person of Christ. As the collective person of Christ, the church is defined as a person rather than an institution. Thus, when Bonhoeffer speaks of the church as *Christus Preasens*, he envisions a church that is a person, the person of Christ.

To be clear, the collective person of Adam and the collective person of Christ are not two options at a human being's disposal to simply choose to be a part of one and not the other. Instead, all partake in the collective person of Adam. It is only through an encounter with Christ—an encounter in which the human is called to responsibility before Christ—that Christ creates the human into the person of Christ, bringing the human into the church, which is the collective person of Christ.[53]

To summarize, persons are formed in an encounter with an other; such an encounter is only possible through Christ who encounters, addresses, and makes a claim upon us. Collective persons are formed when an individual acts on behalf of the species. There are two collective persons, that of Adam, in whom every member is both individual and species in their sinful action, and that of Christ, in whom only Christ acts on behalf of humanity through his vicarious representative action to create the new humanity. Finally, in Christ's action to create the new humanity (which is the church-community), he himself *becomes* the new humanity, *becomes* the church. Thus, Bonhoeffer's concept of person is crucial to his account of ecclesiology. At stake in his concept of person is the structure of the church as the person of Christ, as expressed in Bonhoeffer's account of the church as *Christus Praesens*.

Philip Ziegler has written about Christology and what it implies for a concept of humanity in the theology of Bonhoeffer and John Calvin. Ziegler, Philip Gordon. "The Humanity of Divinity." *Union Seminary Quarterly Review* 65, no. 1–2 (2015): 171–180.

[53] The ongoing capability of those within the church to sin is addressed in chapter 3 and is pertinent both to Bonhoeffer's concept of discipleship (drawn out in chapter 4) and to his ecumenical theology (chapter 5).

Bonhoeffer's Concept of Revelation

The previous section established Bonhoeffer's concept of person and how
it relates to the church. The section described personhood as intrinsically
social, requiring encounter, and how human beings need Christ to open them
up to be able to encounter others, being unable to do so in and of themselves
because of the manner in which sin turns the individual in upon themselves.
It was demonstrated that Bonhoeffer understands the church as a person—
specifically, as the person of Christ, which Christ creates and is through his
vicarious representative action on humanity's behalf. This understanding of
the church as the person of Christ means that Bonhoeffer's understanding of
the church is crucially determined by revelation.

Revelation is concerned with how God is known. It asks, how does God
reveal Godself to humanity? At a fundamental level, this means that the
question of revelation is one that is always important to have in mind when
considering an understanding of the church. How do we know God? How do
we know that any theology is not simply something made up? We know God
because God reveals Godself to us.

The critical question that follows after this is, how does God reveal Godself
to us? God reveals Godself to us in Jesus Christ. God chose to reveal Godself
to us by becoming human in Jesus Christ. Jesus is God, so, in knowing Jesus,
we know God. This is revelation at a basic level.

Revelation is an integral facet of Bonhoeffer's ecclesiology because he
understands the church as the collective person of Christ. If the church is the
collective person of Christ, then the church (understood as person rather than
institution) is the place where Christ reveals himself to be known today. In
Sanctorum Communio, Bonhoeffer writes,

> The concept of the church is conceivable only in the sphere of reality established
> by God. . . . *The reality of the church is a reality of revelation . . . there is no
> relation to Christ in which the relation to the church is not necessarily estab-
> lished as well.*[54]

Put another way, the church is established by God in Christ's vicarious representative action; knowing Christ takes place in an encounter with Christ,
which calls one to responsibility and draws them into the collective person of
Christ; that collective person of Christ is the church that Christ established.
Thus, the church is critically defined by revelation, because it is the place
where God is encountered in Jesus Christ—the place where God reveals
Godself.

---

[54] DBWE 1:127.

In order to grasp the impact of an understanding of the church that is crucially determined by revelation, it is helpful to investigate what revelation requires. Bonhoeffer explores this topic in his second dissertation, *Act and Being*, as he attempts to find an adequate theological solution to what he calls "the problem of act and being"—essentially, the question as to whether human existence derives from act (thinking and doing) or being (from ontology).[55] In Bonhoeffer's estimation, any philosophical solution to the problem of act and being can be tested to see if it is adequate as a *theological* solution to the problem of act and being when that solution is applied to the concepts of God and revelation. Doing so required Bonhoeffer to provide a thorough consideration of the concept of revelation.[56]

Christiane Tietz has rightly asserted that, for Bonhoeffer, a concept of revelation requires a "historical dimension" and a "God-established dimension."[57] Put differently, revelation must be understood to be founded by an action of God and to happen in history. However, to say that Bonhoeffer's concept of revelation necessitates a historical dimension and a God-established dimension does not yet encapsulate the *concreteness* of Bonhoeffer's concept of revelation. Therefore, the section adds two more criteria to Tietz's assessment: Bonhoeffer insists that the revelation must affect human being, and revelation must have continuity.[58] Both of these distinctions contain the historical and God-established dimensions that Tietz identified, adding to those dimensions their necessary concreteness. For Bonhoeffer, these four qualifiers of revelation (historical dimension, God-established dimension, affected human being, and continuity) must all be satisfied for an adequate concept of revelation. While Bonhoeffer did not explicitly provide these in a list of criteria for a concept of revelation, he rejects any concept of revelation in which one or more of these criteria are not satisfied. Ultimately, Bonhoeffer concludes that revelation is to be understood in the church as the revelatory person of Christ.[59]

That Bonhoeffer defines the being of revelation as the person of Christ is clear when he writes, "[t]he being of revelation 'is,' rather, the being of the community of persons that is constituted and formed by the person of Christ and in which individuals already find themselves in their new existence."[60] The chapter's earlier discussion of Bonhoeffer's concept of person illumined

---

[55] DBWE 2:25, 29.
[56] DBWE 2:25–31.
[57] Tietz, Christiane. "Bonhoeffer on the Ontological Structure of the Church." In *Ontology and Ethics: Bonhoeffer and Contemporary Scholarship*, edited by Adam C. Clark and Michael Mawson, 32–46. Pickwick Publications, 2013, 36.
[58] DBWE 2:82; 108.
[59] DBWE 2:110–111.
[60] DBWE 2:113.

that Christ both creates and *is* the new humanity through who he is and his vicarious representative action on behalf of humankind in his death and resurrection; it was thus seen that in the person of Christ, the individual is drawn into the collective person of Christ and that that person of Christ exists in the world today as the church. It is in this same person of Christ that Bonhoeffer identifies his understanding of revelation.[61] But, how does this concept of the church as the person of Christ line up with and satisfy these four criteria for an adequate concept of revelation?

Bonhoeffer's understanding of the church as the person of Christ satisfies the criterion that revelation be God-established both in its being as God's self-revelation in Christ and in Christ's action in creating the new humanity.[62] Simply by claiming the church as the person of Christ, Bonhoeffer posits already the revelation found in the church to be God-established as Christ himself is the revelation of God. Furthermore, Bonhoeffer shows the church as the revelatory person of Christ to be God-established in his assertion that "the church is rather the community of faith created by and founded upon Christ, in which Christ is revealed as the δεύτερος ἄνθρωπος, as the new human, or rather, as the new humanity itself."[63] Put differently, Christ's act of creating the new humanity in his vicarious representative action determines that revelation in the church as the person of Christ is God-established.

Second, Bonhoeffer's concept of revelation in the church as the revelatory person of Christ takes place historically in Christ's presence in the church today. Bonhoeffer claims as much, writing that Christian revelation must

> be thought in the church, for the church is the present Christ, "Christ existing as community." In the proclamation of the community of faith for the community of faith, Christ is the "subject" common to the proclamation (Word and sacrament) and the community of faith alike.[64]

In this quotation, Bonhoeffer identifies that Christ's person is present in the church today both as the church-community itself and as its proclamation through Word and sacrament. As such, revelation maintains its contingent character and satisfies the criterion that revelation take place within history.

Third, that the person of Christ is present as the church-community and as Word and sacrament leads to the manner in which the *continuity* of revelation is upheld in the church as the person of Christ because the continuity

---

[61] DBWE 2:113.
[62] DBWE 2:112.
[63] DDWE 2:112.
[64] DBWE 2:111.

of revelation demands that revelation is "always present."[65] This continual presence is located, for Bonhoeffer, in the collective person of Christ.[66] Specifically, Bonhoeffer argues that "continuity does not lie in human beings, but rather it is guaranteed suprapersonally through a community of persons" which is "Christ's community of faith."[67] In other words, revelation in the church as the person of Christ has continuity due to its being as the collective person of Christ, who is present in the church-community, Word, and sacraments. Thus, the church as the person of Christ upholds the continuity of revelation.

Finally, Bonhoeffer's understanding of the church as the person of Christ fulfils his criterion that revelation *affect human being* in his claim that, in the collective person of Christ, the human being is transformed from the old humanity of Adam to the new humanity of Christ.[68] The chapter's earlier discussion on Bonhoeffer's concept of person clarified that only Christ can encounter human beings in a person-forming way. The same remains true in regard to the person of Christ as revelation; human beings are encountered and formed into the new humanity only through the person of Christ.[69] For Bonhoeffer, the person of Christ truly affects human being as, through participating in the person of Christ, the human being is actually "transposed into a new manner of existence."[70] As such, Bonhoeffer's understanding of the church as the person of Christ satisfies the criterion that revelation affect human being.

Therefore, Bonhoeffer's account of the church as the person of Christ satisfies his criteria for an adequate account of revelation. This concept of revelation in *Act and Being* is consistent with Bonhoeffer's work in *Sanctorum Communio* and "Lectures on Christology." In *Sanctorum Communio*, Bonhoeffer argues that "the New Testament knows a form of revelation, 'Christ existing as church-community.'"[71] Here already, Bonhoeffer understands the church as the revelatory person of Christ. Likewise, in "Lectures on Christology," Bonhoeffer claims that the question at hand is "that of the very revelation of God" and describes Christ's presence in the church as Word, sacrament, and church-community, thus highlighting not only that the

---

[65] DBWE 2:113.
[66] DBWE 2:113–114.
[67] DBWE 2:114.
[68] DBWE 2:113.
[69] DBWE 2:114.
[70] DBWE 2:120.
[71] DBWE 1:141.

person of Christ has to do with revelation but that revelation is understood in the same manner presented in *Act and Being*.[72]

Taken together, Bonhoeffer's concepts of person and revelation reveal what the church *is* in Bonhoeffer's ecclesiology. For Bonhoeffer, the church is the present revelatory person of Christ. The church is a person through Christ's vicarious representative action on humanity's behalf to create the new humanity in himself. As Christ encounters people, they are called to responsibility and drawn into the collective person of Christ; they are broken free from their self-direction to encounter Christ and others and transformed into the collective person of Christ. As the collective person of Christ, the church is revelatory, because it is the place where God reveals Godself in the person of Jesus Christ. This is what the church is for Bonhoeffer. It is not an institution or an agreed-upon set of doctrines. The church is the revelatory person of Christ.

The Church as the Present Christ

Bonhoeffer understands the church as *Christus Praesens*, as Christ's presence. The previous sections developed what the church is in such an understanding—the revelatory person of Christ. As the person of Christ (the revelation of Godself) created through Christ's vicarious representative action on humanity's behalf, the church is the revelatory person of Christ. But this has not yet accounted for *how* Christ is present in the church. If the church is "the presence of Christ on earth" and "has the task of speaking [Christ's] word to the entire world," then it is clear that Christ's presence in the church is central to the structure and activity of Bonhoeffer's account of ecclesiology.[73] In "Lectures on Christology," Bonhoeffer argues that Christ is present in the church in three ways: as Word, as sacrament, and as church-community.[74] Attending to these three ways in which Christ is present in the

---

[72] DBWE 12:308; 314.

    For more on Bonhoeffer's concept of revelation, see Kelly, Geffrey B. "Revelation in Christ: A Study of Bonhoeffer's Theology of Revelation." *Ephemerides Theologicae Lovanienses* 50, no. 1 (May 1974): 39–74.

[73] DBWE 11:358–359.

    Similar but different to Bonhoeffer, who sees the ecumenical movement as church, is the WCC which sees itself as a "fellowship of churches." A big difference here is that, while the WCC asks that member churches recognize *elements* of the "true Church" in all of its members, the WCC does not recognize any particular member church as completely identifiable with the true Church. Constitution, 1; TS: IV.5.

    Garcia also discusses Bonhoeffer's understanding of Christ's presence in the church, doing so to argue that "Bonhoeffer's Christology relies on an intensified participation that is similar to Calvin's." Garcia, *Recovering the Ecumenical Bonhoeffer*, 51–61.

[74] DBWE 12:315.

church draws out Bonhoeffer's account of the church and the activity of those therein.[75]

Before discussing Christ's threefold presence in the church, however, it is important to mention that—although a conception of the church as *Christus Praesens* is crucially determined by Christology—it should not be thought that Bonhoeffer's account of ecclesiology is *purely* Christological (meaning it would be inadequately Trinitarian). Bonhoeffer's understanding of the church as *Christus Praesens* locates his ecclesiology under the doctrine of God. Bonhoeffer's understanding of the origin of the church accounts for each of the three articles of the Trinity.[76] As such, Bonhoeffer's account of ecclesiology does not index ecclesiology to Christology to the *exclusion* of the other two articles of the Trinity.[77] It is worth briefly mentioning the roles of each article of the Trinity in Bonhoeffer's understanding of the church's origin in order to demonstrate that his ecumenical theology is adequately Trinitarian.[78]

Bonhoeffer does not provide a systematic account of the Trinity.[79] In fact, doing so would go against his entire approach to epistemology and revelation. In "Lectures on Christology," Bonhoeffer writes, "It is wrong to derive the God's becoming human from an idea, such as the idea of the Trinity."[80] Bonhoeffer's refusal to systematize an account of the Trinity stems from his conviction that the epistemological access point of theology is revelation, and revelation takes place in an encounter with Christ.[81] Put differently, God is only knowable if God reveals Godself, and God has revealed Godself in Jesus Christ. Such an epistemological access point denies an account of the

---

[75] Bonhoeffer's account of ecclesiology and his approach to the church is also attended to in Moses, "Dietrich Bonhoeffer's Concept of the 'True' Church." See also Tang, Andres S.K. "The Ecclesiology of Dietrich Bonhoeffer: Reflections on *Sanctorum Communio*." *Hill Road* 7, no. 2 (December 2004): 71–80.

[76] Christopher R. J. Holmes has argued that Bonhoeffer's theology would benefit from a more robust account of the Trinity, and he has ventured to supplement Bonhoeffer's account of the doctrine of God. Holmes, Christopher R. J. "Beyond Bonhoeffer in Loyalty to Bonhoeffer: Reconsidering Bonhoeffer's Christological Aversion to Theological Metaphysics." In *Christ, Church and World: New Studies in Bonhoeffer's Theology and Ethics,* edited by Michael Mawson and Philip G. Ziegler, 29–44. London: Bloomsbury T&T Clark, 2016.
Chapter 3 section 1.ii details how each article of the Trinity works in founding the *visible* church.

[77] Pangritz, Andreas. "Who is Christ for Us Today?" In *The Cambridge Companion to Dietrich Bonhoeffer*, edited by John De Gruchy, 134–153. Cambridge: Cambridge University Press, 1999.

[78] "Theological and Historical Background of the WCC Basis." World Council of Churches. https://www.oikoumene.org/en/resources/documents/other/theological-and-historical-background-of-the-wcc-basis (February 20, 2019).

[79] Green has argued that "the doctrine of the Trinity is an unquestioned presupposition of Bonhoeffer's theology." Green, Clifford J. "Trinity and Christology in Bonhoeffer and Barth." *Union Seminary Quarterly Review* 60, no. 1–2 (2006): 1–22.

[80] DBWE 12:355.

[81] DBWE 12:314.

Trinity in the traditional sense because to begin from a systematic account of the Trinity would already be to work around revelation as the epistemological access point of theology. A refusal to systematize an account of the Trinity, however, does not mean that there *is* no Trinity in Bonhoeffer's thought. Indeed, Bonhoeffer's account of ecclesiology necessitates a triune God, even without a systematic account of the Trinity.

Previously, the chapter detailed Bonhoeffer's concept of Christ's vicarious representative action. According to Bonhoeffer's thinking in this concept, Christ both creates and is the new humanity through his vicarious representative action on the cross; this new humanity is the church-community. As such, Bonhoeffer asserts that Christ *realizes* the church.[82] Put differently, in Christ's action of creating the new humanity by his death on the cross and his resurrection, the church becomes a reality—the church as the revelatory person of Christ.[83] While it is certainly true that Christology plays a core role in Bonhoeffer's account of ecclesiology, it would be wrong to imagine any account of the economy (even with regard to the doctrine of appropriations) in which the indivisibility of the Father, Son, and Holy Spirit in the economy was not accounted for.

Bonhoeffer regularly details the work of the Holy Spirit when writing about the origin of the church.[84] Although the church has been *realized* in Christ, it is *actualized* by the Holy Spirit.[85] Put differently, the Holy Spirit makes concretely historical what Christ has made a reality.[86] Two things must be said of the Holy Spirit's activity in Bonhoeffer's account of the

---

[82] DBWE 1:152.

[83] DBWE 1:153.

    Christiane Tietz has argued that Bonhoeffer's theology is directed to and from his account of Chrisology; that his theology is built around Christ's self-revelation. Tietz, Christiane. "The Role of Jesus Christ for Christian Theology." In *Christ, Church and World: New Studies in Bonhoeffer's Theology and Ethics,* edited by Michael Mawson and Philip G. Ziegler, 9–28. London: Bloomsbury T&T Clark, 2016.

[84] Mawson has attended to the relationship of Bonhoeffer's accounts of pneumatology and ecclesiology in his early theology. Although Mawson's interests chiefly concern hamartiology, his work is useful for this discussion of Bonhoeffer's understanding of the Spirit and the founding of the church. Mawson, Michael G. "The Spirit and the Community: Pneumatology and Ecclesiology in Jenson, Hütter and Bonhoeffer." *International Journal of Systematic Theology* 15, no. 4 (October 2013): 453–468.

[85] DBWE 1:152.

[86] Greggs, in the first volume of his *Dogmatic Ecclesiology*, likewise highlights the work of the Spirit in establishing the church. He writes: "A theological account of the church begins with an account of the *Theos* by and through whom the church comes into being. The church is unlike every human community or society in one profound and fundamental way: the church is a community which is a creature of the event of the intensity of the Holy Spirit's economy of grace in redeeming creation. Although the church shares in many—if not all—of the characteristics of other organizations, its primary existence is ultimately distinct from every other expression of human sociality. The church comes into being as an event of the act of the lordship of the Holy Spirit of God who gives the church life." Greggs, Tom. *Dogmatic Ecclesiology Volume 1: The Priestly Catholicity of the Church.* Grand Rapids: Baker Academic, 2019, 2.

origin of the church. First, the Holy Spirit is seen to be integral to the origin of the church. It is the work of the Holy Spirit bringing Christ to the individuals and creating the community that actualizes the church.[87] Second, Bonhoeffer makes explicit that Christ's presence in the church is due to the Holy Spirit.[88] In other words, the Holy Spirit plays a necessary role in creating the church, and that role supports Christ's presence in the church as church-community.

The economy of the Father in the origin of the church is not so easily discerned in Bonhoeffer's writings as that of the Son and the Holy Spirit. In his early writings, Bonhoeffer does not make explicit the precise role of the Father in the origin of the church. Writing on the *visible* church in particular, however, Bonhoeffer identifies the Father as the creator of the visible church.[89] Specifically, he describes the church as "a new act of creation on God's part."[90] Additionally, when Bonhoeffer describes Christ's vicarious representative action, he describes it as being done before the Father for forgiveness. It is clear both in the forgiveness of the Father and in this statement regarding the Father as the creator of the church, that the Father plays an integral and creative—if systematically underdeveloped—role in Bonhoeffer's understanding of the origin and creation of the church. Thus, the account of the church as *Christus Praesens* is attributed to the work of each of the articles of the Trinity.

The account of ecclesiology itself is constructed along the lines of Christ's threefold presence in the church. Narrating Christ's threefold presence in the church establishes Bonhoeffer's account of ecclesiology. More than this, however, Christ's threefold presence in the church forwards three important claims. First, Christ's presence in the church is constitutive of the church, meaning that the church is comprised of Christ's presence. Second, the creation of the church is a work of divine agency, meaning that the church is not created by humans. Finally, Christ's presence in the church and the work of divine agency to create and sustain the church frame the work of the human agent, which is discipleship. In other words, *God acts to create space within God's own acting for humans to act within the church, and the action of the human agent within the church is discipleship.* Because this ecclesiology is the foundation of Bonhoeffer's ecumenical theology, these same claims hold true for his ecumenical theology.

---

[87] DBWE 4:221.
[88] DBWE 4:221.
[89] DBWE 14:442.
[90] DBWE 14:442.

Christ's Presence in the Church as Word

When Bonhoeffer writes about Christ's presence as Word, he does so from a Lutheran understanding of the theology of the Word.[91] This Lutheran understanding of the Word is Christologically focused as Christ's presence and address to the church.[92] In "Lectures on Christology," Bonhoeffer argues that Christ as Word does not indicate a universal concept or an idea, but rather identifies an address between *persons*—specifically Christ's address to the human.[93] He sees this address as Christ's presence in the church's preaching.[94]

The first thing that must be said of Christ's presence as Word is that Christ is present as Word as *person*.[95] Bonhoeffer expresses Christ's presence as Word as an address "between two persons, as speaking and response, responsibility."[96] This starting point of an address between two persons is significant in light of the chapter's earlier discussion of personhood. There, it was demonstrated that Bonhoeffer's understanding of personhood is built upon an encounter with an other—an other who can only be Christ. To phrase Christ's presence as Word as an address between two persons, in which the one addressed is called to responsibility, determines that Christ is present as Word as person in the manner which personhood was previously established.

Christ's presence in the church as Word has three implications. First, the person-forming way in which Christ encounters human beings as Word makes his presence as Word a constitutive factor of the church. If the church

---

[91] DeJonge provides a thorough account of the influence of Luther upon Bonhoeffer's theology. DeJonge, Michael P. *Bonhoeffer's Reception of Luther.* Oxford: Oxford University Press, 2017.
   For more on Bonhoeffer's understanding of the Word, see Ziegler, Philip G. "Dietrich Bonhoeffer: Theologian of the Word." In *Bonhoeffer, Christ, and Culture,* edited by Keith L. Johnson and Timothy Larsen, 17–37. Nottingham: InterVarsity Press, 2013.

[92] For a reading of how the authority of scripture relates to the role of writing biblical commentary—considered alongside Bonhoeffer's commentary of the Sermon on the Mount, see Neumann, Katja. "The Authority of Discipleship: An Approach to Dietrich Bonhoeffer's Commentary on the Sermon on the Mount." *Vision (Winnipeg, Man.)* 13, no. 2 (Fall 2012): 78–86.

[93] DBWE 12:316.

[94] DBWE 12:317.
   Bonhoeffer also discusses Christ's presence as Word in scripture. To summarize, Christ's presence as Word in scripture is a qualified presence. Christ is present as Word in scripture as the Word spoken to His church-community through scripture (DBWE 1:232). The book itself and the words themselves do not subjugate Christ, rather Christ subjugates the words of scripture (DBWE 1:232). Yet Christ is present as Word in scripture (DBWE 1:232). Christ's church-community encounters him in scripture in the simple obedience of discipleship that waits to hear the concrete command of Christ and responds with the obedience of faith (DBWE 4:77).
   For more on Bonhoeffer's approach to scripture, see Kelly, Geffrey B. and F. Burton Nelson. "Dietrich Bonhoeffer's Theological Interpretation of Scripture for the Church." *Ex Auditu* 17 (2001): 1–30; Rochelle, Jay C. "Bonhoeffer: Community, Authority, and Spirituality." *Currents in Theology and Mission* 21, no. 2 (April 1994): 117–122; Plant, Stephen J. *Taking Stock of Bonhoeffer: Studies in Biblical Interpretation and Ethics.* Surrey: Ashgate Publishing Limited, 2014; especially 43–59.

[95] DBWE 12:316.

[96] DBWE 12:316.

is the collective person of Christ and the Word is a place in which the human being encounters Christ and is called into personhood—thereby entering into the collective person of Christ—then it is clear that Christ's presence as Word is a constitutive factor of the church. Indeed, in *Sanctorum Communio*, Bonhoeffer writes, "The church-community is created only through the word and sustained by it."[97]

Second, Christ's presence as Word is a work of divine agency. One way Christ is present in the church as Word is in the sermon.[98] That human beings are encountered by Christ in the sermon means Christ is present as Word in the sermon as the revelatory person of Christ. To say as much is not to say that the preacher makes Christ present in the sermon by their own work; instead, Christ is present in the sermon as Christ *wills to be present* and the preacher is only an instrument of Christ's presence coming through the sermon.[99] Put differently, it is not the case that simply anything the preacher wants to say is the Word of God and the presence of Christ; rather, Christ's presence in the sermon is always due to Christ's will to be present and findable there. The efficacy of the sermon is due to Christ's presence in it as Word. Thus, Christ's presence in the sermon is a work of divine agency. What then is the role of the human agent regarding the sermon? The role of the human agent regarding the sermon is discipleship—to hear and obey Christ as he is encountered in the Word in the sermon.[100] This is the final implication of Christ's presence as Word: it frames the work of the human agent as discipleship. Whether as preacher or as congregant, the role is the same. Both the preacher and those listening to the sermon are called to hear and obey Christ as he is encountered in the sermon.

Christ's Presence in the Church as Sacrament

Writing as a Protestant theologian, Bonhoeffer recognizes the two sacraments of baptism and Eucharist.[101] For Bonhoeffer, Christ is present in the church in both of these sacraments. In "Lectures on Christology," Bonhoeffer relates Christ's presence in sacrament closely to his presence as Word, defining sacrament as the following:

---

[97] DBWE 1:232.

[98] DBWE 1:232.

[99] DBWE 1:235.

[100] Bonhoeffer's approach to preaching is also attended to in Greggs, Tom. "Ecclesial Priestly Mediation in the Theology of Dietrich Bonhoeffer." *Theology Today* 71, no. 1 (April 2014): 81–91. See also Owens, L Roger. "Preaching as Participation: Dietrich Bonhoeffer's Christology of Preaching." *Currents in Theology and Mission* 36, no. 1 (February 2009): 47–54.

[101] DBWE 1:240–247. Christopher Dodson has illumined Bonhoeffer's understanding of sacrament. Dodson, Christopher. "The God Who Is Given: Bonhoeffer's Sacramental Theology and His Critique of Religion." PhD dissertation, University of Aberdeen, 2016.

The sacrament is Word of God, for it proclaims the gospel, not as a wordless action, but as action that is made holy and given its meaning by the Word. The promise of "forgiveness of sins" makes the sacrament what it is.[102]

Soon after, Bonhoeffer expands upon this definition, writing,

Sacrament exists only where God, in the midst of the world of creatures, names an element, speaks to it, and hallows it with the particular word God has for it by giving it its name. Through God's speaking to it, this element becomes what it is.[103]

Taken together, these two statements provide the core of Bonhoeffer's understanding of the sacraments and Christ's presence therein. First, a sacrament is wholly defined, created by, and comprised of Christ. Second, the physical elements of the sacrament have meaning only because God has given it its name—which Bonhoeffer goes on to identify as Jesus Christ.[104] This broad definition of sacrament by Bonhoeffer leads to the same three observations as were made regarding Christ's presence in the church as Word.

Baptism is constitutive of the church-community due to the orientation of baptism toward Christ's work to create the new humanity (the church-community) in his death and resurrection. Specifically, baptism incorporates someone into the church-community, or, as Bonhoeffer writes in *Discipleship*, "Baptism makes us members of the body of Christ."[105] Baptism is therefore one of the ways that the church is built as, in it, people are brought into the new humanity that is the church. To say that baptism is constitutive of the church, however, does not mean that the cultic act of baptism—the sprinkling of, or submerging in, water itself—creates the church.

Bonhoeffer is clear that baptism is a work of divine agency when he calls it a "passive action" on the part of the human agent.[106] Specifically, Bonhoeffer claims that baptism is an offer from Jesus, instead of an act that the human offers God.[107] Bonhoeffer makes this claim on the basis that baptism is baptism into Jesus Christ—that is, into Christ's death and resurrection.[108] At play in this claim is everything that has been discussed regarding Christ as revelatory person. In baptism, the old humanity dies and rises as the new humanity—and it does so on the basis of Christ's own dying and rising, through

---

[102] DBWE 12:318.
[103] DBWE 12:319.
[104] DBWE 12:319.
[105] DBWE 4:216.
[106] DBWE 4:216.
[107] DBWE 4:216.
[108] DBWE 4:207–208.

which Christ both creates and is the new humanity.[109] It is in this way, as revelatory person, that Christ is present in baptism. Thus, it is not the cultic act of baptism that makes it efficacious, but rather it is Christ's vicarious representative action, his presence in baptism, and his sending of the Holy Spirit to dwell with those baptized that make baptism effective.[110]

That said, Bonhoeffer maintains that baptism demands a "visible act of obedience," which is where the role of the human agent in baptism is found.[111] Baptism is an obedient act of stepping into God's call to discipleship, where one is claimed and transformed by Christ into the new humanity—the church-community. The role of the human agent in baptism, therefore, is discipleship. That much is clear when Bonhoeffer writes,

> What the Synoptics describe as hearing and following the call to discipleship, Paul expresses with the concept of *baptism*. . . . The disciple who followed Jesus in the community of the cross received no other gift than the believer who was baptized according to Paul's teaching.[112]

This quotation highlights baptism as a place in which Christ's call to discipleship is heard, and therefore the human agent is called to baptism as an obedient act of discipleship.[113]

In sum, Bonhoeffer's treatment of baptism in *Discipleship* presents it as a passive act of obedient discipleship on the part of human agents, in which they are claimed by Christ's person-forming action on their behalf and transformed into the new humanity (the church-community). As such, baptism is shown to be primarily a work of divine agency, as Christ is present in it as person in his death and resurrection and in the sending of the Holy Spirit to live within those in the church-community. The result is baptism as a place in which Christ is present in the church, further illustrating how Christ's presence is constitutive of the church.

Bonhoeffer's treatment of Christ's presence in the church in the Eucharist bears the marks of the preceding ways in which Christ is present in the church. The manner in which Christ is present in the Eucharist again identifies that, for Bonhoeffer, the origin and efficacy of the subject (in this case the Eucharist) is in the work of divine agency—again specifically Christ;[114]

---

[109] DBWE 4:207–208.
[110] DBWE 4:207–209.
[111] DBWE 4:209–210.
[112] DBWE 4:207–209.
[113] Bonhoeffer goes on to offer infant baptism as an example of the passivity of the human agent in baptism as well as an illustration of the communal form of discipleship in the call to carry the child in a place in which they can claim their baptism for themselves. DBWE 4:211–212.
[114] DBWE 4:217.

the Lord's Supper is shown to be constitutive of the church; and, again, the work of the human agent regarding the sacrament of the Lord's Supper is discipleship.

In "Lectures on Christology," Bonhoeffer writes,

> This is what happens in the Lord's Supper; God hallows the elements of bread and wine by speaking the divine word. But the name of God's Word is Jesus Christ. It is through Jesus Christ that the sacrament is hallowed and given its meaning.[115]

Here, Bonhoeffer identifies the origin and efficacy of the Lord's Supper in Christ. The bread and wine, and the act of taking the bread and wine, are not what confects the sacrament. Instead, the bread and wine and the cultic act of taking the Supper are sacred due *only to Christ's presence in them*.[116] In making this distinction, Bonhoeffer is making explicit that the Lord's Supper has primarily to do with the work of divine agency—the work of Christ in creating and residing in the Eucharist. Bonhoeffer expands upon this claim by expressing that Christ is present in the Eucharist *pro-me* (for me), meaning that Christ is present to be encountered in the Eucharist to those for whom he is for—the church.[117] In other words, the Lord's Supper has its source and efficacy due to Christ's presence in it, and rather than identifying Christ's presence with the elements of bread and wine in and of themselves, he identifies Christ's presence as his presence *pro-me*, a presence directed toward encountering those for whom he is for.

As was the case with Christ's presence in baptism and as Word, Christ's presence in the Eucharist is constitutive of the church. Bonhoeffer voices as much in *Sanctorum Communio* when he claims that Christ gives community with himself in the Lord's Supper and he gives the church-community itself.[118] Christ gave community with himself through his vicarious representative action in his death and resurrection, creating and being the new humanity, which is the community with himself given in the Lord's Supper.[119] As has been stated above, that new humanity is the church-community, which means that Christ also gives the church-community in the Lord's Supper.

---

[115] DBWE 12:319.
[116] DBWE 12:319.
[117] DBWE 12:321.
  Philip Ziegler has discussed the promeity of Christ in Bonhoeffer's thought. Ziegler, Philip Gordon. "Christ for us Today: Promeity in the Christologies of Bonhoeffer and Kierkegaard." *International Journal of Systematic Theology* 15, no. 1 (January 2013): 25–41. John Phillips has also written concerning the promeity of Christ in Bonhoeffer's thought. Phillips, John. *Christ For Us in the Theology of Dietrich Bonhoeffer*. New York: Harper and Row, 1967.
[118] DBWE 1:243.
[119] DBWE 1:243.

This claim is not simply a sociological one; it is a claim to the inherently communal nature of the new humanity that is the church. As such, in the Lord's Supper, one encounters Christ and shares in the church-community that is Christ's body.

There remains the fact that celebrating the Lord's Supper requires a concrete action on the part of the human agent in taking the bread and the wine. This human act, however, is not what makes the Lord's Supper efficacious but rather is an act of obedient discipleship. Bonhoeffer calls this an "obedient symbolic action."[120] Just as in baptism, the act of participating in the cultic act of the Lord's Supper is an act of obedience to Christ's call of discipleship. In this obedient act of discipleship, the disciple is led to a place where Christ is encountered and where his command can be heard.[121]

In sum, Bonhoeffer's understanding of Christ's presence in the Eucharist determines that the Eucharist is primarily a work done by divine agency because Christ's presence makes the sacrament what it is. What is more, the Eucharist is constitutive of the church, as in it Christ gives community with himself and gives the church-community itself, which he does through his death and resurrection. Finally, what is left for the human agent to do is discipleship—here manifested as the obedient act of participating in the Lord's Supper.

Christ's Presence in the Church as Church-Community

Michael Mawson's book on Bonhoeffer's ecclesiology in *Sanctorum Communio* is called *Christ Existing as Community: Bonhoeffer's Ecclesiology* for a reason. From Bonhoeffer's earliest works, his concept of Christ existing as church-community has been determinative of his ecclesiology. One of the key insights from Mawson's book is that the sociological work and development of the concept of person in the early chapters of *Sanctorum Communio* are not that book's climax, but rather that Bonhoeffer develops these in service to the book's true climax: the ecclesiology Bonhoeffer presents in the final chapter.[122] Put differently, the concept of the church as Christ existing as church-community is central to Bonhoeffer's ecclesiology in *Sanctorum Communio*, and the sociological work from the earlier chapters provide supportive content for what that concept entails.

Beyond *Sanctorum Communio*, Bonhoeffer maintains this emphasis on Christ existing as church-community and regularly attends to the church in

---

[120] DBWE 1:244.

[121] For more on Christ's presence as Word and sacrament in Bonhoeffer's thought, see Mawson, *Christ Existing in Community*, 151–169.

[122] Mawson, *Christ Existing as Community*, 71.

terms of Christ's presence therein (as the chapter previously demonstrated).[123] Of the three ways in which Christ is present in the church, his presence as church-community is perhaps the most significant for the purposes of grasping his ecumenical theology. Christ's presence in the church as church-community is Christ's revelatory and personal presence in the church *as the church-community itself.* While Christ's presence as Word and sacrament maintains a presence that is revelatory and even a presence that is personal, it is Christ's presence as church-community that brings others into the church and binds them together in true community. So, what does Bonhoeffer's concept of Christ existing as church-community mean and how is it impactful for his ecumenical theology?

Christ existing as church-community brings together all that was discussed regarding Bonhoeffer's concepts of person and revelation. Christ exists as church-community as person, creating the collective person of Christ through his vicarious representative action. And Christ exists as church-community as revelation, being God's chosen form of self-revelation. Bonhoeffer puts it this way in *Act and Being*:

> The Protestant idea of the church is conceived in personal terms—that is, God reveals the divine self in the church as person. The community of faith is God's final revelation as "Christ existing as community [Gemeinde]." . . . Here Christ has given Christ's own self to the new humanity in Christ so that the person of Christ draws together in itself all whom Christ has won, binding and committing Christ to them and them to one another. The "church" is, therefore, not a human community [Gemeinschaft] to which Christ then comes or not, nor is it a gathering of such persons as those who (as individuals) seek Christ or think they have Christ and now wish to cultivate this common "possession." The church is rather the community of faith created by and founded upon Christ, in which Christ is revealed as the δεύτερος ἄνθρωπος, as the new human, or rather, as the new humanity itself.[124]

Christ's presence in the church as church-community establishes the connectedness and social relations of those within the church. The church's personal form is a *communal* form. As the collective person of Christ, the church is just that—a collective. But, more than just being a collective, the collective person of Christ is a *community.* The collective person of Adam

---

[123] Literature written on Bonhoeffer's concept of Christ existing as church-community includes McBride, Jennifer M. "Christ Existing as Concrete Community Today." *Theology Today* 71, no. 1 (April 2014): 92–105; Leahy, Breandan. "'Christ Existing as Church-Community': Dietrich Bonhoeffer's Notion of Church." *Irish Theological Quarterly* 73, no. 1–2 (2008): 32–59.

[124] DBWE 2:112.

is still a collective in spite of its being a collective of isolated individuals closed off from one another.[125] The collective person of Christ, in contrast, is a collective person of those who are not only bound and open to Christ but bound and open to each other as well.[126] The collective person of Adam is characterized by isolation; the collective person of Christ is characterized by community.[127] It is this presence in the church-community *as* church-community as the collective person of Christ that determines social relations for those within the church.

In *Sanctorum Communio*, Bonhoeffer narrates this community founded by Christ's presence as church-community in terms of "being-with-each-other" and "being-for-each-other." The "being-with-each-other" of the church is the fact that Christ has bound the new humanity to himself and to each other. Bonhoeffer expresses it thus:

> The church-community is so structured that wherever one of its members is, there too is the church-community in its power, which means in the power of Christ and the Holy Spirit . . . and in every situation and problem of life *the church-community is with this individual* . . . and wherever the church is, there the individual member is also. . . . Now where the church-community is, there is Christ.[128]

Bonhoeffer articulates the "being-with-each-other" of the church in terms of the whole of the church being with the individual, and the individual being with the whole of the church. Significant here is that the church is communal, meaning that those within it are to be understood as *communal* every bit as much as they are to be understood as individual. It is not that individuality is vanquished within the church, but that it subsists in community within the church. This much was demonstrated in the chapter's earlier treatment of the collective person of Christ, where it was illustrated that the individual who finds themselves within the collective person of Christ, finds themselves as

---

[125] DBWE 1:121.

[126] DBWE 1:150.

[127] Further literature on Bonhoeffer's approach to community includes Zerner, Ruth. "Bonhoeffer on Discipleship and Community." *Lutheran Forum* 30, no. 2 (May 1996): 35–38; McBride, "Christ Existing as Concrete Community Today"; Hooton, "Community and Christology in the Theology of Dietrich Bonhoeffer;" Green, Clifford J. "Human Sociality and Christian Community." In *The Cambridge Companion to Dietrich Bonhoeffer*, edited by John W. De Gruchy, 113–133, Cambridge: Cambridge University Press, 1999; Tang, Andres S K. "Confucianism and Bonhoeffer on Individualism and Community: From the Perspective of the Way of Humanization." *Ching Feng* 1, no. 1 (2000): 97–103; Marsh, Charles. "Human Community and Divine Presence: Dietrich Bonhoeffer's Theological Critique of Hegel." *Scottish Journal of Theology* 47, no. 4 (1992), 127–148.

[128] DBWE 1:178–182.

"being already in the community of Christ."[129] This communal form means that wherever the whole of the church is, there also is each individual member, and wherever the individual member is, there also is the whole of the church.[130] This is the "being-with-each-other" of the collective person of Christ in Christ's presence as church-community.

This "being-with-each-other" that characterizes Christ's presence as church-community does not only make the claim that those within the church are part of a collective as much as they are individuals. It also determines how those within the church relate to one another. Those in the church are *bound* to Christ and *bound* to one another. In the same way that Christ is to be encountered in the Word and the sacraments, Christ is to be encountered in one another in the church-community. It is through Christ's presence as church-community that those who are turned in upon themselves are broken open to encounter Christ in the other. As Bonhoeffer writes in *Sanctorum Communio*:

> The person living in the community of the I-You-relationship is given the assurance of being loved, and through faith in Christ receives the power to love also, in that this person, who in Christ is already in the church, is led into the church. For that person the other member of the church-community is essentially no longer claim but gift, revelation of God's love and heart. Thus the You is to the I no longer law but gospel, and hence an object of love. The fact that my claim is met by the other I who loves me—which means, of course, by Christ—fulfills me, humbles me, frees me from bondage to myself, and enables me—again, of course, only through the power of faith in Christ—to love the other, to completely give and reveal myself to the other.[131]

Christ's presence in the church as church-community is the establishment of this community characterized by love. Those within the church as *Christus Praesens* no longer encounter others as a curse, but instead, they encounter them as a gift. Christ's presence as church-community binds those within the church together in such a way that those within the church are freed from their self-direction—broken open to encounter the other in love. And, in the church-community, the other becomes the locus of Christ's presence. It is in and through other people that Christ's claim comes to the individual. Thus, in Christ's presence in the church as church-community, there is a "being-with-each-other" of the church, in which those within the church are bound to one another, liberated from their self-bondage to encounter Christ in each other. This restructures their sociality as they are freed to truly reveal their selves

---

[129] DBWE 2:155.
[130] DBWE 1:178 182.
[131] DBWE 1:166.

to one another as Christ's command, and God's very self is revealed through Christ's presence in the church as church-community.

In addition to the "being-with-each-other" established through Christ's presence as church-community, there is a "being-for-each-other" that is likewise established. The "being-with-each-other" of the church details the boundedness of those within the church to each other through Christ's presence and how that affects their relationships with one another. The "being-for-each-other" of the church describes ways that those who are bound to each other in Christ act for and toward one another. Bonhoeffer depicts what he intends by the "being-for-each-other" of the church, writing:

> *Three great, positive possibilities of acting for each other* in the community of saints present themselves: *self-renouncing, active work for the neighbor; intercessory prayer; and, finally, the mutual forgiveness of sins* in God's name. All of these involve giving up the self "for" my neighbor's benefit, with the readiness to do and bear everything in the neighbor's place, indeed, if necessary, to sacrifice myself, standing as a *substitute* for my neighbor. Even if a purely vicarious action is rarely actualized, it is intended in every genuine act of love.[132]

Bonhoeffer does not narrate the interactions of those within the church along the lines of agreement on doctrine or the relation of ministerial offices to one another.[133] Instead, the interactions of those within the collective person of Christ are characterized by self-renouncing acts of love, prayer, and forgiveness. At the base of all three of these acts is Bonhoeffer's idea of vicarious representative action (*Stellvertretung*). It is the willingness to give up oneself for the sake of the neighbor—to make sacrifices for each other. This activity is, of course, different from Christ's (in scope and efficacy), but it still defines the activity of those within the church toward one another. In other words, Christ's vicarious representative action creates the church-community as Christ's presence therein and also defines the way in which those within the church-community relate to one another.

The three possibilities for acting for each other in the church that Bonhoeffer highlights are illuminating. One way those within the church-community act

---

[132] DBWE 1:184.

[133] George Lindbeck's cultural-linguistic approach to doctrine and his account of its impact upon ecumenism is a landmark text regarding doctrine and ecumenism and bears referencing here, despite the way in which it differs from Bonhoeffer's understanding of the place of doctrine regarding church and church unity. Lindbeck, George A. *The Nature of Doctrine: Religion and Theology in a Postliberal Age.* Louisville: Westminster John Knox Press, 1984.

For more on the missiological dimensions of Bonhoeffer's ecclesiology, see Sundermeier, Theo. "Der Kirchenbegriff von Dietrich Bonhoeffer—Eine missiologische Perspektive. Mission und Religion in der Theologie Bonhoeffers." *Interkulturelle Theologie. Zeitschrift für Missionswissenschaft* (no. 4/2016) *Dietrich Bonhoeffer zu Mission und Okumene*: 331–350.

for each other is intercessory prayer. In a most basic sense, this can mean setting aside oneself to lift up the needs of the other to God in prayer. And yet,
Bonhoeffer intends something further reaching than an individualistic view
of intercession in which prayer is seen as an individual elevating another
individual's need to God. An understanding of the church as the presence
of Christ determines that the life of the church can be seen as a communal
whole—or, as Bonhoeffer puts it: "The church-community leads *a single
life*."[134] This means that "even the most personal prayer no longer belongs to
the individual, but to the church."[135] The prayer and need of the individual
are the prayer and need of the church because the church is bound together in
Christ. The one who prays for their neighbor, therefore, actually lifts up their
own prayer in doing so. The church-community leads a single life, and so the
need and burden carried by the neighbor become one's own need and burden.

Under this approach, Bonhoeffer sees intercession as "God's most power-
ful means for organizing the entire church-community toward God's own
purpose."[136] What he means by this is that in intercessory prayer, one seeks
God's will for the other; seeking God's will for the other opens one's eyes to
the need of the other and the command of Christ that comes from the other.
As the church-community seeks God's will for each other through prayer, it
becomes more aware of the need of the other and the burden they carry and
more aware of how to act to and for the other. Thus, as the church-community
prays for each other, Christ and Christ's commands are encountered in each
other and actively obeyed. In intercessory prayer, therefore, the church-
community acts for each other as the present person of Christ as it leads a
single life, praying the prayers of those within the community and bearing
each other's burdens, which in turn leads to awareness of the need of others
and Christ's commands in response to those needs.

A second way those within the church-community act for each other is
through the mutual forgiveness of sins. Bonhoeffer recognizes that only
Christ is able to forgive sins because only Christ has taken each sin upon
himself and eliminated it.[137] And yet, the church-community is the present
person of Christ. For Bonhoeffer, therefore, those who are in Christ are
capable of bearing the sin of their neighbor upon themselves, because ultimately, they lay that burden upon Christ. As the collective person of Christ,
the church-community is able to bear the sins of each other and forgive one

---

[134] DBWE 1:185.
[135] DBWE 1:185.
[136] DBWE 1:100.
[137] DBWE 1:189.

another, because it is Christ who carries those sins and through Christ that forgiveness comes.[138]

Finally, the third possibility for acting for each other in the church is self-renouncing, active work for the neighbor. Christ's presence in the church as church-community determines that self-renouncing work characterizes the work those within the church-community do for one another. Being in Christ means being bound to each other in such a way that demands the willingness to sacrifice one's own advantages for each other. Bonhoeffer gives the examples of Exodus 32:32, in which Moses expresses a desire to be removed from the book of life together with his people, and Romans 9:3, in which Paul expresses that he would desire to be cut off from Christ if it helped his people have community with God.[139] Paradoxically, such desires actually bring one into intimate relation with God, because the desire to go even to the darkest place of damnation for the sake of the other is precisely the heart of God found in Jesus Christ. It is Jesus Christ who goes to the darkest place of damnation for the sake of the other. Although Christ's self-renouncing work—Christ's vicarious representative action—is the first and ultimate self-renouncing work, those within the church also act for each other through self-sacrificial works for the other.

Both intercession and mutual forgiveness represent this kind of self-renouncing work. And yet, self-renouncing work for the neighbor is not restricted to these two activities. As Bonhoeffer puts it: "We are called to advocate vicariously for the other in everyday matters, to give up possessions, honor, even our whole lives."[140]

To summarize, Christ's presence in the church as church-community dictates the social relations of those within the church in the "being-with-each-other" and "being-for-each-other" of the church-community. The "being-with-each-other" of the church-community describes the boundedness of those within the church-community to each other as Christ restructures their sociality, breaking them open from their self-direction to encounter and be encountered by Christ and the other. The "being-for-each-other" of the church-community describes the self-sacrificial acts of love that characterize how those within the church-community relate to one another. Taken together, Christ's presence as church-community establishes a community of people bound together and open to each other in Christ—people who act toward each other in self-sacrificial active works of love, prayer, and forgiveness.

---

[138] DBWE 1:190.
[139] DBWE 1:184-185.
[140] DBWE 1:184.

So, what? What is the significance of Christ's presence in the church as church-community for his ecclesiology and ecumenical theology? Christ's presence as church-community is the third and final manner in which Bonhoeffer understands Christ's presence in the church, rounding out his account of the church as Christ's presence. This manner of Christ's presence in the church maintains and enriches the implications observed in the description of Christ's presence as Word and sacrament: Christ's presence as church-community depicts a church created through the work of divine agency; Christ's presence as church-community is constitutive of the church itself, establishing Bonhoeffer's ecclesiology; and, the work of the human agent in the church as it relates to Christ's presence in the church as church-community once again proves to be discipleship.

As the previous discussions of Christ's presence in the church as Word and sacrament demonstrated, Christ's presence in the church as church-community reinforces the idea that the creation of the church is the work of divine agency. Rather than repeat what was said in those discussions, it is significant to articulate ways that this form of Christ's presence in the church adds to what has been said. As has been stated regarding Christ's presence as Word and sacrament, Christ's presence in the church as church-community depicts a church created by divine agency through Christ's vicarious representative action to create and be the church-community—the collective person of Christ. This form of Christ's presence enriches and builds upon the previous discussions by demonstrating the fact that Bonhoeffer envisions a church "which is simultaneously a historical community and one established by God."[141] To this point, the reality that the church is established by God has been clear enough. That said, Bonhoeffer's understanding that the church is a historical community finds its strongest expression in Christ's presence in the church as church-community.

In describing Christ's presence in the church as church-community, Bonhoeffer does not envision a church that is the collective person of Christ in only a spiritual or immaterial sense. Rather, he envisions a church that is the collective person of Christ *concretely*—within history. In Christ's presence as church-community, Bonhoeffer presents a church that is both God-established *and* historical. The two are held together. The church is the reality of God's self-revelation in the person of Jesus Christ who creates the church-community in himself as the collective person of Christ, and, at the same time, that church-community includes those who are in Christ and their active works of discipleship in the world.[142] This understanding of the church simultaneously as historical and God-established reinforces the claim that

---

[141] DBWE 1:126.

[142] Space does not permit an exploration of all that it means that the church is "simultaneously a historical community and one established by God," but Mawson dedicates the final two chapters of his book to doing just this. Mawson, *Christ Existing as Community,* 121–175.

the church is created through divine agency and makes explicit the fact that the church that is created through God's work also takes up real space in the world—it is concrete.

The second implication that is bolstered through Christ's presence in the church as church-community is that Christ's presence is constitutive of the church. Indeed, of the three manners in which Christ is present in the church, it is perhaps Christ's presence as church-community that is most clearly constitutive of the church. This is because, according to Bonhoeffer, the church *is* the present person of Christ. The concept of Christ existing as church-community describes the church *as* Christ's presence. For Bonhoeffer, Christ's presence is what makes the church what it is. The church is the revelatory person of Christ—the new humanity, the collective person of Christ. As such, Christ's presence in the church as church-community establishes the church itself. Christ's action to create the new humanity in himself as the collective person of Christ determines that Christ's presence constitutes the church because the church itself is understood to be present person of Christ. Christ's presence as church-community means that the community of the church, how those within the church relate to one another and are bound together, and the very being of each person within the church are characterized by Christ's presence. Thus, Christ's presence as church-community fundamentally constitutes the church for Bonhoeffer.

The final implication of Christ's presence in the church as church-community is that it yet again forwards discipleship as the work of the human agents who are within the church. The entire discussion of Christ's presence as church-community and the "being-with-each-other" and "being-for-each-other" that accompanies it detailed an understanding of the action of those within the church that is characterized by discipleship. As humans encounter Christ and are freed from their own self-direction to encounter others, they encounter Christ and Christ's command in the other which calls them to responsible action—discipleship.[143] Put simply, the triune God creates the church and sustains the church, and the activity of those who are within the church is discipleship. As Christ encounters people, he breaks them open from themselves and they encounter the command of Christ and are called to responsibility (to discipleship);[144] as those who are in Christ encounter the command of Christ in the other, they are continually called to obedience to the command. Bonhoeffer writes,

> It is the Spirit's work that, by my seeking nothing but to be obedient to God, that is, by pursuing purely an end that as such is something other than the

---

[143] DBWE 4:57.
[144] DBWE 1:48.

community, I completely surrender my will, so that simultaneously I truly love
my neighbor.[145]

This is discipleship—hearing and doing the command of God. This discipleship is the activity of those who are within the church.

Drawing all of the preceding conversations together, Bonhoeffer's account
of ecclesiology is built upon Christ's presence—it is an account of the church
as *Christus Praesens*. The church is the revelatory person of Christ created
by Christ's action on humanity's behalf, creating the church in himself as
the new humanity, the collective person of Christ.[146] Christ is present in the
church as Word, sacrament, and church-community. Christ's presence constitutes the church. As such, the church is created and sustained by the triune
God, and yet it is a concrete community within history. The work of those
within the church is discipleship—the active obedient response to encountering Christ and Christ's command. In short, the church is the revelatory person
of Christ, and the work of those within the church is discipleship. This work
of the human agent does not create the church; this work of the human agent
is done *within* the work of the divine agent of creating the church. The work
of divine agency in creating the church frames the work of the human agent
within the church.[147]

Herein lies the core of Bonhoeffer's ecumenical theology. In his claim that
ecumenical work emerges from a concept of the church as *Christus Praesens*
and has the task of proclaiming Christ's commands to the world, Bonhoeffer
intends the account of the church that has been presented in this chapter as
the framework and foundation of his ecumenical vision.[148] According to this
vision, the ecumenical movement understands itself to be church (as *Christus
Praesens* as articulated to this point and not as institution) and understands
the role of the human agent within ecumenism to be discipleship.[149] By

---

[145] DBWE 1:262.

[146] For more on Christian formation in terms of being formed into the person of Christ in Dietrich
Bonhoeffer's theology, see McGarry, Joseph. "Con-Formed to Christ: Dietrich Bonhoeffer and
Christian Formation." *Journal of Spiritual Formation & Soul Care* 5, no. 2 (Fall 2012): 226–242;
VandenBerg, Mary. "Bonhoeffer's Discipleship: Theology for the Purpose of Christian Forma-
tion." *Calvin Theological Journal* 44, no. 2 (November 2009): 333–349.

[147] Philip Ziegler has attended to the priority Bonhoeffer attributes to the work of divine agency
in soteriology. Ziegler utilizes *Act and Being* and *Ethics* to argue that moral knowledge is only
gained through a constant focus upon Christ, and therefore, "a human life 'in Christ' is subjected
to the relentless gracious activity of the living God of our salvation." Put otherwise, priority is
given to the work of divine agency regarding the ethical life, as the human agent is ever focused
upon Christ. Ziegler, Philip G. "'Completely Within God's Doing:' Soteriology as Meta-Ethics
in the Theology of Dietrich Bonhoeffer." In *Christ, Church and World: New Studies in Bonhoeffer's Theology and Ethics,* edited by Michael Mawson and Philip G. Ziegler, 101–118. London:
Bloomsbury T&T Clark, 2016.

[148] DBWE 11:360–369.

[149] DBWE 11:358–359.

detailing this account of ecclesiology, this chapter has provided the foundation of Bonhoeffer's ecumenical theology.

ADDRESSING CONCERNS

Christ and the Church Over-identified?

In drawing the chapter to a close, it is worth addressing and dispelling a potential issue Bonhoeffer's account of ecclesiology as *Christus Praesens* may seem to present. This account of ecclesiology poses the question of whether or not Bonhoeffer over-identifies Christ and the church.[150] Is Bonhoeffer claiming that the church is literally and indistinguishably Christ? Put otherwise, is there a distinction between Christ and the church? Indeed, there are Bonhoeffer scholars who have levied this claim against him.[151] Foremost among these is Ernst Feil, whose criticism is aimed solely at Bonhoeffer's theology in *Sanctorum Communio*.[152] Feil argues that—in *Sanctorum Communio*—Bonhoeffer's construction of "Christ existing as church-community" is too abstract Christologically, such that Christology is collapsed into ecclesiology;[153] this collapse of Christology into ecclesiology, Feil argues further, results in an account of the church that not only lacks a robust Christology but also places the church beyond criticism in its close identification with Christ.[154] If Feil's suspicions are correct, Bonhoeffer's account of the church is idealized and unrealistic, not taking sin in the church seriously, and thereby not truthfully testifying to the concrete church as it exists in the world.[155]

That Bonhoeffer had no intention of completely equating Christ and the church is evident as he writes in *Sanctorum Communio*, "A complete

---

[150] Craig L. Nessan considers Bonhoeffer's understanding of the church as the body of Christ alongside the understandings held by Hauerwas and Jensen. Nessan, Craig L. "What if the Church Really is the Body of Christ?" *Dialog* 51, no. 1 (2012): 43–52.

[151] Pangritz, Andreas. "Who is Christ for Us Today?" In *The Cambridge Companion to Dietrich Bonhoeffer*, 134–153. Cambridge: Cambridge University Press, 1999, 151; Bethge, Eberhard. *Dietrich Bonhoeffer: A Biography*. Minneapolis: Fortress Press, 2000, 84; McBride, Jennifer M. *The Church for the World: A Theology of Public Witness*. Oxford: Oxford University Press, 2012, 123; Feil, *The Theology of Dietrich Bonhoeffer*, 61–67.

[152] Feil maintains that Bonhoeffer's later works provide a more adequate and robust account of Christology. Feil, *The Theology of Dietrich Bonhoeffer*, 62.

[153] Feil, *The Theology of Dietrich Bonhoeffer*, 61–64.

[154] Feil, *The Theology of Dietrich Bonhoeffer*, 9.

  For a detailed discussion on—and refutation of—Feil's claims concerning Bonhoeffer's Christology in *Sanctorum Communio*, see Michael Mawson, *Christ Existing as Community*, 145–149.

[155] Barker, Gaylon. *The Cross of Reality: Luther's Theologia Crucis and Bonhoeffer's Christology*. Minneapolis, MN: Fortress Press, 2015.

identification between Christ and the church-community cannot be made."[156] He comes to this conclusion on the basis that "Christ has ascended into heaven and is now with God and we still await Christ's coming."[157] Essentially, Bonhoeffer claims that Christ and the church cannot be completely equated on the basis that Christ has ascended to heaven and the church has not, thereby signifying a distinction between the two. He further argues that the church cannot be completely identified with Christ by virtue of the fact that the church is not pure, thus acknowledging the necessity for distinguishing the two to faithfully testify to the church as it exists in the world.[158]

Not only does Bonhoeffer explicitly claim that Christ and the church cannot be completely equated, but his concept of "Christ existing as church-community" also distinguishes the two. Bonhoeffer locates the distinction between Christ and the church in his concept of revelation, writing, "One must not think of a second incarnation of Christ, but rather a form of revelation that may be called 'Christ existing as church-community.'"[159] In other words, the church is not the body of Christ in a literal flesh and blood sense, but rather the church is the body of Christ as the revelation of Christ in the world today. The church is not the revelation of Christ because of its physical, institutional existence; rather, the church is the revelation of Christ because of Christ's work in creating the new humanity (the church), which the church participates in by following Christ and proclaiming Christ's commands. In this way, Bonhoeffer not only explains how Christ and the church are not over-identified with one another in the concept of "Christ existing as church-community" but also reinforces that the concept inheres both spiritual and concrete aspects in its understanding of the church as revelation.

Finally, the distinction between Christ and the church is also established in Bonhoeffer's understanding of Christ's lordship over the church. Christ's Lordship over the church designates the church as disciple, capable and culpable of sin, whose only objective is to follow after Christ and proclaim his commands. It is as disciple that the distinction between Christ and the church is evinced in Bonhoeffer's conception of the church as *Christus Praesens*.

Does Ecclesiology Undermine Ecumenism?

Bonhoeffer repeatedly pushes the ecumenical movement to understand itself as church.[160] This chapter has detailed what that account of church entails.

---

[156] DBWE 1:140.
[157] DBWE 1:140.
[158] DBWE 1:138 fn. 29.
[159] DBWE 1:138 fn. 29.
[160] DBWE 14:399.

It is not that Bonhoeffer wants the ecumenical movement to form a new institutional church—or a "super-church" as the World Council of Churches calls such an approach—but rather he pushes the ecumenical movement to understand that it *is* church and therefore can operate as such.[161] The church as *Christus Praesens* that gathers on Sunday morning is the same church as *Christus Praesens* that gathers in the ecumenical movement.[162] Such a strong ecclesiological foundation for ecumenical theology begs a question: If ecumenism is so closely identified with ecclesiology, such that the ecumenical theology is built on a self-identity as church and what it means practically to exist within that church, has ecumenism itself been undermined as a theological category?

The answer must be no. The question raises an excellent point. It is true that Bonhoeffer's ecumenical theology consists of an ecclesiological foundation as the church as the revelatory person of Christ, with an operative theological content of discipleship. In this way, this account of ecumenical theology could be seen simply as an account of the church and what it means to be within that church. Yet, is that not what ecumenical theology ought to be doing when it is properly understood?

The original use of the qualifier "ecumenical" in the church relates to the early ecumenical councils. These councils were concerned with codifying the chief theological statements of the church as a whole. As such, they were concerned at a basic level with the entire church (ecclesiology) and the beliefs and actions therein. What we find in Bonhoeffer's ecumenical theology is a very Protestant (but not anti-Roman Catholic) approach to that original type of ecumenism. Just as the early councils were concerned with the whole church, so, too, is Bonhoeffer. He is not interested in an ecumenical theology which only describes the actions or gatherings of a select few, but with a theology that can be inclusive of the church as a whole, and only as such be truly ecumenical.

---

[161] TS: III.1; III.3.

[162] Bonhoeffer's thought has had an impact on the WCC's early thought on the organization's self-understanding of its ecclesiality. Willem Visser't Hooft—Bonhoeffer's friend, and the first secretary of the WCC—has claimed as much in his article, "Dietrich Bonhoeffer and the Self-understanding of the Ecumenical Movement." Visser't Hooft admits that Bonhoeffer's thought in "The Confessing Church and the Ecumenical Movement"—particularly Bonhoeffer's emphasis that the ecumenical movement be church—was influential to his own claim that "Representatives of churches can never meet without at least attempting to live up to their main obligation, which is to *be the church*, and to announce the Lordship of Jesus Christ over the world." Thus, as Visser't Hooft claims, Bonhoeffer's thought *did* have an influence on the early thought of the WCC in bringing what Visser't Hooft calls a "church-consciousness" to the WCC. Even with this church-consciousness and Bonhoeffer's influence upon it, there remains a distinction between the WCC's conception a fellowship of churches and Bonoeffer's understanding of the ecumenical movement as church as *Christus Praesens*. Visser't Hooft, "Dietrich Bonhoeffer and the Self-Understanding of the Ecumenical Movement," 198–203.

What emerges is an ecumenical theology that, yes, is deeply and inherently ecclesiological; but it is also a theology that is crucially ecumenical. The ecumenicity of the ecumenical theology is not undermined or dissolved by the emphasized account of ecclesiology, but rather is bolstered as the ecclesiology presented is truly and fundamentally ecumenical—including the whole of the church. As such, ecumenism is not undermined as a theological category by Bonhoeffer's ecclesiology.

CONCLUSION

In conclusion, Bonhoeffer sets before us a dynamic account of the church as the revelatory person of Christ in the world today—the church as *Christus Praesens*. The church is a person because it subsists in the person of Christ. The church is revelatory because the person of Christ is the form of God's self-revelation in Christ. This account of the church is structured around Christ's threefold presence in the church as Word, sacrament, and church-community. To understand the church as the present person of Christ is to understand it as a living and active presence within the world. To understand the church as a *person*—namely, the person of Christ—is to understand it as a relational entity. This entity is founded in Christ's person-forming encounter with human beings, forming them into the collective person of Christ. Those within the church, then, encounter Christ in the Word and sacrament of the church. And they also encounter Christ in each other and in the other in whom Christ's command is found. This is not an account of church built upon institutional terms but rather built upon Christ's living and active presence within the world—the living and active Christ who is with and for the humanity he came to save.

The church as *Christus Praesens* is the conception of church within which Bonhoeffer grounds his ecumenical theology.[163] By grounding ecumenical theology in a self-understanding of the ecumenical movement as church, Bonhoeffer indicates a foundation to ecumenical work defined by the work of divine agency, as the triune God creates, realizes, and actualizes the church. It is this revelatory person of Christ, the new humanity, that Bonhoeffer sees as the ecumenical church. The work that is left to those who are within the church is discipleship. The book now moves to discuss the fact that this revelatory person of Christ is—and can only be—one.

---

[163] DBWE 11:358–359.

Chapter 2

Church Unity

Church unity has been a central topic for ecumenical discourse since the ecumenical movement emerged around a century ago. While the ecumenical councils of the early church focused upon the topic of orthodox doctrine, the contemporary ecumenical movement has had to grapple with the plurality of denominations, which, in turn, has made the church's unity itself a question of significance.[1] Much contemporary ecumenical work focuses upon *visible* unity. Indeed, the World Council of Churches has identified its primary purpose as calling "one another to visible unity."[2] Before *visible* church unity can be defined, however, an investigation of church unity in general is needed.

For Bonhoeffer, church unity is a given reality of the church as *Christus Praesens*. If the church is the person of Christ, and Christ's person can only be one, then the church itself must be one.[3] In other words, church unity already

---

[1] A few significant documents produced by the WCC on the topic of unity include *The New Delhi Report: The Third Assembly of the World Council of Churches, 1961*, edited by W.A. Visser't Hooft. London: SCM, 1962, especially 116–125; "What Unity Requires." In *Breaking Barriers, Nairobi 1975: Official Report, Fifth Assembly, World Council of Churches,* edited by David M. Paton, 59–64. Geneva: WCC, 1976; http://www.oikoumene.org/en/resources/documents/assembly /2013-buas/adopted-documents-statements/unity-statement, 2013; "Called to Be One Church." In *God, in Your Grace: Official Report of the Ninth Assembly of the World Council of Churches,* 255–261. Geneva: WCC, 2006; "Towards Unity in Tension." In *Documentary History of Faith and Order 1968-1993,* edited by Gunther Gassmann, *Faith and Order paper no. 159,* 144–147. Geneva: WCC, 1993.

See also Castro, Emilio. "The Unity of the Church." In *A Passion for Unity: Essays on Ecumenical Hopes and Challenges,* edited by Emilio Castro, 1–13. Geneva: WCC Publications, 1992; Tanner, Mary. "On Being Church." *The Ecumenical Review* 53, no. 1 (2001): 64–71.

[2] Constitution, 1.

[3] The authors of "Called to be One Church" articulate the unity of the church in Christ in a similar way, writing, "the Church is called to manifest its *oneness in rich diversity.* . . . We affirm that the apostolic faith of the Church is one, as the body of Christ is one. Yet there may legitimately be different formulations of the faith of the Church." "Called to Be One Church." In *God, in Your*

exists and it is complete. It is not something that must be achieved by those within the church, and it is not something created by those within the church. The church—as the revelatory person of Christ—is one. The unity of this church is created by Christ as he creates the new humanity through his life, death, and resurrection. What all of this signifies is that Bonhoeffer's account of the church as *Christus Praesens* carries his account of church unity within it. In other words, Bonhoeffer's account of church unity is *part* of his account of the church. Although the account of church unity is being given its own chapter, it should not be thought that this account itself is separate from the account of the church or that Bonhoeffer's account of the church is being rent asunder. Bonhoeffer's understanding of church unity is absolutely part of his account of the church. In order to develop this account of church unity fully, therefore, this chapter *builds on* the account of the church as *Christus Praesens* developed in chapter 1, with the basic claim that this understanding of the church—which was identified as the foundation of Bonhoeffer's ecumenical theology—inheres church unity.[4] In providing this account of church unity, the book continues to establish the theological presuppositions undergirding the theology Bonhoeffer articulated in his ecumenical works.

The chapter examines Bonhoeffer's account of church unity and demonstrates that this account is consistent with—and inherent to—his account of the church as *Christus Praesens*. Over the course of this study, three implications of this account of church unity are observed: (1) the church is intrinsically united in its being the revelatory person of Christ; (2) church unity is understood to be a work of divine agency; and (3) the unity of the church is both a spiritual reality *and* a concrete, historical reality—even today in the time before the eschaton.[5] In other words, the church is inherently united, its unity is created by God, and that unity is a concrete reality today.

Grace: Official Report of the Ninth Assembly of the World Council of Churches, 255–261. Geneva: WCC, 2006.

[4] Bonhoeffer's account of church unity is attended to in broad strokes in Moses, "Dietrich Bonhoeffer's Prioritization of Church Unity (Oekumene)."

[5] The claim that the church is intrinsically united is not a controversial one. A near universal majority of thought on church unity agrees with this claim, typically stemming from the Nicene affirmation of "*One*, Holy, Catholic, and Apostolic Church." Even the second claim that church unity is a work of divine agency is not one that would be refuted by the vast majority of thought on the subject. That said, while most ecumenical literature begins from a place of describing the church as intrinsically united as a gift of God, the texts then tend to move to discuss the role of the human agent in realizing this unity, thus attributing a decisive role to the work of human agency in the creation of church unity. One such example is found in the New Delhi Statement on Unity from the WCC's 3rd Assembly in 1961: "It is in Jesus Christ, God's Son and our only Mediator, that we have union with God. It is he who has given this gift to us through his coming into our world. Unity is not of our making, but as we receive the grace of Jesus Christ we are one in him. . . . The fact that we are living in division shows that we have not realized God's gift of unity and we acknowledge our disobedience before him. . . . But as Christ has come visibly into this world and has redeemed men of flesh and blood this union must find visible expression." There is an immediate turn from a given

BONHOEFFER'S ACCOUNT OF CHURCH UNITY

Bonhoeffer discusses church unity in the final chapter of *Sanctorum Communio*.[6] He begins the discussion decisively in the following passage:

> The unity of spirit of the church-community is a fundamental synthesis willed by God; it is not a relation that must be produced, but one that is already established (iustitia passiva! [passive righteousness]), and that remains hidden from our eyes. Neither unanimity, uniformity, nor congeniality makes it possible, nor is it to be confused with unity of mood. . . . Christ has created, out of two, a single new person in himself. . . . The decisive passages in the New Testament do not say: *one* theology and *one* rite, *one* opinion on all matters public and private, and *one* kind of conduct. Instead they say: *one* body and *one* Spirit, *one* Lord, *one* faith, *one* baptism, *one* God and father of us all (Eph. 4:4ff.; 1 Cor. 12:13; Rom. 12:5); various gifts—*one* Spirit, various offices—*one* Lord, various powers—*one* God (1 Cor. 12:4ff.) . . . the objective principle sovereignly establishes unity, unites the plurality of persons into a single collective person.[7]

To what conception of church does Bonhoeffer attribute church unity in this passage? At two separate points of this quotation, he indicates that the conception of church he is referring to is the same that was articulated in chapter 1 of this book—the church as *Christus Praesens*. In both instances, this indication is discernible in his use of person language. He writes of Christ creating "a single new person in himself" and of uniting "the plurality of persons into a single collective person."[8] In doing so, it is clear that Bonhoeffer is referring to the church he understands to be the collective person of Christ, the new humanity—what this book has been calling the revelatory person of Christ.

This account of church unity, therefore, corresponds with Bonhoeffer's account of the church as *Christus Praesens*. But what is he actually claiming about church unity? Two implications concerning Bonhoeffer's account

---

unity to an unrealized unity that the human agent is responsible for producing. The present chapter argues that the unity of the church is a given of the church and that that unity is completely an act of divine agency, without recourse to the work of human agency in any constitutive way. The primary point of distinction on this topic would be that Bonhoeffer does not identify visibility as the goal of discipleship, which he identifies instead with a sole focus on hearing and doing Christ's commands. *The New Delhi Report: The Third Assembly of the World Council of Churches, 1961.* edited by W.A. Visser't Hooft. London: SCM, 1962.

[6] DBWE 1:192–208.

[7] DBWE 1:192–193.

[8] DBWE 1:192–193.

of church unity can be drawn from this excerpt: (1) unity is inherent to the church and (2) church unity is created as a work of divine agency.[9]

Bonhoeffer describes church unity as "a fundamental synthesis willed by God."[10] Moreover, he describes the church as "a single new person" and "one body."[11] What do these descriptions signify? These descriptions signify that Bonhoeffer understands unity to be intrinsic to the church. As Christ is one, so too is the collective person of Christ that is the church. Unity is a given fact of the church's existence as the revelatory person of Christ. Bonhoeffer himself claims as much, writing,

> The personal unity of the church [Kirche] is "Christ existing as church-community [Gemeinde]". . . . The unity of the church as a structure *is* established "before" any knowing and willing of the members; it is not ideal, but real.[12]

In other words, conceiving of the church in terms of *Christus Praesens* inheres unity.[13]

---

[9] The introduction of this chapter claimed that Bonhoeffer's account of church unity has three implications. In this first section, the third implication—that the unity of the church is a spiritual and concrete reality, even today—is not articulated. The reason for this is that Bonhoeffer appears less settled on his account of the visible church in *Sanctorum Communio* than he is in the works that followed after his dissertation. At all times, he is seeking to avoid identifying the institutional forms of the empirical church with what the church essentially is. He is always careful to emphasize the "hiddenness" of the church, as he does in the above excerpt. Shortly after, he writes, "The unity of the church as a structure *is* established 'before' any knowing and willing of the members; it is not ideal, but real. It is a reality as truly as the church is the church of Christ, and as truly as the body of Christ *never becomes fully manifest in history*" (DBWE 1:199. Italics added for emphasis). In this quotation, Bonhoeffer's tension on this matter is on display. On the one hand, he speaks here and elsewhere about the unity of the church being "real"; on the other hand, he claims that the body of Christ does not fully manifest in history. The reason for this tension is that Bonhoeffer wants to make abundantly clear that the creation of—or production of—church unity is not attributed to the work of human agency or attributed to the political structures of the institutional church. Furthermore, Bonhoeffer is being careful to parse out that the church is not visible to us and that the church is beyond our assessment. In his lecture, "The Visible Church in the New Testament," Bonhoeffer says, "The space of Christ in the world is occupied by the *church; it is the present Christ*. It is to be understood as a person, as a human being, not as a multiplicity, but as a unity" (DBWE 14:446). It is clearer in the works after *Santorum Communio* that Bonhoeffer understands the unity of the church as a spiritual and concrete reality. For more on Bonhoeffer's account of the visible church, see chapter 3 of this book.

[10] DBWE 1:192.

[11] DBWE 1:192–193.

[12] DBWE 1:199.

[13] Philip J. Hefner agrees with the claim that the church is intrinsically united, but wrestles with the institutional disunity of the empirical church and its meaning for church unity, concluding that, "the unity of the church is too important to be dealt with indifferently. If there is not unity in the Eucharist and ministry or in works of love for the world, one may reasonably ask whether a basic article of the church's faith and life has not been abandoned." The point of divergence between Hefner and this chapter is that Hefner ultimately understands the church's unity in institutional terms, emphasizing the shared practice of the Eucharist and ministry as integral to unity, while Bonhoeffer does not understand these as constitutive of the church's unity (insofar as these are

These statements which outline the inherent unity of the church also demonstrate the second implication of Bonhoeffer's account of church unity—
that church unity is created through the work of divine agency. In the first
quotation, Bonhoeffer states, "[unity] is not a relation that must be produced,
but one that is already established," and "Neither unanimity, uniformity,
nor congeniality makes [unity] possible, nor is it to be confused with unity
of mood";[14] instead, "Christ has created, out of two, a single new person in
himself."[15] These statements together demonstrate that the unity of the church
is not only an intrinsic feature of its existence but that such unity has been
created by Christ—meaning it is a work of divine agency.

It can, therefore, be said positively that church unity is created through the
work of divine agency; conversely, it can also be said negatively that church
unity is *not* created through the work of human agency. Bonhoeffer is clear
that when he speaks of unity, he does not intend unanimity or uniformity of
doctrine;[16] nor does he mean congeniality between denominations.[17] Instead,
Bonhoeffer intends a unity that is created by Christ and already established
and inherent to what the church is at a fundamental level.[18]

What, then, *can* be said of the work of the human agent regarding the
unity of the church? The human agent does not have any creative role in the
founding or sustaining of the church's unity. What the human agent *does* do
regarding church unity is only discipleship. Bonhoeffer indicates as much,
writing, "Faith is possible only in the church-community, within its unity; it
is in fact the practice of this unity."[19] Bonhoeffer's use of the term "faith" here

---

cultic rituals). Hefner, Philip J. "The Church." In *Christian Dogmatics: Volume 2,* edited by Carl E.
Braaten and Robert W. Jenson, 183–253. Philadelphia: Fortress Press, 1984, 203–205.

[14] DBWE 1:192.

[15] DBWE 1:192.

[16] For more on Bonhoeffer's approach to doctrine, see Harasta, Eva. "The Responsibility of Doctrine:
Bonhoeffer's Ecclesiological Hermeneutics of Dogmatic Theology." *Theology Today* 71, no. 1
(April 2014): 14–27.

[17] DBWE 1:192.

[18] The steadfast commitment of this book to the claim that the church's intrinsic unity is solely an
act of divine agency runs in contrast to some voices who initially claim unity as a work of divine
agency, but ultimately turn to view unity as a work of human agency. For instance, Harding Meyer
states: "the unity that is a gift to us also becomes a *unity that is a task for us.*" Likewise, Brian E.
Daley argues, "The aim of what we call ecumenism . . . is not to create a unity among Christians
where none presently exists . . . but to allow the unity that already exists among us as God's gift
. . . to become *more fully evident in the way Christians look upon each other, articulate their faith,
carry out their worship, and act in the world.*" In isolation, Daley's stance has the appearance of
Bonhoeffer's ecumenism of discipleship, but Daley's account of the visible church is much more
institutionally informed than Bonhoeffer's. Meyer, Harding. *That they May All Be One: Perceptions and Models of Ecumenicity.* Translated by William G. Rusch. Grand Rapids: Eerdmans, 1999,
12; Daley, Brian E. "Rebuilding the Structure of Love: The Quest for Visible Unity Among the
Churches." In *The Ecumenical Future,* edited by Carl E. Braaten and Robert W. Jenson, 73–105.
Grand Rapids, Eerdmans 2004, 74.

[19] DBWE 1:202.

corresponds with his conception of discipleship, as can be deduced from his words, "Faith, by its nature, is exclusively directing oneself to God."[20] Thus, the human agent *participates* in the church's unity in the active discipleship of its members to Christ. It is not that discipleship produces, creates, manifests, or establishes the church's unity. Rather, through discipleship, the human agent participates in the already established unity inherent to the church.[21]

In its presentation of this account of church unity, the section has claimed that this account of church unity is consistent with the account of ecclesiology provided in chapter 1. This claim must now be made thoroughly.

LOCATING BONHOEFFER'S ACCOUNT OF CHURCH UNITY IN HIS ACCOUNT OF THE CHURCH AS *CHRISTUS PRAESENS*

The introduction to this chapter claimed that Bonhoeffer's account of the church as the revelatory person of Christ as *Christus Praesens* carries within it his account of church unity. Put otherwise, Bonhoeffer's account of church unity is consistent with and derivative of his account of ecclesiology. A return to the concepts of person and revelation and their combination in Bonhoeffer's understanding of the church as the revelatory person of Christ bears this out and further emphasizes the implications that unity is intrinsic to the church, a creation of divine agency, and both a spiritual and concrete reality today.

Person and Church Unity

The church that Bonhoeffer understands as united *is* the church as *Christus Praesens*. To be clear, this church is not to be completely identified with the institutional forms of the empirical church.[22] For this reason, Bonhoeffer's

---

[20] DBWE 1:202.

[21] Willem Visser't Hooft—inspired directly by Bonhoeffer—likewise argues that there is already a real unity of the church. Visser't Hooft, Willem. *The Pressure of Our Common Calling*. Garden City, NY: Doubleday, 1959, especially 16–30.

[22] Much ecumenical work is in agreement with Bonhoeffer—at least to some degree—that the unity of the church is not completely identifiable with the empirical church. That said, it is common for ecumenical approaches to emphasize either convergence of thought or conciliarism such that the empirical forms of the church are given a prioritized place regarding discussion of church unity. For example, the authors of "The Unity of the Church as *koinonia*" write "The goal of the search for full communion is realized when all the churches are able to recognize in one another the one, holy, catholic, and apostolic church in its fullness. This full communion will be expressed on the local and universal levels through conciliar forms of life and action. In such communion churches are bound in all aspects of their life together at all levels in confessing the one faith and engaging

understanding of church unity is not detailed in institutional terms. In *Discipleship*, Bonhoeffer writes, "While we are used to thinking of the church as an institution, we ought instead to think of it as a *person*."[23] The church does not subsist in its empirical forms—as institution; the empirical and institutional forms of the church are *incidental* to the church as *Christus Praesens*. The church's unity, therefore, does not subsist in the empirical forms of the church; rather, the church's unity subsists in the revelatory person of Christ as *Christus Praesens*.

Chapter 1 demonstrated that Bonhoeffer's concept of person is instrumental to his account of the church as *Christus Praesens*. This concept of person is, likewise, instrumental to his account of *church unity*. Indeed, it is in his articulation of person that Bonhoeffer establishes how the church is united and that that unity is intrinsic to the church.[24]

The facet of Bonhoeffer's concept of person that is particularly significant for his account of church unity is his understanding of collective persons—specifically his understanding of Christ's ability to act as vicarious representative and what this act affects. Bonhoeffer claims that Christ is able to act as vicarious representative for humanity because he is fully God and fully human.[25] Because Jesus is fully human, he is able to represent humanity;[26] because Jesus is fully God, he is able to act on behalf of humanity in such a way that creates the new humanity and enables the inclusion of other humans within this new humanity.[27] Because Jesus is fully God, he is the head of the new humanity he has created—the church;[28] because Jesus is fully human and standing in humankind's place before the Father, "he *is* the new humanity . . . he *is* the church-community."[29] In other words, due to his being fully God and fully human, Christ can and does create, rule over, and *be* the new humanity through his vicarious representative action.[30] It is through Christ's vicarious representative action that the church is the collective person of Christ. Constructing Christ's vicarious action in this way has two weighty implications for his account of church unity.

First, Bonhoeffer's articulation of the church as the collective person of Christ via Christ's vicarious representative action implies unity as a given

---

in worship and witness, deliberation and action." "The Unity of the Church as *koinonia*: Gift and Calling." In *Documentary History of Faith and Order 1968-1993,* edited by Gunther Gassmann, 3–5. Geneva: WCC, 1993.

[23] DBWE 4:218.

[24] DBWE 1:157; DBWE 1:190.

[25] DBWE 12:315.

[26] DBWE 1:146; 155–157.

[27] DBWE 1:146; 155–157.

[28] DBWE 12:315.

[29] DBWE 12:315.

[30] DBWE 1:147.

reality of the church. The church is inherently united. This intrinsic unity of the church in Bonhoeffer's account is made evident in Bonhoeffer's lecture on the "The Visible Church in the New Testament," when Bonhoeffer is recorded saying,

> The space of Christ in the world is occupied by the *church; it is the present Christ*. It is to be understood as a person, as a human being, not as a multiplicity, but as a unity. The καινὸς ἄνθρωπος [new humanity] is the unity of the church.[31]

Moreover, in *Discipleship*, Bonhoeffer writes, "The church is one . . . [the church] is the 'new human being' . . . the 'new human being' is one, not many. . . . *The church is one; it is the body of Christ*."[32] In both of these examples, Bonhoeffer makes clear that his concept of person and its relation to the church implies unity as a given for the church.[33] Unity is a fact of the church as the collective person of Christ, as the new humanity, as *Christus Preasens*.

Second, unifying the church-community as the collective person of Christ through Jesus' vicarious representative action implies that church unity is an act of divine agency. Put differently, establishing the church-community as the collective person of Christ means that the work of actually creating church unity is purely a work of divine agency, attributing no role in its creation to the work of human agency. Bonhoeffer's concept of personhood and its relation to the church, thus, promotes a church that is inherently united in a unity established by God's Godself.

Revelation and Church Unity

In *Sanctorum Communio*, Bonhoeffer asserts, "Only the concept of revelation can lead to the Christian concept of the church."[34] He comes to this conclusion by tying together his concepts of revelation and person in Christ.[35] Essentially, the way in which Bonhoeffer constructs his concepts of revelation and the collective person of Christ (specifically in Christ's vicarious representative action) determines that the church is the revelatory person of Christ. As the constitutive nature of these two concepts for Bonhoeffer's ecclesiology was

---

[31] DBWE 14:446–447.
    Donald Fergus has addressed Bonhoeffer's understanding of the space of the church. Fergus, Donald Murdoch. "Lebensraum: Just What is This 'Habitat' or 'Living Space' That Dietrich Bonhoeffer Claimed for the Church?" *Scottish Journal of Theology* 67, no. 1 (2014): 70–84.
[32] DBWE 4:218–220.
[33] DBWE 14:446–447.
[34] DBWE 1.134.
[35] DBWE 2:111–112.

explored in chapter 1, the present discussion focuses on the implications of Bonhoeffer's concept of the church as revelation for his account of church unity. This exploration of the concept of revelation further displays that unity is both intrinsic to the church and established through divine agency.

Chapter 1 introduced the four criteria Bonhoeffer requires of an adequate conception of revelation.[36] The current section looks specifically to the God-established dimension of Bonhoeffer's concept of revelation to identify what impact this concept has upon his account of church unity.

The God-established dimension of Bonhoeffer's concept of revelation is satisfied in his account of Christ's vicarious representative action on behalf of humanity. As fully God and fully human, Christ acts on behalf of humanity in his life, death, and resurrection and stands in humanity's place before God, thereby creating, ruling, and existing as the new humanity, the collective person of Christ, the church as *Christus Praesens*.[37] Detailing the creation of the church in this way determines that, for Bonhoeffer, the church as *Christus Praesens* is the form of revelation;[38] this form is inherently united by virtue of its being as the person of Christ; moreover, the creation of this unity that is inherent to the church as *Christus Praesens* is evinced to be a work of divine agency, as it is created by Christ through his vicarious representative action. Therefore, the concept of revelation that is constitutive of Bonhoeffer's account of the church contributes to his account of church unity as, in it, unity is demonstrated to be intrinsic to the form of revelation that is the person of Christ and that unity is demonstrated to be a work of divine agency because of Christ's work to establish it.

Following the architecture of the argument of chapter 1, the chapter now completes its consideration of Bonhoeffer's account of church unity by examining his understanding of the church as *Christus Praesens*—the church as the revelatory person of Christ.

The Revelatory Person of Christ and Church Unity

As chapter 1 demonstrated, the concepts of person and revelation combine to form Bonhoeffer's understanding of the church as the revelatory person of Christ—the church as *Christus Praesens*. When the account of church unity adherent to that account of church is examined, the same two implications for Bonhoeffer's account of church unity hitherto demonstrated in the concepts of person and revelation are again present—unity as intrinsic to the church and unity as a work of divine agency. It adds to these, however, a third

---

36 DBWE 2:108–109.
37 DBWE 1:146· 155· 157·
38 DBWE 2:109–116.

implication. It could be argued that to this point, the account of church unity that has been presented accounts for a spiritual unity of the church but does not account for a unity that is concrete and historical. Studying the account of church unity adherent to an understanding of the church as the revelatory person of Christ yields this historical concretion. For Bonhoeffer, the church is united concretely in space-time.[39]

To be clear, the argument is *not* that the church is united in the world today as a uniform institution with uniform beliefs;[40] to say so would be patently false and would be to completely contradict the account of church unity that has been developed to this point. The argument, instead, is that the church as *Christus Praesens* exists within space-time, and therefore the unity that is inherent to the church must also exist within space-time. The argument is also *not* that discipleship creates, manifests, expresses, or has any other sort of creative role at all in the church's unity. The argument, instead, is that the existence of the human beings who exist within this revelatory person of Christ is characterized by discipleship—the practical content of which is concrete acts of obedience to Christ's commands. Thus, because the human agent's existence within this revelatory person of Christ is characterized by discipleship and because this revelatory person of Christ is inherently one, the concrete discipleship of the human agent within the revelatory person of Christ evinces a church unity that is concrete and present within spatio-temporality.

---

[39] The claim that the united church is already present and complete in spatio-temporality is one that would be refuted in some ecumenical thought. Much of the reason for this disagreement stems from a conception of the church and its concrete unity in terms of the institutional forms of the empirical church. One example of this stance is found in *In One Body Through the Cross: The Princeton Proposal for Christian Unity*, the authors of which write: "Therefore, the quest for a deeper unity among Christians is a discipline internal to the life of faith. It has two fundamental assumptions: a) that Christian unity is an intrinsic part of the transformed life God works among those who live in the faith of Jesus, and b) that it is a goal yet to be fully achieved in concrete, visible terms. . . . The gift of the church's unity remains, in Christ, a promise for the future. The fulfillment of this promise is a common life of shared worship, joint witness, agreed conviction, and mutual care, expressing the single vocation Scripture calls 'the one hope of your calling' and rooted in 'one Lord, one faith, one baptism.'" *In One Body Through the Cross: The Princeton Proposal for Christian Unity.* Edited by Carl E. Braaten and Robert W. Jenson. Grand Rapids: Eerdmans, 2003, 14–15. Bonhoeffer does not articulate the united church in these institutional terms and is thereby able to make the claim that the church *is* concretely united even now. The point of distinction remains that the authors of the *Princeton Proposal* understand church unity as subsisting in the institutional forms of the church, while Bonhoeffer posits a church unity that subsists in Christ's person as the new humanity.

[40] The authors of the WCC's "Unity Statement" from 2013 write: "The unity of the Church is not uniformity; diversity is also a gift, creative and life-giving. But diversity cannot be so great that those in Christ become strangers and enemies to one another, thus damaging the uniting reality of life in Christ . . . our disunity undermines our witness to the good news of Jesus Christ and makes less credible our witness to that unity God desires for all." In this way, the authors of the "Unity Statement" agree that unity is not uniformity. When they write of disunity, it does not refer to a disunity in Christ, but a significant and violent disunity between empirical churches when they see each other as strangers or enemies http://www.oikoumene.org/en/resources/documents/assembly /2013-buas/adopted-documents-statements/unity-statement, 2013.

In discussing the presence of church unity in spatio-temporality, the section enters into the territory of the topic of church visibility, which is the subject of chapter 3. The topic must be discussed in this chapter as it relates to church unity. Bonhoeffer expounds on this matter in *Sanctorum Communio*, writing:

> The church is God's new will and purpose for humanity. God's will is always directed toward the concrete, historical human being. But this means that it begins to be implemented *in history*. God's will must become visible and comprehensible at some point in history. But at the same point it must already be completed. Therefore, it must be revealed. Revelation of God's will is necessary because the primal community, where God speaks and the word becomes deed and history through human beings, is broken. Therefore God must personally speak and act, and at the same time accomplish a new creation of human beings, since God's word is always deed. *Thus the church is already completed in Christ, just as in Christ its beginning is established.*[41]

In these words, Bonhoeffer states that the church must "be implemented *in history*" and "must already be completed."[42] Put otherwise, for Bonhoeffer, the church must be concretely present in spatio-temporality, and it must be so in the totality of all that the church is. This claim holds immense significance for Bonhoeffer's account of church unity.

The claim that the church must be present concretely within history in the full sense of the meaning of the church as *Christus Praesens* means that the intrinsic unity of the church is a fact of the church's existence not simply in an abstract, spiritual way, but that the church is united within spatio-temporality. When Bonhoeffer in "The Visible Church in the New Testament" states,

> The space of Christ in the world is occupied by the *church; it is the present Christ.* It is to be understood as a person, as a human being, not as a multiplicity, but as a unity. The καινὸς ἄνθρωπος [new humanity] is the unity of the church,

the entirety of this quotation pertains to the church as it exists concretely within space-time. [43]

In Bonhoeffer's thinking, "the church is one"[44]—"[the church] is to be understood . . . as a unity."[45] The church as *Christus Praesens* is present in the world and it is united as a fact of its existence as the new humanity. The

---

[41] DBWE 1:141–142.
[42] DBWE 1:141–142.
[43] DBWE 14:446–447.
[44] ΠΠWΓ ⅃ ?1Ω
[45] DBWE 14:446–447.

church as it exists in the world even today is united, and *it cannot be other-wise*. To say that the church as it exists in the world is not united is incongru-ous and untenable in Bonhoeffer's account of the church.[46]

These statements are not to say that the church-community is perfect, nor is it to ignore the very real (and sometimes violent) disagreements between denominations or church-communities.[47] Instead, Bonhoeffer's account of church unity forces these issues to be called by a name other than ecclesial disunity.[48] Regarding the impurity of the church, Bonhoeffer maintains a firm stance that there is sin in the church and that those within the church remain capable of sin. Issues of doctrinal difference, denominational conflict, and the expansive variety of ways in which the empirical church orders itself institutionally do not factor in to Bonhoeffer's understanding of church unity, and thus, they do not signify ecclesial disunity.[49] For Bonhoeffer, the unity

---

[46] This may feel like an idealistic account of church unity given the plurality of denominations, but it is not. The authors of "Towards Unity in Tension" "resolutely refuse any too easy forms of unity," and yet concede that "forces of division are finally overcome in the unity which Christ creates and gives, as he leads all things to unity in himself." While these authors identify a need of the church to "work for unity" that Bonhoeffer does not include, they are largely in agreement that the unity of the church is created and given in Christ, and that this account of unity is not "too easy." "Towards Unity in Tension." In *Documentary History of Faith and Order 1968-1993,* edited by Gunther Gassmann, *Faith and Order paper no. 159,* 144–147. Geneva: WCC, 1993.

[47] Jose Miguez Bonino insists that the lines of division be taken seriously as "the basic reference for our discussion of unity." He argues that "the search for unity is the struggle of the Church as it strives to take shape in the quest for a new kind of human life in a new society." Bonhoeffer is not opposed to such sentiments, nor does he ignore the downtrodden. He bases his account of church unity in the person of Christ and emphasizes the work of discipleship, which will engender a new kind of human life and a new society. Bonino, Jose Miguez. "A Latin American Attempt to Locate the Question of Unity." In *What Kind of Unity?* Faith and Order Paper no. 69, 51–60. Geneva: WCC, 1973.

[48] In the 1932 catechism he wrote with Franz Hildebrand, Bonhoeffer laments the fact that there are so many denominations, writing: "Why, then, are there so many churches? We really should be *one* church. Due to our *inexplicable disunion,* we insist on a new community of all Christians. To have such a new community is never possible for us as human beings other than in expectation and in a faith that is faithful to God's Church." This quotation appears to equate the multiplicity of denominations with disunity; Bonhoeffer's next statements, however, imply otherwise. He goes on to identify the "true church" as there where Christ is present in Word, sacrament, and church-community, thereby highlighting the same ecclesiology he has maintained since at least as early as *Sanctorum Communio*. This ecclesiology is united as a basic fact of its existence. Language of "inexplicable disunion" must, therefore, be understood as an instance in which Bonhoeffer is still learning to explicate his understanding of the relation between church unity and church visibility. DBWE 11:265, emphasis added.

[49] Many disagree with this assertion that institutional disunity does not factor into the concrete unity of the church in the world. Michael Root, for example, grapples with the perception that there is an essential unity of the church and an apparent disunity in its institutional reality, as evinced in the many denominations. Root's entire narration of church unity runs along the lines of the work of human agency in the practices by which he claims churches participate in the church's being. He argues that there are practices which the churches have in common and other practices in which participation is a joint endeavor—for example, that the denominations ordain ministers for their own denominations but not for others. Underpinning all of Root's thought is the idea that unity has principally to do with the cultus acts and institutional organization of the church. Bonhoeffer's stance does not articulate church unity in such institutional terms. Root, Michael. "Essential Unity

of the church subsists in the unity of the revelatory person of Christ, who is concretely present in the world today as church as *Christus Praesens.*[50]

That the church as *Christus Praesens* is concretely present in spatio-temporality is exceedingly significant for those within the church in the world. The church as the revelatory person of Christ in the world means that Christ truly encounters people;[51] the church as the revelatory person of Christ in the world means that Christ truly transforms people into the new humanity;[52] the church as the revelatory person of Christ in the world means that Christ truly calls people to discipleship in the world.[53]

It is this last claim that begins to involve the work of the human agent in Bonhoeffer's account of church unity. As this chapter has demonstrated, Bonhoeffer attributes the creation of the church's unity to the work of divine agency. The discipleship of the human agent does nothing to create church unity. That said, inclusion in the collective person of Christ entails an encounter with Christ—an encounter in which one is called to discipleship.[54] The existence of those within the collective person of Christ is, therefore, characterized by discipleship. As Bonhoeffer put it in *Discipleship*, "Christianity without the living Jesus Christ remains necessarily a Christianity without discipleship; and a Christianity without discipleship is always a Christianity without Jesus Christ."[55] Although the discipleship of the human agent does not create church unity, there is no being in the collective person of Christ for the human agent without discipleship. To be a disciple is what it means to be in the church as *Christus Praesens.*

The content of discipleship is hearing and doing the commands of Christ;[56] as Bonhoeffer writes, "The call to discipleship has no other content than Jesus Christ himself, being bound to him, community with him."[57] Being bound to Christ and having community with him is exactly what it means to be in the church as the revelatory person of Christ.[58] What does the discipleship of the human agent have to do with Bonhoeffer's account of church unity? If the existence of the human agent within the church as the revelatory person of Christ is characterized by discipleship, and the church as the revelatory person

---

and Lived Communion: The Interrelation of the Unity We Have and the Unity We Seek." In *The Ecumenical Future,* edited by Carl E. Braaten and Robert W. Jenson, 106–125. Grand Rapids: Eerdmans, 2004.
50 DBWE 14:446–447.
51 DBWE 2:82.
52 DBWE 1:140–143.
53 DBWE 4:57–64; 4:74; 4:87; 4:111–112; 4:178–182; 4:215; 4:232; 4:247; 4:280; 4:281; 4:287–288.
54 DBWE 4:57.
55 DBWE 4:59.
56 DBWE 4:47.
57 DBWE 4:74.
58 DBWE 2:112.

of Christ is concretely present within space-time, it follows that the existence of those within the church as the revelatory person of Christ in the world—and therefore the concrete presence of the revelatory person of Christ in the world writ large—is characterized by discipleship.[59] How is the church that is inherently united as *Christus Praesens* concretely present in the world today? It is present in the world in the active discipleship of the church.

A more concrete example of what it means that discipleship is the work of the human agent regarding church unity can be found in a 1940 correspondence between Bonhoeffer and Bethge. Bonhoeffer is musing over the possibility of coming together with the Catholic Church, when he writes:

> One more word on the Catholic question: How did we Lutherans come together with the Reformed? Actually quite untheologically . . . [We came together] by two things: by the "guidance" of God (Union, Confessing Church), and by the recognition of what is objectively given in the sacrament—Christ is more important than our thoughts about him and about his presence. Both are theologically questionable foundations, and yet the church made a decision for fellowship of the altar—that is, for church fellowship. It made a decision to recognize the Union as God's guidance; it made a decision to subordinate its thinking and doctrine of Christ to the objectivity of Christ's presence (even in the Reformed Lord's Supper). But it came to no sort of theological unity. . . . *It seems to me as if churches unite not primarily theologically but rather through faith-based decisions*, in the sense above. That is a dangerous sentence, I know! One could make anything of it! But isn't this how we have acted, practically speaking, in the Confessing Church? Of course, the guidance was more visible then. I am not suggesting all this could take place tomorrow or the next day, but I would like to keep my eyes open in this direction![60]

The content of Bonhoeffer's words here stray into the realm of a discussion of church visibility but is significant for the purposes of this chapter because it demonstrates what Bonhoeffer intends regarding the role of the human agent in church unity. Bonhoeffer states that "churches unite not primarily theologically but rather through faith-based decision."[61] By articulating "faith-based decision" as the core of united action, Bonhoeffer

---

[59] Germanos of Thyateira provides an Orthodox perspective on unity from the early involvement of the Orthodox Church in the ecumenical movement, describing unity as a call. Germanos of Thyateira. "The Call to Unity." In *Faith and Order: Proceedings of the World Conference, Lausanne 1927,* edited by H.N. Bate, 18–23. London: SCM, 1927.

[60] DDWE 16,01 06,

[61] Ibid.

is identifying discipleship as that core.[62] In *Discipleship*, when Bonhoeffer identifies Christ's presence in the church as the place at which Christ's commands can be heard, he writes that discipleship "is always a *decision* for or against Jesus Christ."[63] This decision is the answer of the disciple to Christ's command. This decision is what Bonhoeffer intends in his language of a "faith-based decision" as the work of the human agent regarding church unity. This decision does not create unity. This decision is the obedient response of discipleship—an obedient response that (as chapter 3 explains) results in ecclesial visibility as an inevitable by-product of (but not a goal of) discipleship to Christ.

CONCLUSION

The preceding discussion demonstrates that church unity is an inherent part of Bonhoeffer's understanding of the church as *Christus Praesens*. If the church is the revelatory person of Christ, and if the person of Christ is one, then the church, too, must be one. Such an account of church unity funds three significant claims. First, church unity is intrinsic to the church. For Bonhoeffer, that the church is one is not a matter of debate but simply a fact of the reality of the church. Second, an account of church unity adherent to an understanding of the church as *Christus Praesens* implies that the unity of the church is a work of God. Church unity, for Bonhoeffer, is not something those within the church strive to create or to sustain. Rather, the unity of the church is created and sustained by God's action. Finally, Bonhoeffer—in his account of church unity—claims that the unity of the church is complete and concretely present today. Over against the idea of a mystical church unity that does not find expression in the world, Bonhoeffer posits that the revelatory person of Christ is *present* in the world in the church. Therefore, the unity inherent to the revelatory person of Christ is likewise present in the world. Having traced Bonhoeffer's account of church unity and having come to this third claim of the concrete unity of the church, it is necessary for the next chapter to address Bonhoeffer's account of the *visible* unity of the church.

---

[62] In Bonhoeffer's essay, "Lecture on the Path of the Young Illegal Theologians," he expands upon this approach to unity regarding the concrete situation of the results of Dahlem. He stresses that those who adhered to Dahlem acted on behalf of the entire church, while those who did not became *false* churches. He writes: "Unity exists only in the unity of faith, expressed in *confession*. Dahlem has called the church to unity on the basis of the word: Everyone therefore who acknowledges me before others, I also will acknowledge before my Father in heaven. From this position, Dahlem claimed—for the new and true church leadership—the validity of the entire church." This is an example of making a faith-based decision. DBWE 15:423.

[63] DBWE 4:202, emphasis added.

Chapter 3

The Visible Church

The visible unity of the church is a chief topic of interest within the ecumenical movement. Any ecumenical theology of quality must be able to give an account of the practicability of church unity. Bonhoeffer's ecumenical theology is no exception. The previous chapter came to the profound conclusion that unity is intrinsic to the church and that church unity is a concrete reality today. One could be forgiven for questioning whether the church is visibly united in the world. It is one thing to say that the church is united but quite another to posit that unity as a practical and concrete reality. Many within the church are comfortable to say the former, while the latter becomes a point of great contention. The contentious nature of the church's visible unity is fairly reasonable when one considers the empirical church as it exists now and as it has existed throughout time.

A jaded church historian might rightly point to the seemingly innumerable times in which the empirical church has perpetrated heinous acts of violence and hate, such as during the Crusades. A more ecclesiologically optimistic thinker might present the counterargument that those were really *political* affairs and that the *true* church was not actually involved. Then one must consider the plurality of denominations and the (sometimes violent) church schisms seen throughout history. As such, the present state of the institutional church and its fractious history leave many to wonder how anyone could possibly think the church is *visibly* united. A popular approach to the question of church visibility has been to articulate a distinction between the visible and invisible church, in which the visible church (the institutional, empirical church) is flawed and fallen, while the invisible church (the hidden reality of the true church) is pure.[1] Bonhoeffer rejects this approach.

---

[1] Martin Luther is generally pointed to as an early proponent of this idea. Some of these invisible church and visible church ideas can be seen in his approach to the ban. Luther, Martin. *Luther*

73

As chapter 2 illumined, Bonhoeffer understands the church to be inherently united and to be so *concretely within history even today*. That said, Bonhoeffer does not identify the church with its institutional forms. What Bonhoeffer offers is a different account of church visibility than is generally thought of along the lines of a visible/invisible church distinction. Attending to Bonhoeffer's account of church visibility offers rich potential for contemporary ecumenical discourse.

Bonhoeffer is consistently concerned with the visibility of the church as he articulates his ecclesiology. Indeed, he even explicitly teaches on the subject at Finkenwalde in a lecture series titled "The Visible Church in the New Testament."[2] As such, the topic of visibility retains a significant place within Bonhoeffer's ecclesiology. Drawing this account out serves an accurate depiction of both Bonhoeffer's ecclesiology and the ecumenical theology that is built upon that ecclesiology.

Bonhoeffer's account of church visibility, like his account of church unity, emerges from his understanding of the church as *Christus Praesens*. The chapter argues that, for Bonhoeffer, the visible church is created by the triune God and that visibility is a by-product of the active work of discipleship. The church is not visible as an institution or a set of cultic practices or doctrines,[3] nor is the church visible in a program for social justice or humanitarian efforts; instead, for Bonhoeffer, the church is visible and takes up concrete space in the world through the active obedience of discipleship. Pursuant to this argument, this chapter details Bonhoeffer's understanding of visibility itself, presents his account of church visibility, and concludes with a discussion of sin in the church.

BONHOEFFER'S UNDERSTANDING OF "VISIBILITY"

Accounts of the visible church are wide and varying. The Roman Catholic Church conceives of church visibility within the hierarchical structure of its

---

Works, Volume 39: Church and Ministry I. Edited by Eric E. Gritsch. Philadelphia: Fortress Press, 1970, 7–8.

[2] DBWE 14:434–476.

[3] Robert Jenson argues that "the basic flaw in ecumenical theology" is that a vast majority of ecumenical work begins with the question of the "basic difference" between doctrinal stances of different denominations, when they should instead start with the acknowledgment that the churches have never fully developed a doctrine of God. In other words, the churches have a shared flaw rather than a basic difference. While Bonhoeffer agrees with Jenson that the doctrine of the church is indexed to the doctrine of God, the two differ greatly on their ecumenical theology. They differ because Jenson identifies the church principally in its institutional form in the various denominations, and thus sees the church as divided. Bonhoeffer does not do so and therefore diverges at the outset from the ecumenical understanding of Jenson. Jenson, Robert W. *Unbaptized God: The Basic Flaw in Ecumenical Theology.* Minneapolis: Fortress Press, 1992.

offices.[4] Essentially, in this view, the church is present and visible where the pope, cardinals, bishops, priests, on down to the laity are present and visible. In the World Council of Churches, there are many different understandings of church visibility among its member churches.[5] For instance, there are those that have an institutional view of church visibility that is similar to that of the Roman Catholic Church, while there are those that understand the church as visible in the convergence of doctrine between denominations; others understand the church as visible in the service of its members to the community; still others understand visible church unity as the collaborative efforts of denominations in both service and the convergence of doctrine; and among all of these is the possibility of viewing church visibility as some combination of these views. Along with these differing understandings of how the church is visible are the differing understandings of what such visibility means regarding church unity. Does the visibility of the church attest to the unity of the church? Are the unity and visibility of the church connected, synonymous, entirely separate, or related only vaguely to each other?

Bonhoeffer approaches church visibility differently from these positions. For him, the unity of the church is a fact of its being the revelatory person of Christ as *Christus Praesens*, and the visibility of the church is a by-product of obedient discipleship; the church that is visible is the church as *Chrstus Praesens*—meaning that the complete unity of the church is not divorced from its visibility—and that church is visible and concrete in the active works of discipleship. This construction of church visibility means that Bonhoeffer does not understand church visibility in institutional terms, doctrinal terms, or even service-oriented terms.[6] Visibility is not a goal to which disciples aspire. Disciples focus only on hearing and doing the commands of Christ,

---

[4] For example, the authors of Lumen Gentium write: "They are fully incorporated in the society of the Church who, possessing the Spirit of Christ accept her entire system and all the means of salvation given to her, and are united with her as part of her visible bodily structure and through her with Christ, who rules her through the Supreme Pontiff and the bishops." Vatican Council. *Dogmatic Constitution on the Church: Lumen Gentium, Solemnly Promulgated by His Holiness, Pope Paul VI on November 21, 1964.* Boston: St. Paul Editions, 1965, 14; See also Rahner, Karl. *Bishops: Their Status and Function.* Compass Books 5. London: Burns & Oates, 1964. Especially chapter 6.

[5] TS: III.5.

[6] This approach stands over against Protestant viewpoints that would posit church visibility in Luther's famous seven marks of the church, by which Luther suggests that the church is visible and findable in its cultic acts and institutional form. The authors of *Marks of the Body of Christ* embrace this idea, narrating each of the seven marks of the church. Although Bonhoeffer does write on the topics of the seven marks in his lecture series on the visible church, these marks are located downstream from the central work of the visible church being created and founded through the work of divine agency; furthermore, when Bonhoeffer *does* eventually touch on each of these topics, he re-narrates them. As such, Bonhoeffer is clear that the visible church does not subsist in these marks. *Marks of the Body of Christ.* Edited by Carl E. Braaten and Robert W. Jenson. Grand Rapids. Eerdmans, 1999. DBWE 14:434–475.

and in doing this, *the church is concretely visible as a matter of course.*[7] But how does Bonhoeffer construct his account of ecclesial visibility and reach these conclusions?

Before grasping *how* the church is visible, it is important to note *to whom* the church is visible in Bonhoeffer's thought. For Bonhoeffer, the church is not visible to those within the church.[8] Stated differently, those within the church are unaware of their own visibility. Bonhoeffer puts it this way in *Discipleship*:

> The incarnate, the crucified, and the transfigured Christ takes on form in indi-
> viduals because they are members of his body, the church. . . . Since we have
> been formed in the image of Christ, we can live following his example. . . . Here
> simple obedience to the word takes place. I no longer cast even a single glance
> on my own life, on the new image I bear. For in the same moment that I would
> desire to see it, I would lose it. For it is, of course, merely the mirror reflection
> of the image of Jesus Christ upon which I look without ceasing. The followers
> look only to the one whom they follow. But now the final word about those who
> as disciples bear the image . . . is that they are called to be "imitators of God."
> The follower of Jesus is the imitator of God.[9]

This quotation is found at the end of *Discipleship* in Bonhoeffer's treatment of the *imago Dei*. In the first sentence of this excerpt, Bonhoeffer's stance that "Christ takes on form" in the church indicates that he is writing about the church as *Christus Praesens* and the disciple within the church as has been detailed in the first two chapters of this book.[10] This first sentence, thus, determines that when Bonhoeffer is writing about the individual disciple's inability to look upon their own visibility without losing it, the same holds true for the church as a whole.[11] Any attempt by those in the church to evaluate their own visibility results in that visibility being lost. Therefore, the church is not capable of seeing or assessing its own visibility.

So, to whom *is* the church visible? The church is visible to those not in the church, and to Christ.[12] Bonhoeffer's introduction to his chapter on the Sermon on the Mount in *Discipleship* demonstrates this distinction. There, Bonhoeffer describes the point of view of three different groups present for the sermon: the crowd, the disciples, and Jesus.[13] He expresses that when the

---

[7] DBWE 4:287–288.
[8] DBWE 4:288.
[9] DBWE 4:287–288.
[10] DBWE 4:287.
[11] DBWE 4:287–288.
[12] DBWE 4:100–102.
[13] DBWE 4:100–102.

crowd looks at the disciples, they see that the disciples have left everything to follow Jesus: "Something has happened to [the disciples] which has not happened to the others. This is an extremely unsettling and offensive fact, which is *visibly evident* to the crowd."[14] In these words, Bonhoeffer expresses that the church is visible to those outside the church.

The church is likewise visible to Christ: "*Jesus sees:* his disciples are over there. They have *visibly* left the people to join him. . . . They have only him."[15] In addition to being visible to those outside the church, the church is visible to Christ. The reason for the church's hiddenness from itself and visibility to Christ and those outside the church becomes clear with an understanding of *how* the church is visible in Bonhoeffer's account.

Bonhoeffer does not understand visibility in terms of institution but in terms of discipleship. The church is not visible due to its structures or institutions; rather *it is visible through discipleship as a matter of course*. The ethical content of discipleship is characterized by hearing and doing the concrete commands of Christ, or as Bonhoeffer puts it: "The disciple's answer is not a spoken confession of faith in Jesus. Instead, it is the obedient deed . . . everything depends upon call and deed directly facing each other."[16] It is in this deed of obedient discipleship that the church is visible; this deed of obedient discipleship is visible and concrete, evincing the way in which the church is visible and takes up space in the world. Visibility is not a goal of the disciple, whose goal is to "look only to their Lord,"[17] instead, visibility is a by-product—an inevitable result—of the obedient and concrete deed of discipleship.[18] Thus, ecclesial visibility, in Bonhoeffer's account, is deeply connected to discipleship.[19]

BONHOEFFER'S ACCOUNT OF THE VISIBLE CHURCH

Bonhoeffer's account of the visible church—like his account of church unity—is part of his ecclesiology. For Bonhoeffer, there is no difference between the church and the visible church—the two are one and the same; in speaking of the visible church, Bonhoeffer is simply detailing how it is that the church is concretely present and visible in the world.[20] Between

---

[14] DBWE 4:100. Italics added.
[15] DBWE 4:101. Italics added.
[16] DBWE 4:57.
[17] DBWE 4:251.
[18] DBWE 4:66.
[19] DBWE 4:287–288.
[20] Put otherwise, Bonhoeffer rejects the notion of an invisible/visible church distinction. Mawson makes this same observation in his analysis of *Sanctorum Communio*, writing, "The real church is not something that stands above or apart from the actual church in its concrete, empirical form.

November 11, 1935, and February 27, 1936, Bonhoeffer gave a lecture series at Finkenwalde on "The Visible Church in the New Testament."[21] From the start of this series, Bonhoeffer is clear that he is not seeking to articulate an entity called "the visible church," which is separate from the church, but rather he is seeking to articulate both that the church *does* take up physical space in the world and *how* the church takes up space in the world.[22] The result is an understanding of the visible church as the church as *Christus Praesens*, created through the work of divine agency, the role of whose members is discipleship. It is helpful, therefore, to construct the account of the visible church along these lines: first by narrating the activity of God in creating the visible church, and only then attending to the activity of those within the visible church.

Founding the Visible Church: The Work of God

Bonhoeffer begins his lecture series "The Visible Church in the New Testament" with a lecture on the founding of the visible church.[23] The entire first lecture is dedicated to detailing the way in which the visible church is founded in the work of divine agency. Structuring the lecture this way instantly clarifies that the creation and sustenance of the church is a matter of the work of divine agency and not human agency, even when discussing the visible church. The content of this first lecture attends to the work of each article of the Trinity in the founding of the visible church.[24] In doing so, Bonhoeffer situates his account of the visible church under the doctrine

---

In other words, the church is not an ideal that the existing community must either direct itself towards or strive to embody. . . . On the other hand, Bonhoeffer's clear insistence upon the existing or empirical church as the place of God's word or revelation should not be too closely identified with attempts to emphasize the 'visible church' in Christian theology and ethics . . . it is only the church as a *sinful* . . . community, for Bonhoeffer, that is the body of Christ as the place of God's revelation." Mawson, *Christ Existing as Community*, 151–153.

This stance goes against other proponents of Bonhoeffer scholarship who *do* emphasize the concrete, institutional, congregation in Bonhoeffer's theology. Such proponents include Hauerwas, Stanley. *Performing the Faith: Bonhoeffer and the Practice of Nonviolence.* Grand Rapids: Brazos Press; SPCK, 2004; McClendon, James. *Systematic Theology: Ethics,* vol 1. Nashville: Abingdon Press, 2002, 188–208; Nation, *Bonhoeffer the Assassin.*

This chapter is also consistent with Mawson's conclusions about Bonhoeffer's understanding of sin in the church.

21 DBWE 14:434–476.

22 DBWE 14:438.

23 DBWE 14:438–446.

24 Colin E. Gunton has also addressed church visibility and the being of the church by indexing ecclesiology to the doctrine of God and exploring what the doctrine of the Trinity signifies for church visibility. Gunton, Colin E. "The Church on Earth: The Roots of Community." In *On Being the Church: Essays on the Christian Community,* edited by Colin E Gunton and Daniel W Hardy, 48–81. Edinburgh: T&T Clark, 1989.

of God—just as he does with his account of ecclesiology as a whole.[25] More specifically, he attributes the founding of the visible church to the work of the Trinity. Doing so establishes the work of divine agency as a key factor in the founding of the visible church.[26]

As was true of Bonhoeffer's account of the founding of the church in general, he identifies God as the creator of the visible church. Specifically, he claims the visible church as "a new act of creation on God's part."[27] Thus, the work of creating the visible church is attributed to divine agency.

Christ's role in founding the visible church is realizing the visible church in his life, death, and resurrection.[28] Christ's realization of the church is consistent with the account of the church as *Christus Praesens* detailed in chapter 1. Christ creates, is Lord over, and *is* the new humanity—the church—in his life, death, and resurrection.[29] In this, the visible church is realized but not yet actualized.

Bonhoeffer attributes the *actualizing* of the visible church to the work of the Holy Spirit.[30] It is through the actualizing role of the Holy Spirit that Bonhoeffer's concept of Christ existing as church-community becomes effectual in the visible church.[31] Or, as Bonhoeffer puts it, "The space of Christ

---

[25] Bonhoeffer is not alone in making this theological move. John Webster also identifies ecclesiology as a derivative doctrine under the doctrine of God. Webster, John. "'In the Society of God': Some Principles of Ecclesiology." In *Perspectives on Ecclesiology and Ethnography*, edited by Pete Ward, 200–222 (especially 205–206). Cambridge, UK: William B. Eerdmans Publishing Company, 2012. See also Greggs, Tom. "Proportion and Topography in Ecclesiology: A Working Paper on the Dogmatic Location of the Doctrine of the Church," in *Theological Theology: Essays in Honour of John Webster*, edited by R. David Nelson and Darren Sarisky, 89–106. London: Bloomsbury T&T Clark, 2015.

[26] Recent Trinitarian discourse might lead one to expect the use of Trinitarian terms in describing the visible church to indicate a social Trinitarian or relational Trinitarian account. However, Bonhoeffer's use of Trinitarian language here falls under neither of these categories. He does not view the relationships that the members of the Trinity have with each other as analogous or exemplary of human relationships with each other, as social Trinitarians do. Neither does he posit that humanity is swept up into the movements of love between the members of the Trinity, as relational Trinitarians do. Bonhoeffer's use of Trinitarian language assumes relationships between the members of the Trinity, but these relationships are not the driving force of his use of Trinitarian language. See Volf, Miroslav. *Exclusion and Embrace: A Theological Exploration of Identity, Otherness, and Reconciliation.* Nashville: Abingdon Press, 1996, 127; Fiddes, Paul S. *Participating in God: A Pastoral Doctrine of the Trinity.* London: Darton, Longman & Todd; Westminster John Knox, 2000.

[27] DBWE 14:442.

[28] DBWE 11:305. Bonhoeffer does not explicitly articulate Christ's action in founding the visible church as "realizing" the visible church, but his articulation of the church as "the present Christ" and "as a person," along with his statement, "Christ is the church, church-community, the new human being" (DBWE 14:446–448), makes clear that his understanding of Christ's role in the founding of the visible church is consistent with his understanding of Christ's founding of the church articulated elsewhere in his corpus as "realizing" the church (DBWE 1:157). The section uses this term "realizing" in order to distinguish it from the role of the Holy Spirit of "actualizing" the visible church.

[29] DBWE 14:449–455.

[30] DBWE 14:455.

[31] DBWE 14:455.

existing as church-community is thus simultaneously the space of the Holy Spirit in the believer. Only as such is the space of Christ—*real* church."[32] Here, it is clear that the role of the Holy Spirit in the founding of the visible church is integral to Bonhoeffer's account of the visible church as the Holy Spirit brings Christ to those in the church and actualizes the present person of Christ in the world.

In sum, Bonhoeffer locates the creation and sustenance of the visible church in the divine work of the Trinity.[33] This account of God creating the visible church, Christ realizing the visible church, and the Holy Spirit actualizing the visible church matches his account of the work of the Trinity in creating the church that was provided in chapter 1. Furthermore, Bonhoeffer's articulation of the roles of the articles of the Trinity in the founding of the visible church accentuate the fact that this Trinitarian construction does not signify discontinuity with the account of the church as *Christus Praesens*; once again, the church is still understood as the revelatory person of Christ as Christ's presence in the world today;[34] the Trinitarian language does not show two distinct accounts of the church—one which is purely Christological and one which is Trinitarian—but rather a single account of the church as *Christus Praesens* that includes the active working of each article of the Trinity. In speaking of the founding of the church—visible or in general—Bonhoeffer intends his understanding of the church as *Christus Praesens*; in discussing visibility, Bonhoeffer merely concerns himself with detailing the visibility of that account of ecclesiology.

The Work of Human Agency in the Visible Church

This treatment of the role of divine agency in creating and sustaining the visible church frames the role of the human agent in the church. The role of the human agent in the visible church is discipleship. It is important to be clear regarding the work of divine and human agency—and their interrelation—in Bonhoeffer's concept of the visible church. It is *not* the case that church visibility has only to do with the work of divine agency to the *exclusion* of any work of the human agent; and it is likewise *not* the case that the work of the human agent *creates* church visibility; instead, church visibility is created and sustained through the work of divine agency, and the work of divine agency *creates space within its own work* in which the human agent is called to active

---

[32] DBWE 14:455.
[33] DBWE 14:438–458.

Although Philip Hefner is in agreement with Bonhoeffer regarding the Trinitarian locus of the church, he nevertheless ultimately narrates church visibility through an explication of Luther's seven marks of the church—a more Bonhoeffer never makes. Hefner, "The Church," 223–238.

[34] DBWE 14:438.

work identifiable as discipleship. The point is that church visibility has *principally* to do with the work of divine agency, and yet there remains an active role for the human agent. This active role of the human agent does not create church visibility; it works within the work of divine agency.

In other words, the roles of divine and human agency are asymmetrical. It is true that both divine and human agents have active roles. Even so, it is the work of divine agency that is constitutive of the visible church and frames the work of human agency.

Bonhoeffer's treatment of sanctification and works in *Discipleship* is particularly useful for a discussion of the role of human agency in church visibility because it displays how the work of the human agent relates to the visibility of the church. This treatment of sanctification and works identifies discipleship as the active role of human agency in his account of the visible church.[35]

Bonhoeffer's treatment of sanctification and works is found in his chapter "The Saints" in *Discipleship*.[36] Significant for the purposes of the present discussion, "The Saints" is the chapter immediately following the chapter "The Visible Church-Community." While in "The Visible Church-Community," Bonhoeffer addresses the creation of the visible church along the lines of *Christus Praesens* and expounds upon the work of the members of the Trinity in creating the visible church, of which God makes humans members as disciples (precisely what has just been demonstrated through examining "The Visible Church in the New Testament"),[37] in "The Saints," Bonhoeffer attends to the works of the human agent within the visible church.

That Bonhoeffer writes these as two distinct chapters emphasizes the significance of understanding the church and the visible church as principally

---

[35] Greggs also considers sanctification when investigating the topic of visible church unity—doing so from a Methodist perspective through a sermon of John Wesley. Greggs and Bonhoeffer agree that visible unity is concerned with sanctification, and that it does *not* rest upon polity or doctrine. The difference between these two is that Greggs highlights a visibility in Wesley's sermons that is recognizable between believers, while Bonhoeffer stresses the hiddenness of visibility from the church. Greggs, Tom. "The Catholic Spirit of Protestantism: A Very Methodist Take on the Third Article, Visible Unity and Ecumenism." *Pro Ecclesia*, 26, no. 4 (Fall 2017): 353–372; 365.

For more on Bonhoeffer and sanctification, see Knight, M. J. "Christ Existing in Ordinary: Dietrich Bonhoeffer and Sanctification." *International Journal of Systematic Theology* 16, no. 4 (October 2014): 414–435.

[36] DBWE 4:254–280.

The aim of this section is not to provide a comprehensive account of Bonhoeffer's treatment of sanctification and all of its implications. Instead, the section attends to Bonhoeffer's account of sanctification merely to demonstrate the role of the human agent in the visible church. For a more detailed study of Bonhoeffer's treatment of sanctification, see Joseph McGarry's doctoral dissertation, which draws out the theological doctrines in which Bonhoeffer's account of sanctification rests in order to consider Bonhoeffer's accounts of justification and sanctification as they relate to spiritual disciplines (p. 105). McGarry, Joseph. "Christ Among a Band of People: Dietrich Bonhoeffer and Formation in Christ." Ph.D. diss., University of Aberdeen, 2013.

[37] DBWE 4:225–253.

concerning the work of divine agency. The work of the human agent does
not create the church or the visible church, and therefore it is not detailed
at length in the chapter concerning the visible church. Instead, Bonhoeffer
details the work of the human agent in the visible church in the chapter immediately following the chapter on the visible church. Following Bonhoeffer's
lead, this section attends to the work of the human agent in the visible church,
emphasizing that this work in no way *creates* the visible church; instead, a
close reading of Bonhoeffer's treatment of sanctification and works demonstrates discipleship as the role of the human agent in the visible church, a role
which relates to church visibility in that the church is visible in the concrete
obedience of discipleship, making visibility a by-product of discipleship.[38]

Bonhoeffer describes sanctification as a realm of preservation, writing
that sanctification is a reality created through Christ and preserved by God
through the seal of the Holy Spirit.[39] This realm of preservation is the church
as *Christus Praesens*. This much is clear in Bonhoeffer's claim that justification brings people into the body of Christ, and sanctification preserves
them in that body.[40] Sanctification still concerns holiness—the holiness
of the church and its members—but in this construction of sanctification,
Bonhoeffer clarifies that the holiness and righteousness of the church is the
holiness and righteousness of God, which the church has only by virtue of its
being in Christ;[41] as such, Bonhoeffer does not understand sanctification as

---

[38] One of the WCC's significant statements regarding visible church unity is found in "What Unity
Requires," from its Fifth Assembly held in Nairobi in 1975. In this text, the WCC seeks to express
what church unity is and what it requires. The authors conclude that visible church unity requires
"conciliar" unity. The authors discuss their intentions in using the term "conciliar fellowship" to
express "a unity which is publicly manifested when the representatives of these local churches
gather together for a common meeting." Even so, the authors describe the current councils being
held as "not councils in this full sense, because they are not yet united by a common understanding
of the apostolic faith, by a common ministry, and a common Eucharist." As such, the authors of
this text present a church unity which is visible in conciliar form, and yet they further state that that
very conciliar form is presently inadequate and present the need for visible unity as expressed in a
unity of "a common understanding" of faith, ministry, and Eucharist. It should be noted that when
the WCC speaks of "manifesting" church unity, they are speaking of being what they already are—
which is similar to Bonhoeffer's understanding of the visible church being what it has already been
made into. That said, having a *goal* of manifesting church unity—particularly doing so through
"a common understanding" of faith, ministry, and Eucharist—is different from Bonhoeffer, who
understands this manifestation of unity as a byproduct of discipleship. "What Unity Requires." In
Breaking Barriers, Nairobi 1975: Official Report, Fifth Assembly, World Council of Churches,
edited by David M. Paton, 59–64. Geneva: WCC, 1976.

[39] DBWE 4:254.

[40] DBWE 4:259.

[41] DBWE 4:257–260.
  Wolfhart Pannenberg expresses a similar sentiment regarding sanctification and righteousness:
"Since the ontic sharing of believers in Christ's righteousness rests on union with Christ 'beyond
the self,' the question arises as to how this matter relates to the empirical reality of believers 'in
themselves.' What we read of here are only initial effects of faith fellowship with Christ and his
righteousness in the lives of believers. In their empirical existence, then, believers share in the
righteousness that is theirs in Christ outside themselves only inasmuch as there is imputed to them,

the gradual or progressive increase in the holiness of the individual disciple but rather as the disciple being what they have already been created into—the collective person of Christ as *Christus Praesens*—and thereby being holy by virtue of being *Christus Praesens* and having God's holiness.[42]

Bonhoeffer offers three hallmarks of sanctification. Attending to these three hallmarks reveals his understanding of discipleship as the work of the human agent within the church and how that work relates to the visible church. He introduces the three implications of sanctification for the church-community as follows:

> *First,* [the church-community's] sanctification will manifest itself *in a clear separation from the world.* Its sanctification will, *second,* prove itself through *conduct* that is *worthy* of God's realm of holiness. And, *third,* its sanctification will be *hidden in waiting* for the day of Jesus Christ.[43]

To understand the relation of Bonhoeffer's treatment of sanctification to his understanding of church visibility, it is helpful to begin by considering the third hallmark of sanctification. The hallmark of hiddenness informs the hallmarks of separation from the world and worthy conduct. This hallmark of hiddenness is consistent with Bonhoeffer's approach to visibility. While there is separation of the church from the world, and while there are concrete works being done, these are not visible to the church itself.[44] Instead, the sanctification of the church is hidden until Christ's return.[45]

Bonhoeffer's insistence on the hiddenness of sanctification determines that the "clear separation from the world" does not imply that the visible church subsists in its institutional forms.[46] His statements that sanctification is "possible only within the visible church-community" and that "the church-community's claim to a space of its own within this world, and the concomitant separation from the space of the world, attests that the church-community is in the state of sanctification" are not statements that equate the

---

as regards their empirical constitution, that which they are in Christ." Bonhoeffer is consistent with Pannenberg in his understanding that the righteousness of the church is Christ's righteousness. Pannenberg, Wolfhart. *Systematic Theology, Volume 3.* Grand Rapids: Eerdmans, 2009, 317–318.

[42] DBWE 4:263.

McGarry's thesis attends to this idea of sanctification in its exploration of spiritual disciplines and Bonhoeffer's works. "The community does not become more holy through faithful life, for the community has been made completely holy in Christ's body. Consequently, Bonhoeffer's formal theological structure does not treat holiness as something into which one incrementally grows. It is, instead, God's granted identity to which the community lives faithfully." McGarry, "Christ Among a Band of People," 108.

[43] DBWE 4:261.

[44] DBWE 4:276.

[45] DBWE 4:276–277.

[46] DBWE 4:261.

institutional forms of church with the visible church.[47] To say as much would be inconsistent with his previous chapter on the visible church and his final chapter on the *imago Dei*.[48]

Moreover, to say as much would put the first and the third hallmarks of sanctification at odds with each other. This apparent inconsistency is negotiated in Bonhoeffer's understanding of the church as *Christus Praesens*. As chapter 1 illumined, the account of the church as *Christus Praesens* posits Christ as present in the church as Word, sacrament, and church-community. Under this construction, it is not the cultic acts of preaching or performing the sacraments and it is likewise not the act of congregating that makes Christ present in the church in these three ways; it is because Christ acts as vicarious representative on behalf of humanity and wills to be present in the church as Word, sacrament, and church-community that he is present in the church in these ways.[49]

In order to hear and obey Christ's commands (the content of discipleship), the disciples must go where Christ is present—Word, sacrament, and church-community;[50] in order to go to the place where Christ is present, therefore, the disciples must congregate and provide a space where the preaching and sacrament can take place. Again, it is not the congregating or the performative acts of preaching and sacrament that *make* Christ present, but rather it is because Christ *wills to be present* as Word, sacrament, and church-community and because the pursuit to hear the command of Christ leads the disciples to the places where Christ is present, that the institutional forms of the church come to exist. Therefore, designating the clear space of the institutional church within the world as a hallmark of sanctification is not an indication that the visible church subsists in its institutional forms, but rather that such institutional forms—places in which the disciples can hear the sermon, partake in the sacraments, and have community—will manifest as a result of discipleship to Christ.

What Bonhoeffer is attempting to state in the hallmark of separation from the world is that sanctification is communal.[51] He is attempting to demonstrate that sanctification does not principally concern individuals but the community that is the collective person of Christ in the church as *Christus Praesens*. It is not his intention to equate the institutional forms of church with the visible church.

---

[47] DBWE 4:261.

[48] DBWE 4:236; DBWE 4:287–288.

[49] Tom Greggs details Bonhoeffer's account of religion, placing it in conversation with that of Karl Barth. Greggs, Tom. *Theology Against Religion: Constructive Dialogues with Bonhoeffer and Barth.* London: T & T Clark International, 2011.

[50] DBWE 4:202.

[51] DBWE 4:262.

Considering the first and third hallmarks of sanctification together reveals a consistency in which the sanctification of the church is hidden even while discipleship to Christ yields clear physical spaces in the world where disciples congregate to hear the word, partake in the sacraments, and be in community.[52] But these two hallmarks of sanctification have not yet illumined the role of the human agent in the visible church. It is in the second hallmark of sanctification—worthy conduct—that this role is found.

Taken in isolation, the designation of worthy conduct as a hallmark of sanctification appears to be a gateway to virtue ethics and the reduction of discipleship to a program, formula, or system. When considered alongside the hallmark of hiddenness, this hallmark must take on a different meaning, or the two hallmarks would be inconsistent with one another. It is only in holding these two hallmarks together that Bonhoeffer can say both that "good works is the goal of being a Christian" and "our good work is thus completely hidden from our eyes";[53] the statement that bridges these two is Bonhoeffer's assertion that "our goal is to do the good work which God demands."[54]

Put otherwise, the goal of the disciple is to hear and obey Christ's commands;[55] Because Christ's commands demand concrete action, it can be said that good works are the goal of being a disciple but only insofar as those works are the specific works demanded in the command of Christ; finally, because discipleship's goal of hearing and obeying Christ's commands precludes self-assessment as to the visibility of one's own—or the church's own—good works, the good work of the disciples is hidden from their eyes.[56]

Thus, when Bonhoeffer designates worthy conduct as a hallmark of sanctification, he is not stating that good works create the visible church, and he is not promoting pietism or virtue ethics; instead, he is highlighting good works as a hallmark of sanctification because the practical content of obedience to Christ's commands can only be good works. Bonhoeffer uses the following allegory of a tree and its fruits to illustrate the relation of the good works commanded by Christ and visibility:

> What is the meaning of fruit? The "works" of the flesh are many, but there is only one "fruit" of the Spirit. Works are accomplished by human hands, but the fruit sprouts and grows without the tree knowing it. Works are dead, but fruit is

---

[52] McGarry also observes this account of visibility and hiddenness, and the fact that visibility is not the goal of discipleship but a byproduct of it. McGarry, Joseph. "Formed While Following: Dietrich Bonhoeffer's Asymmetrical View of Agency in Christian Formation." *Theology Today* 71, no. 1 (April 2014): 106–120. 114–115.

[53] DBWE 4:278–279.

[54] DBWE 4:278.

[55] DBWE 4:271.

[56] DBWE 4:279; 287–288.

alive and the bearer of seeds which themselves produce new fruit. Works can exist on their own, but fruit cannot exist without a tree. Fruit is always something full of wonder, something that has been created. It is not something willed into being, but something that has grown organically. The fruit of the Spirit is a gift of which God is the sole source. Those bearing this fruit are as unaware of it as a tree is of its fruit. The only thing they are aware of is the power of the one from whom they receive their life. There is no room for praise here, but only the ever more intimate union with the source, with Christ. The saints themselves are unaware of the fruit of sanctification they bear. The left hand does not know what the right hand is doing. If they become curious to know something in this matter, if they decide to engage in self-contemplation, then they would have already torn themselves away from the root and their time of bearing fruit would have passed.[57]

In distinguishing between works and fruits, Bonhoeffer is distinguishing between an understanding of good works in universalized terms and an understanding of good works in terms of the specific works commanded by Christ. In saying, "works are dead" and "works can exist on their own," Bonhoeffer is referring to—and rejecting—an account of good works in which certain works are good in and of themselves;[58] works are worthless, argues Bonhoeffer, unless they are the specific works ("fruits") commanded by Christ.

What is more, Bonhoeffer deepens this understanding of good works within sanctification in his assertions that the "fruits" are neither willed into being by the tree (the disciple) nor visible to the tree. In the first assertion, Bonhoeffer designates the creation of good works to the work of divine agency, who wills that the works commanded by Christ be done.[59] In the second assertion, Bonhoeffer highlights that the good works are not visible to the ones doing them.

If sanctification's second hallmark of worthy conduct is characterized by good works willed by God and performed by the human agent within the church in such a way that precludes self-assessment of such conduct, it

---

[57] DBWE 4:266–267.

[58] DBWE 4:266–267.

[59] John Webster's account of sanctification is largely in harmony with Bonhoeffer's. The only distinction between Webster and Bonhoeffer here would be that Bonhoeffer understands sanctification as received and complete, whereas Webster sees it as "not simply a received and completed condition, but a summons actively to reiterate the death of the old nature and to perform the new, to die and rise again not only once for all but also continually." Regardless, both arrive at essentially the same conclusion—that sanctification is principally a work of divine agency and that that work of divine agency calls forth activity from the human agent. Webster, John. "Communion with Christ: Mortification and Vivification." In *Sanctified by Grace: A Theology of the Christian Life*, edited by Kent Eilers & Kyle Strobel. London: Bloomsbury, 2014, 122.

must be concluded that the worthy conduct—the work of the human agent in the visible church—can only refer to discipleship. The sole goal of discipleship is to hear and do the concrete commands of Christ;[60] this sole goal precludes self-evaluation as to the successful accomplishment of that goal; nevertheless, hearing and doing the concrete commands of Christ inevitably results in obedient deeds that are visible and concretely done in the world. Bonhoeffer put it this way earlier in *Discipleship* in his discussion of the Sermon on the Mount:

> The better righteousness of the disciples should not be an end in itself. Of course, what is extraordinary does have to become visible. Although the visibility of discipleship does have a necessary reason, which is the call of Jesus Christ, it is never a goal in itself. If it were, then the focus would no longer be on discipleship itself.[61]

Here, Bonhoeffer is adamant that discipleship will be visible by virtue of the practical reality of following Christ. That visibility is not the goal of discipleship;[62] obediently following after Christ and Christ's commands is the goal of discipleship. *Visibility is a by-product of following after Christ.* As disciples follow after Christ, the church *will be visible* through the concrete acts of discipleship. This is how the church is visibly united in the world today.

The visible unity of the church is not a goal of those within the church, it is not something those within the church strive for or create. The visible church is created through the work of the triune God creating, realizing, and actualizing the church as *Christus Praesens*. And that church can be seen by God and those outside the church in the active discipleship of those within the church, doing the good works created and commanded by Christ. Church visibility is not a goal but a by-product. It is a by-product of God creating the church and disciples following after Christ within that church. This is Bonhoeffer's account of the visible church.

---

[60] DBWE 4:287–288.

[61] DBWE 4:149.

[62] The claim that visibility is not a goal to which the church strives goes against some ecumenical thought. For instance, the authors of *In One Body Through the Cross: The Princeton Proposal* argue: "The manifest imperfection of our unity, in worship and in the articulation of apostolic faith, reveals the goal and vocation of the whole Christian people. . . . If Christians are to realize the unity for which Jesus prayed, they need structures, institutions, and regular practices by which their communion in faith is expressed and formed." *In One Body Through the Cross*, 16. These authors posit the necessity of "structures, institutions, and regular practices" in order to make church unity visible. Bonhoeffer, by contrast, develops an account of theology in which visible unity is not a goal—which is only to hear and do Christ's commands—but is an inevitable byproduct.

SIN AND BONHOEFFER'S ACCOUNT
OF THE VISIBLE CHURCH

This chapter has presented Bonhoeffer's account of the visible church and concluded that he understands the church as *Christus Praesens*, which is concretely visible in the world in the obedience of discipleship. The emphasis of this approach to church visibility upon the disciple hearing and doing the commands of Christ may at first glance appear to be too optimistic regarding the ability of the human agents to hear and faithfully do the commands of Christ. Indeed, in his "Address to the Fano Conference" in 1934, Bonhoeffer goes so far as to say, "Only the one great Ecumenical Council of the Holy Church of Christ over all the world can speak out so that the world, though it gnash its teeth, will have to hear."[63] To speak of the church in such terms and to claim that the church is capable of proclaiming together is a rather optimistic perspective. Such an approach to church visibility prompts a couple of questions. Is Bonhoeffer's formulation of church visibility as a by-product of simple obedience to Christ's commands unrealistic? Does this formulation present an idealization of the church rather than a truthful and accurate depiction of the church in the world today? In a word, no. The longer answer to these questions lies in Bonhoeffer's understanding of sin and the church.[64]

Bonhoeffer's ecumenical vision of a church that is visible in the world through concrete discipleship is not, to use Ephraim Radner's words, a "hallucinogenic fantasy."[65] Bonhoeffer does not see the church as a community of sinless individuals but as the collective person of Christ, whose members

---

[63] DBWE 13:304.

[64] Secondary literature on Bonhoeffer's conception of sin and sin in the church include Wilkes, Nicola J. "Private Confession of Sin in the Theology of Dietrich Bonhoeffer." *Tyndale Bulletin* 66, no. 2 (2015): 317–320; Harasta, Eva. "One Body: Dietrich Bonhoeffer on the Church's Existence as Sinner and Saint at Once." *Union Seminary Quarterly Review* 62, no. 3–4 (2010): 17–34; Harasta, Eva. "Adam in Christ? The Place of Sin in Christ-Reality." In *Christ, Church and World: New Studies in Bonhoeffer's Theology and Ethics,* edited by Michael Mawson and Philip G. Ziegler, 61–76. London: Bloomsbury T&T Clark, 2016; Greggs, "Bearing Sin in the Church: The Ecclesial Hamartiology of Bonhoeffer"; Tietz, Christiane. "The Mysteries of Knowledge, Sin, and Shame." In *Mysteries in the Theology of Dietrich Bonhoeffer: A Copenhagen Bonhoeffer Symposium,* edited by Kirsten Busch Nielsen, Ulrik Nissen, and Christiane Tietz, 27–48. Gottingen: Vandenhoeck & Ruprecht, 2007.

[65] Radner, Ephraim. *A Brutal Unity: The Spiritual Politics of the Christian Church.* Waco: Baylor University Press, 2012, 108. Radner is concerned that Bonhoeffer has an unrealistic hope regarding the church and the ecumenical movement—specifically in his hope that the ecumenical movement could speak with one voice. The problem with Radner's assessment of Bonhoeffer's words is that Radner sees the church in institutional terms—particularly in terms of denominations with competing ideologies. Bonhoeffer, on the other hand, is speaking of the church in terms of *Christus Praesens,* and he is speaking of that church proclaiming Christ's commands in the concrete and specific manner in which he understands the command. This idea is not unrealistic.

remain capable of and vulnerable to sin.[66] The church remains capable of committing atrocities—capable of sinning. Bonhoeffer addresses this in his lecture at Ciernehorske Kupele in 1932:

> Rather, when the church really has a commandment of God, it must proclaim this in the most concrete form out of the fullest knowledge of the matter and call others to obedience. . . . Now, however, there arises a tremendous difficulty. If the church must know the situation in detail before it can command . . . there is always the danger that the church in its commandment will nonetheless over-look this or that objective point of view or underestimate it, and therefore the church will be made completely uncertain in its commandment. Therefore, the commanding church's understanding of the subject matter is, on the one hand, the precondition of a real commandment and, on the other hand, makes every one of its commandments uncertain, again and again, because it is dependent on the complete knowledge of reality. Fundamentally, there are two ways to face this insoluble dilemma . . . namely, *either* a conscious and qualified silence of ignorance, *or* the commandment is dared in every conceivable concretion, exclusivity, and radicalism . . . *out of the clear recognition that it is possible therewith to take the name of God in vain, that the church is in error and is sinful, but it may speak it in faith in the word of the forgiveness of sins that holds true for the church as well.* Thus, however, the proclamation of the com-mandment is founded in the proclamation of the forgiveness of sins. The church cannot command unless it itself stands in the belief in the forgiveness of sins and without directing all those whom it commands to emphasize this proclamation of the forgiveness of sins.[67]

These words illumine a critical facet of Bonhoeffer's ecumenical theology. Bonhoeffer does not envision the church as a perfect community of sinless people whose words and deeds are infallible. He understands the church as the collective person of Christ, whose members remain vulnerable to sin;[68] he understands that the commands of that church are likewise vulner-able to error.[69] Nevertheless, he argues that the church is called to obedient

---

[66] Jennifer McBride has argued that Bonhoeffer's concept of collective persons results in neglect for the problem of sin in the church. This section disagrees with McBride's assessment. McBride, Jennifer. *The Church for the World*, 120. Greggs's account of the individual and corporate nature of sin is helpful here, even though this book does not explore this topic in depth. Greggs, "Bearing Sin in the Church," 80–84.

[67] DBWE 11:361. Italics added.

[68] Mawson also articulates the individual and communal aspects of sin in Bonhoeffer's thought. Mawson, *Christ Existing as Community*, 107–118.

[69] Harasta's pieces on Bonhoeffer's understanding of sin and the church are illuminating. The cur-rent book broadly agrees with Harasta's assessment but would point out one point of distinction. Harasta focuses on Bonhoeffer's concept of "Christ-reality" in *Ethics* and—in doing so—focuses

discipleship and must therefore proclaim Christ's commands in the world, knowing full well that its perception and transmission of those commands may be in error and therefore in sin. When the church finds its proclamations to be anything other than Christ's command, then it must repent and seek the forgiveness of sins "that holds true for the church as well."[70]

This understanding of sin and the church is consistent with Bonhoeffer's wider corpus. For example, Bonhoeffer puts it this way in *Discipleship*:

> The community of saints is not the "ideal" church-community of the sinless and the perfect. It is not the church-community of those without blemish, which no longer provides room for the sinner to repent. Rather it is the church-community that shows itself worthy of the gospel of the forgiveness of sins by truly proclaiming God's forgiveness, which has nothing to do with forgiving oneself. It is the community of those who have truly experienced God's costly grace, and who thereby live a life worthy of the gospel which they neither squander nor discard.[71]

Furthermore, in *Sanctorum Communio*, Bonhoeffer states, "The reality of sin and the communio peccatorum remain even in God's church-community,"[72] and, in *Act and Being*, he claims,

> Sin and death, therefore, reach even into the community of faith of Christ. But they do so in such a way that now the community of faith bears my sin and death with me, and I no longer see sin and death in the community of faith, that is, in Christ, but only forgiveness and life.[73]

In each of these cases, it is clear that Bonhoeffer does not understand the church as a pure community incapable of sin. But this fallibility does not

---

more heavily upon Christ's transformative affect upon all of creation. The result is that Harasta reduces Bonhoeffer's account of the church to his understanding of it as a confessing community. Though Harasta still narrates Bonhoeffer's ecclesiology in terms of person and revelation, the depth and implications of Bonhoeffer's understanding of the church as the revelatory person of Christ are lost. Harasta, "One Body"; Harasta, "Adam in Christ?"

[70] DBWE 11:361.

For more on Bonhoeffer and repentance, see McBride, Jennifer M. "Thinking Within the Movement of Bonhoeffer's Theology: Towards a Christological Reinterpretation of Repentance." In *Religion, Religionlessness and Contemporary Western Culture: Explorations in Dietrich Bonhoeffer's Theology,* edited by Stephen Plant and Ralf K. Wustenberg, 91–109. Peter Lang, 2008; Fortin, Jean-Pierre. "The Church as Confessing Community: Dietrich Bonhoeffer's Theology of Forgiveness and Reconciliation." *Touchstone* 34, no. 3 (October 2016): 14–24.

[71] DBWE 4:269.

[72] DBWE 1:124.

[73] DBWE 2:123.

preclude common action and common proclamation.[74] Bonhoeffer's account of the visible church as a by-product of discipleship is not undermined by his understanding of sin in the church; rather, his account of the visible church is demonstrated to be a truthful depiction of the church in the world with realistic expectations of what church visibility entails. The church is to follow after Christ and proclaim his commands, and, in so doing, the church is visible in the world. The church is to obey and proclaim these commands in the full knowledge that it is possible that they speak erroneously—sinfully—and that, in such cases, the church is called to repentance.

CONCLUSION

In a time of declining interest in traditional ecumenism, it is important to continually be thinking through what church visibility means. Unity does not mean uniformity. Visible church unity is not principally concerned with getting the denominations to agree on as many doctrines as possible. Visible church unity is about obediently following after Christ in the world. Those within the church neither create this visibility nor strive for it; the visibility of the church is a by-product of discipleship to Christ. This is a message which must be heard again and again within ecumenical circles. The visible unity of the church is found in our discipleship to Christ. How discipleship is ecumenical remains to be seen. Chapter 4 attends to Bonhoeffer's concept of discipleship and its place in his ecumenical theology.

---

[74] Greggs discusses Bonhoeffer's thought in *Ethics* that "the church has a vicarious role in accepting the sin of those outside of the church . . . the church as Christ existing as community shares in the work and power of Christ in accepting vicariously the sins of those outside of the community which exists in Christ." Space does not allow for a full account of this aspect of Bonhoeffer's thought, but the present book would not refute Greggs' conclusions. Greggs, "Bearing Sin in the Church," 93.

Chapter 4

Discipleship in Bonhoeffer's Ecumenical Works

The savvy Bonhoeffer scholar will arch an eyebrow at the claim that Bonhoeffer's concept of discipleship is the operative theological content of his ecumenical theology. In a way, this skepticism is warranted. After all, Bonhoeffer never once uses the word "discipleship" in any of his ecumenical works. Moreover, his ecumenical works predate his 1937 publication of *Discipleship*. Even so, a careful investigation of the theology present in these works reveals the surprising truth that Bonhoeffer's concept of discipleship is, indeed, their operative theological content. Providing such an investigation is the aim of this chapter.

In order to perform this investigation, it is necessary, first, to clarify Bonhoeffer's concept of discipleship itself. Once this concept is established, it is possible to inspect the theological content of each of Bonhoeffer's ecumenical works diachronically. To this end, the chapter identifies and explicates four key components of Bonhoeffer's concept of discipleship. These components are then highlighted across Bonhoeffer's ecumenical works. As such, the chapter argues that discipleship is demonstrably the operative theological content of Bonhoeffer's ecumenical theology, meaning that the ecumenism presented therein should be understood as an ecumenism of discipleship.

To be clear, the argument is *not* that *Discipleship* is a precursor which structures his ecumenical works. This would be a chronological fallacy. The argument is that the same components that structure his concept of discipleship also structure his earlier articulation of his ecumenical theology. As such, Bonhoeffer's ecumenical theology can be most accurately described as an ecumenism of discipleship.

BONHOEFFER'S CONCEPT OF DISCIPLESHIP

Unsurprisingly, *Discipleship* provides the most exhaustive account of Bonhoeffer's concept of discipleship. As such, the text is superlative as a source for examining this concept in depth. Drawing chiefly from this text, therefore, the section identifies and details four key components of Bonhoeffer's concept of discipleship: (1) discipleship's Christological orientation, (2) Christ's command and the disciple's obedience, (3) the inherently ecclesiological nature of discipleship, and (4) the disciple's sinfulness and need for the forgiveness of sins. Each of these components must now be attended to in order that the full significance of Bonhoeffer's ecumenism of discipleship may be understood.

The Christological Orientation of Discipleship

The original, German title that Bonhoeffer gave *Discipleship* is *Nachfolge*, a literal translation of which is "following after."[1] This title captures the essence of the ethic prescribed in the text; at the heart of *Discipleship* is the ethical demand to "follow after." But the words "follow after" leave the question open as to the subject being followed. Bonhoeffer identifies this subject as Christ, writing, "We desire to speak of the call to follow Christ."[2] The entire text is organized around this desire, and in this desire, we find Bonhoeffer's emphasis on a Christological orientation for discipleship.[3]

The call to discipleship becomes a binding ethical imperative because it is Christ who calls.[4] Bonhoeffer argues, "Because Jesus is the Christ, he has authority to call and to demand obedience to his word. Jesus calls to

---

[1] DBWE 4:4.

[2] DBWE 4:38.

[3] David Fergus' article "'To Do What is Good is to Take the Form of Jesus Christ:' Dietrich Bonhoeffer's Approach to a Dynamic Ethic" provides an excellent account of Bonhoeffer's ethics within the work *Ethics*. Fergus discusses the Christological orientation of ethics, which he then equates with discipleship. Fergus draws out Bonhoeffer's account of Christ's presence in the church as well as the disciple's work of seeking to hear and do Christ's commands. The article is a good representation of the presence of Bonhoeffer's concept of discipleship within *Ethics*. Fergus, Donald Murdoch. "'To Do What is Good is to Take the Form of Jesus Christ:' Dietrich Bonhoeffer's Approach to a Dynamic Ethic." *The Bonhoeffer Legacy* 3, no. 1 (2015): 57–68.

John Howard Yoder also attends to the relation of discipleship and Christology in Bonhoeffer's theology. Furthermore, Mawson has illumined the important distinctions between Yoder and Bonhoeffer. Yoder, John H. "The Christological Presuppositions of Discipleship." In *Being Human, Becoming Human: Dietrich Bonhoeffer and Social Thought,* edited by Jens Zimmermann and Brian Gregor, 127–151. Cambridge: James Clarke & Co., 2010; Mawson, Michael. "The Politics of Jesus and the Ethics of Christ: Why the Differences between Yoder and Bonhoeffer Matter." In *The Freedom of a Christian Ethicist: The Future of a Reformation Legacy,* edited by Brian Brock and Michael Mawson, 127–143. London: T&T Clark, 2016.

[4] DBWE 4:57.

discipleship, not as a teacher and a role model, but as the Christ, the Son of God."[5] He further states, "Because Christ exists, he must be followed."[6] As such, "Jesus is the only content" of discipleship.[7]

The binding nature of Christ's call is illumined by the material from chapter 1 on personhood and revelation.[8] There, it was explained that Bonhoeffer conceives of personhood in terms of encounter.[9] In encountering someone else, the I is transcended and called to responsibility.[10] Furthermore, it was explained that, due to sin, human beings are turned in upon themselves;[11] because of this, only Christ—being both God and human—is able to encounter the human being in such a way that transcends them.[12] Encountering the person of Christ calls the one encountered to responsibility.[13] This is what Bonhoeffer intends in *Discipleship* when he speaks of Christ having the authority to call to discipleship because he is the Christ.[14] The encounter with Christ calls to responsibility—and that responsibility is discipleship. The "following after" of discipleship is, therefore, a following after Christ and his call. As such, discipleship necessarily has a Christological orientation.[15]

In other words, Jesus is capable of demanding discipleship in a binding manner due to his being fully God and fully human. Thus, Bonhoeffer posits Christ himself as the focus of discipleship. The action of the disciple, who is focused solely on Christ, is "obedience toward the Son of God."[16]

Concrete Command and Simple Obedience

The Christological orientation of discipleship leads to the second component of discipleship for Bonhoeffer: Christ's concrete command and the disciple's

---

[5] DBWE 4:57.
[6] DBWE 4:59.
[7] DBWE 4:59.
[8] This book is not alone in noting a consistency between Bonhoeffer's work in *Discipleship* and his dissertations. Michael DeJonge writes, "Bonhoeffer has in place an account of discipleship that formally mirrors his account of 'being in Christ' in *Act and Being* . . . his description of Christian existence in *Discipleship* is formally consistent with his description in *Act and Being*." DeJonge, *Bonhoeffer's Theological Formation*, 130–136; especially 133–134.
[9] DBWE 1:54–57.
[10] DBWE 1:54–57.
[11] DBWE 2:144–147.
[12] DBWE 1:54–55.
[13] DBWE 12:301.
[14] DBWE 4:57.
[15] Ernst Feil also notes the Christological basis of Bonhoeffer's concept of discipleship. Though this book agrees with Feil that the concept has a Christological basis, this book would argue that Feil's account lacks an adequate representation of the concept's rich ecclesiological implications. Feil, *The Theology of Dietrich Bonhoeffer*, 76–81.
[16] DBWE 4:74.

obedience.[17] According to Bonhoeffer, the command comes from Christ. The disciple's only appropriate response to this command is "the obedient deed."[18] But what is the command and what does obedience to the command entail?

The command is not a nebulous idea or universal principle. Bonhoeffer is adamant that Christ always commands concretely, by which he means that Christ's command demands a specific action in a specific context.[19] Bonhoeffer uses the biblical examples of Christ commanding Peter to step out of the boat and the command to the rich young ruler to give up his possessions to illustrate that Christ's command is always concrete.[20] When Christ commands Peter to step out of the boat, the specific obedient response demanded is stepping out of the boat; when Christ commands the rich young ruler to give up his possessions, the specific obedient response demanded is to give up his possessions. Thus, Christ commands concretely. The response to this command is what Bonhoeffer terms "simple obedience."[21]

Simple obedience means single-mindedly doing what is commanded. Again, Peter's simple obedience is stepping out of the boat; the rich young ruler's simple obedience should have been giving up his possessions. This simple obedience is the ethical content of discipleship.[22] Simple obedience is purely action—specifically, obedient action in response to the command of Christ. Bonhoeffer writes:

> If you anxiously ask again whether or not I should know and consider ahead of time how to act, there is only the advice that I cannot know or think about it except by already acting, by already knowing myself to be challenged. I can only learn what obedience is by obeying, not by asking questions.[23]

Simple obedience is not a system, principle, or formula.[24] Therefore, discipleship—the content of which is simple obedience—likewise cannot be expressed as a system, principle, or formula. Furthermore, simple obedience—and discipleship by extension—does not include evaluation beyond

---

[17] Joseph McGarry also highlights simple obedience to Christ's command as "the driving concept in *Discipleship*." McGarry, "Formed While Following," 108. See also McGarry, Joseph. "Con-Formed to Christ: Dietrich Bonhoeffer and Christian Formation." *Journal of Spiritual Formation & Soul Care* 5, no. 2 (Fall 2012): 226–242.

[18] DBWE 4:57.

[19] DBWE 4:66.

[20] DBWE 4:66–76.

[21] DBWE 4:77.

[22] DBWE 4:77–83.

[23] DBWE 4:70.

[24] DBWE 4:59.

what is commanded.[25] Put otherwise, discipleship is not concerned with judging either the command or the results of obedience.[26] Discipleship is concerned solely with being obedient to Christ's command, with no thought of results. In this way, discipleship is consistent with Bonhoeffer's understanding of church visibility as expressed in chapter 3; the disciple simply acts in obedience with no thought of the visibility of the act. The act will be visible, but this visibility is the result of obedience rather than the goal of obedience.

The ethical content of Bonhoeffer's account of discipleship is simple obedience—actively doing what is commanded by Christ.[27] As such, Christ's concrete command and the disciple's simple obedience always belong together in discipleship. The sole focus of the disciple is to hear and obey Christ's commands.[28] But where is the command heard?

Ecclesiology and Discipleship

Bonhoeffer claims that Christ's commands can only be heard where Christ is present.[29] This leads the section to the third component of Bonhoeffer's

---

[25] DBWE 4:76.

[26] Marsh likewise notes the immediacy of Christ's call and the obedient deed in *Discipleship*. Such obedience precludes self-assessment, as has been discussed regarding church visibility. Marsh, *Reclaiming Dietrich Bonhoeffer,* 106–108.

[27] Clifford Green writes, "the Christ of *Discipleship* is an overwhelming power of 'absolute authority' who demands total submission to his commands and the complete renunciation of any independent human will. The power of Christ is set over against the power of the self; the self-centered man renounces the ambition of his autonomous ego and is obedient to Christ in the service of the church." The present book does not agree with Green's conclusion. Although Bonhoeffer's concept of simple obedience *does* intend strictly doing what is commanded by Christ, the will and activity of the human agent has not been snuffed out. Brian Gregor explains this nicely in drawing out a dialectic of faith and obedience in *Discipleship* in order to argue for both passivity and activity on the part of the human agent. To use Gregor's words: "The call creates the new situation, but this situation still requires an active response. . . . Bonhoeffer organizes his description of obedience around this image of the *first step,* which is the active response of obedience. The disciple continues to be a human agent." Green, *Sociality,* 170–179, especially 172; Gregor, Brian. "Following-After and Becoming Human: A Study of Bonhoeffer and Kierkegaard." In *Being Human, Becoming Human: Dietrich Bonhoeffer and Social Thought,* edited by Jens Zimmermann and Brian Gregor, 152–175. Cambridge: James Clark & Co., 2010; especially 161–168.

[28] DBWE 4:181.
    For more on Bonhoeffer's understanding of Christ's command, see Ziegler, Philip Gordon. "Graciously Commanded: Dietrich Bonhoeffer and Karl Barth on the Decalogue." *Scottish Journal of Theology* 71, no. 2 (2018): 127–141.

[29] DBWE 4:202.
    Nation, Siegrist, and Umbel's preoccupation with nonviolence along with their Anabaptist presuppositions cause them to err in their representation of Bonhoeffer's account of Christ's command in *Discipleship*. Though the authors are correct to identify the central importance Christ's command and the disciple's obedience, they mistakenly argue that Bonhoeffer posits Christ's commands strictly in the scriptural words of Christ—particularly those recounted in the Sermon on the Mount. Bonhoeffer himself specifically rejects this approach. In his ecumenical lecture at Ciernohorské Kúpele, Bonhoeffer illustrates why the command is to be found and states, "even the Sermon on the Mount may not become a literal law for us." Instead, Bonhoeffer locates the

concept of discipleship: its ecclesial nature. Chapter 1 detailed the church as the locus of Christ's presence. That material is revisited here in order to exhibit the ecclesiological nature of Bonhoeffer's concept of discipleship. In *Discipleship*, Bonhoeffer states that Christ is present in the church in its preaching and sacraments, writing:

> If we want to hear [Jesus'] call to discipleship, we need to hear it where Christ himself is present. It is within the church that Jesus Christ calls through his word and sacrament. The preaching and sacrament of the church is the place where Jesus Christ is present. To hear Jesus' call to discipleship, one needs no personal revelation. Listen to the preaching and receive the sacrament![30]

Discipleship is, thus, tied to ecclesiology. Discipleship is not a solo activity for the individual believer but rather always carries ecclesiology with it. Although the call to discipleship goes to the individual, discipleship to Christ brings one into the church.[31] By locating Christ's command in his presence in the church, Bonhoeffer is able to avoid an overly subjective account of divine command that would identify Christ's command with the disciple's conscience—meaning that one cannot simply identify whatever one wishes as the command of Christ.[32] Instead, the command is heard in the church, not by virtue of the institution itself, nor by its doctrine, but because the church is where Christ is present, and he is present in the church as Word and sacrament.[33] But Christ is present in the church in a third way as well.

Christ is also present in the church as the church-community itself.[34] Christ is present as church-community by virtue of his vicarious representative action (*Stellvertretung*) on the cross on behalf of humanity, thus creating the new humanity of those who are in Christ as opposed to those in Adam.[35] That new humanity is the church.[36] Significant for ecumenical discussion is the fact that by identifying the church as the new humanity, Bonhoeffer posits an

---

command in Christ's contingent commanding where he is present—the church. Nation, Mark, Anthony G. Siegrist, and Daniel P. Umbel. *Bonhoeffer the Assassin?: Challenging the Myth, Recovering His Call to Peacemanking.* Grand Rapids: Baker Academic, 2013, 143–160; DBWE 11:362–363. For a contradictory voice to Nation, Siegrist, and Umbel, see DeJonge, Michael P. *Bonhoeffer on Resistance: The Word Against the Wheel.* Oxford: Oxford University Press, 2018.

[30] DBWE 4:202.
[31] DBWE 4:99.
[32] DBWE 4:99.
[33] DBWE 4:202.
[34] DBWE 4:217–218.
[35] DBWE 4:217.
[36] DBWE 4:217.
  Brian Gregor has also noted the relationship of discipleship and the new humanity. Gregor, "Following-After and Becoming Human," 152–175.

inherent unity of the church.[37] When Bonhoeffer writes, "the church is one," it is not a statement about the church as an institution but as *person*—the person of Christ.[38]

This ecclesiological statement becomes explicitly related to discipleship in the final chapter of *Discipleship* on the image of Christ. Here, Bonhoeffer illumines that in following after Christ, the disciple bears Christ's likeness. Or, as Bonhoeffer states it:

> We are to be like Christ because we have already been shaped into the image of Christ. Only because we bear Christ's image already can Christ be the "example" whom we follow. . . . Since we have been formed in the image of Christ, we can live following his example. On this basis, we are now actually able to do those deeds, and in the simplicity of discipleship, to live life in the likeness of Christ. Here simple obedience to the word takes place.[39]

Discipleship is the way in which disciples participate in the new humanity. It is not that the disciples *make* the new humanity, which only Christ does, but that the disciples *participate* in that new humanity through discipleship. Thus, if Christ is the new humanity, and the church is the new humanity by virtue of its being in Christ,[40] then discipleship as participation in the new humanity implies that discipleship has an ecclesial tenor.[41]

This ecclesial tenor, it must be said, means that discipleship carries the church with it in a particular way. Discipleship means an ordering of the church within itself and toward the world of *Stellvertretung* (vicarious representative action); it is not only Christ who works as a vicarious representative actor on behalf of the church but also disciples who act with and for each other, and with and for the world through its discipleship. This ecclesiology that is carried with discipleship is, therefore, not merely a mystical or immaterial reality but rather a concrete reality demanding concrete actions—the specific command of Christ goes not only to individual disciples but also to the church-community as a whole. If Bonhoeffer's concept of discipleship is to be understood correctly, discipleship must be understood as an ecclesial activity.[42]

---

[37] DBWE 4:217.
[38] DBWE 4:217.
[39] DBWE 4:287.
[40] DBWE 4:217.
[41] DBWE 4:287.
[42] For an account of Bonhoeffer's approach to community in *Sanctorum Communio, Discipleship, Ethics,* and *Letters and Papers from Prison,* and what implications that approach to community has for ethics and communal responsibility see ecclesiological discussion, see Clements, Keith. "Community in the Ethics of Dietrich Bonhoeffer." *Studies in Christian Ethics* 10, no. 1 (April 1997): 16–31.

Ecclesial Sinfulness and the Forgiveness of Sins

It could be argued that the accounts of both discipleship and the church that have been presented to this point are naïve and idealistic. This would be true if Bonhoeffer did not account for sin within the church. Thus, the fourth and final component of Bonhoeffer's concept of discipleship is ecclesial sinfulness and the forgiveness of sins.

As chapter 3 illustrated, Bonhoeffer does not understand the church as a pure and sinless community.[43] He instead acknowledges that those within the church remain capable and culpable of sin.[44] The sinfulness of the church does not destroy an account of ecumenical discipleship but rather grounds it in a truthful understanding of the church in the world, thereby preventing an idealistic account of ecclesiology. Bonhoeffer stresses the disciple's need for repentance and for the forgiveness of sins.[45] By acknowledging the possibility of the disciple to sin and the disciple's need for the forgiveness of sins, his concept of discipleship as hearing and doing the commands of Christ remains entirely realistic and concrete.

To recap, the section has identified and attended to four key components of Bonhoeffer's concept of discipleship. Considering these components as a whole, discipleship for Bonhoeffer means hearing and doing the command of Christ, and repenting of sinfulness, all of which is understood to be ecclesial—both communal and individual.

DISCIPLESHIP IN BONHOEFFER'S ECUMENICAL WORKS

Having established Bonhoeffer's concept of discipleship, the chapter now moves to consider this concept in light of his ecumenical works. This section argues that the four components previously shown to be the rudiments of Bonhoeffer's concept of discipleship are also the rudiments of the theology presented in his ecumenical works. This argument is made through a diachronic study of the ecumenical works. This study reveals the ubiquity of discipleship throughout Bonhoeffer's ecumenical corpus from which it must be deduced that his ecumenism is an ecumenism of discipleship.

---

[43] DBWE 4:269.
[44] DBWE 4:279.
[45] DBWE 4:268–269.

Discipleship in "On the Theological Foundation of the Work of the World Alliance"—July 1932

Bonhoeffer's earliest significant ecumenical work is his 1932 lecture "On the Theological Foundation of the Work of the World Alliance." The lecture is among his most extensive pieces of ecumenical writing, and the whole of Bonhoeffer's ecumenical thought can be found within it. As chapter 1 indicated, this lecture he gave in Ciernehorske Kupele should be considered the Rosetta Stone of Bonhoeffer's ecumenical theology. A close reading of the text highlights that the same four components demonstrated to be the rudiments of Bonhoeffer's concept of discipleship are also the rudiments of the ecumenical vision Bonhoeffer promotes in this text. The ecumenism forwarded by Bonhoeffer in this lecture should, therefore, be understood as an ecumenism of discipleship, wherein discipleship is understood to be its operative theological content. Put otherwise, discipleship is the content of ecumenical work—it is the active work done by those within the church.

Bonhoeffer famously begins this lecture with the words, "There is still no theology of the ecumenical movement."[46] His goal in this lecture is to suggest such a theology—an ecumenical theology emerging from an account of the church, within which human activity is defined as hearing and doing the command of Christ. This is the critical center of Bonhoeffer's ecumenical theology, and it can be observed as Bonhoeffer writes:

> The work of our World Alliance—consciously or unconsciously—is grounded in a very distinct conception of church. The church as the one church-community of the Lord Jesus Christ, who is the Lord of the world, has the task of speaking his word to the entire world . . . under which authority does the church speak, when it proclaims this claim of Christ on the world? Under the only authority in which the church is in a position to speak, in the authority of the Christ who is present and living in it. The church is the presence of Christ on earth; the church is *Christus Praesens*.[47]

In the first sentence of this quotation, Bonhoeffer claims that ecumenical work emerges from a conception of church; in the quotation's final sentence, he identifies that conception of church, namely, the church as Christ's presence in the world—the church as *Christus Praesens*.[48] Thus, Bonhoeffer intends the same ecclesiology found in discipleship in the ecumenical theology presented in this lecture—that of the church as the revelatory person of

---

[46] DBWE 11:356.
[47] DDWE 11:358–359.
[48] DBWE 11:358–359.

Christ.[49] The task of this church, adds Bonhoeffer, is to speak Christ's "word to the entire world."[50] Put differently, the church's task is to hear Christ's command and to proclaim that command to the world in word and deed. As such, the church's task in ecumenism is identical to discipleship's task—hearing and doing Christ's commands.[51] Finally, in this quotation, Bonhoeffer insists that the church has the authority to proclaim Christ's commands by virtue of Christ's presence within it. This is the same authority under which the disciple operates.[52]

Therefore, within this quotation, several components of Bonhoeffer's concept of discipleship are clearly present within his ecumenical theology as well. First, ecumenical work is oriented toward Christ because it is from Christ that the command is heard and under Christ's authority that the command is proclaimed. Second, the content of ecumenical work is proclaiming Christ's commands, or what is the same, obediently doing Christ's commands. Third, ecumenical work is inherently ecclesial in nature as it emerges from a conception of the church as the present person of Christ.[53] What remains to be seen is whether the command of Christ is understood in the same concrete terms as it is in discipleship and whether ecclesial sinfulness and the need for the forgiveness of sins are expressed here as they were in Bonhoeffer's concept of discipleship.

That Bonhoeffer intends the commands proclaimed by the ecumenical movement to be concrete is evident when he states,

> When the church really has a commandment of God, it must proclaim this in the most concrete form . . . and call others to obedience. A commandment must be concrete or it is not a commandment. God's commandment demands something absolutely particular now from us.[54]

In other words, Christ's command demands a specific action in a specific context. Thus, Bonhoeffer's understanding of Christ's concrete command and the

---

[49] DBWE 4:217–219.

[50] DBWE 11:358–359

[51] DBWE 4:57.

[52] DBWE 4:57.

[53] Clements has highlighted the ecclesiological emphasis of Bonhoeffer's ecumenical theology: "Bonhoeffer . . . had a definite theology of the church which was at the same time his ecumenical theology: the church is Christ existing as church-community. . . . But the church for Bonhoeffer is not a religious body; it is nothing less than the *new humanity* created in Christ. In a world of conflict, it is at the international level that community in Christ, the new humanity, must be most decidedly revealed. That is what the ecumenical movement is for. To take it seriously means attaching incredibly high expectations to it. For this reason, Bonhoeffer will ever be a challenge to the ecumenical movement, or at any rate he will be well ahead of it for as long as we can see at present." Clements, *Dietrich Bonhoeffer's Ecumenical Quest* 289–290.

[54] DBWE 11:360.

obedient response to it is the same in both the ecumenical theology presented in this lecture and his concept of discipleship.

Finally, Bonhoeffer's ecumenical theology in this lecture maintains the emphasis on the church's sinfulness and need for the forgiveness of sins that was also seen in his concept of discipleship. This emphasis is clear in Bonhoeffer's claim that the ecumenical movement must proclaim Christ's commands

> out of the clear recognition that it is possible therewith to take the name of God in vain, that the church is in error and is sinful, but it may speak [the command] in faith in the word of the forgiveness of sins that holds true for the church as well.[55]

This quotation demonstrates that Bonhoeffer's ecumenism retains the same acknowledgment of the church's sinfulness that was illustrated in his concept of discipleship, and Bonhoeffer again urges the doing of the command in spite of the church's sinfulness, with the assurance that the church can repent and seek the forgiveness of sins if the command it makes turns out to be anything other than the actual command of Christ.[56]

Thus, the four fundamental components of Bonhoeffer's concept of discipleship prove to be the same fundamental concepts at the core of the ecumenical theology that Bonhoeffer presents in his 1932 lecture in Ciernehorske Kupele: (1) a Christological orientation, (2) hearing a concrete command from Christ and simply obeying that command, (3) the ecclesiological nature of discipleship, and (4) the sinfulness of the church and the need for forgiveness. It should be concluded, therefore, that discipleship is the operative theological content of the ecumenical theology presented in this lecture. The result is an ecumenical theology emerging from an understanding of the church as the present person of Christ in which discipleship is the active ecumenical work of the human agent.

Discipleship in "Address in Gland"—August 1932

Only a month after his lecture in Czechoslovakia, Bonhoeffer gave an address in Gland at an international youth conference.[57] The content of this address is essentially a truncated version of what he presented the previous month. Indeed, some scholars have suggested that since Bonhoeffer was asked to speak in Czechoslovakia on such short notice that he constructed

---

[55] DBWE 11:361.
[56] DBWE 11:361.
[57] DBWE 11:375.

his lecture from the material he was preparing for this address in Gland.[58]
As such, Bonhoeffer makes largely the same points in this address as he did
in Ciernehorske Kupele; the ethical conclusion he gives is once again that
the ecumenical movement needs to proclaim peace as Christ's command.[59]
Again, a close examination of how Bonhoeffer constructs his argument
demonstrates that the rudiments of the ecumenical theology that Bonhoeffer
presents mirror the rudiments of his concept of discipleship, further demonstrating that Bonhoeffer's concept of discipleship is the operative theological
content of his ecumenical theology.

Bonhoeffer begins his address with a bit of drama: "Dear friends," he says,
"'The Church is dead,' a serious German man said to me recently."[60] From
this start, he rhetorically asks his listeners whether or not the church is dead—
whether or not the church has anything left to say to the world. In doing so,
Bonhoeffer immediately frames his address as a statement concerning what,
precisely, the church *does* have to say to the world for that time. His conclusion is that the church must proclaim peace as the command of Christ for that
time.[61] But what is the theology undergirding this conclusion? A close reading of the following excerpt reveals that Bonhoeffer's concept of discipleship
funds and forms the ecumenism he suggests:

> We are not a purely functional organization of church business but rather a
> distinct form of the church itself. . . . Indeed, in everything we say and do,
> it is a matter of nothing more than Christ. . . . We come together in order to
> hear Christ! The World Alliance is the community of those who want to hear
> the Lord as they anxiously cry to the Lord in the world on earth, in the night,
> and do not flee from the world, but rather want to hear the call of Christ obe-
> diently in faith within it, and know that through this call they are responsible
> to the world. . . . Christ must again become present among us in preaching
> and sacrament. . . . The church forsakes obedience whenever it sanctions war.
> The church of Christ stands against war in favor of peace among the peoples,
> between nations, classes, and races. . . . With the proclamation of peace, how-
> ever, the church imparts the message of a new humanity, of the holy fellowship
> in Christ. . . . Certainly this is something quite different than an international
> friendship on the basis of the old world . . . brethren in the hearing of the word of
> the *Lord*. . . . It is not those who are so overzealously admirable but rather—tax
> collectors and prostitutes will sooner enter the kingdom of heaven than these
> —the community of those who repent and carry their guilt of not hearing the

---

[58] Clements, *Dietrich Bonhoeffer's Ecumenical Quest*, 78–79.
[59] DBWE 11:378–381.
[60] DBWE 11:375.
[61] DBWE 11:378–381.

commandments of God as they should, even though the kingdom of heaven is near. . . [t]he call goes out to us, to the church.[62]

Here, all four components of Bonhoeffer's concept of discipleship are demonstrably present, further evincing that discipleship is the operative theological content of Bonhoeffer's ecumenical theology. First, the Christological orientation of discipleship is seen in the repeated claim that the work of the ecumenical movement is "to hear Christ"[63] and the statement that every word and action of the World Alliance is "a matter of nothing more than Christ."[64] This is the same Christological orientation Bonhoeffer forwards in his concept of discipleship.[65]

Second, that Christological orientation leads to obedience to the concrete command of Christ. Bonhoeffer states that the World Alliance wants to hear the command of Christ "obediently"[66] and identifies sanctioning war with forsaking "obedience"[67] and peace as a "commandment."[68] In each of these instances, Bonhoeffer emphasizes the concrete command and the obedience such a command requires. This is directly in line with Bonhoeffer's words in *Discipleship*: "The call goes out, and without any further ado the obedient deed of the one called follows."[69]

Moreover, this Christological orientation and obedience are located within an ecclesiology. From the start, Bonhoeffer articulates that the World Alliance "is a distinct form of the church itself."[70] That Bonhoeffer here intends the same ecclesiological nature found in his concept of discipleship becomes more evident through the rest of the quotation; he defines the church in terms of Christ's presence and argues that the proclamation of the church carries with it "the message of a new humanity, of the holy fellowship in Christ."[71] After all, it is to "the church"—and not the individual—that Bonhoeffer claims the call goes out.[72] Bonhoeffer ties the ecumenical act of hearing and proclaiming the command of Christ to ecclesiology in the same way he ties discipleship to ecclesiology.[73] In both instances, a command is heard and proclaimed from within the context of the new humanity, in which

---

[62] DBWE 11:377–381.
[63] DBWE 11:377.
[64] DBWE 11:377.
[65] DBWE 4:38.
[66] DBWE 11:378.
[67] DBWE 11:380.
[68] DBWE 11:378.
[69] DBWE 4:57.
[70] DBWE 11:377.
[71] DBWE 11:380.
[72] DBWE 11:381.
[73] DBWE 4:217.

the church is understood as *Christus Praesence* through "Christ existing as church-community."

Finally, the ecclesial sinfulness and need for the forgiveness of sins that is a component of Bonhoeffer's concept of discipleship is also present in his ecumenical theology as presented in his address in Gland. Specifically, he highlights the sinfulness of the church and its need for forgiveness when he calls it "the community of those who repent and carry their guilt of not hearing the commandments of God as they should."[74] This claim parallels the emphasis Bonhoeffer places on the disciple's sinfulness and need for repentance in *Discipleship.*[75] In each case, the church must be truthful about its sinfulness and its continued capability to sin and repent when it finds itself to be in sin.

Thus, again, the four components demonstrated to be fundamental to Bonhoeffer's concept of discipleship are also fundamental to the ecumenical theology forwarded by Bonhoeffer in his address in Gland. This conclusion reinforces the claim that Bonhoeffer's concept of discipleship should be considered the operative theological content of his ecumenical theology. This trend would continue in his address in Fano.

Discipleship in "Address to the Fano Conference: English Transcription"—1934

By the time of the conference in Fano in 1934, the church struggle in Germany had begun, and tensions were already high concerning the ramifications it would have on the ecumenical landscape.[76] Although Bonhoeffer's responsibilities at the conference mostly had to do with the youth conference, he still presented a paper and gave an address which has come to be known as his "Peace Sermon."[77] The paper, entitled, "The Church and the Peoples of the World," is no longer extant, but Bonhoeffer's outline for the paper survives.[78] The full transcription of his "Peace Sermon" remains, and it is to that address that the chapter now turns its attention.[79]

With Hitler's rise to power and the emergence of the church struggle, Bonhoeffer's ecumenical exhortations for the ecumenical movement to identify as church and proclaim the command of peace sharpened in their specificity, and as these ecumenical exhortations sharpened, they became the main

---

[74] DBWE 11:380.
[75] DBWE 4:268–269.
[76] Clements, *Dietrich Bonhoeffer's Ecumenical Quest,* 139.
[77] Clements, *Dietrich Bonhoeffer's Ecumenical Quest,* 140–141.
[78] DBWE 13:304–306.
    Clements also discusses this paper. Clements, *Dietrich Bonhoeffer's EcumenicalQuest,* 142.
[79] For more on the historical and biographical details surrounding the conference in Fano, see Clements, *Dietrich Bonhoeffer's Ecumenical Quest,* 127–148.

thrust of his ecumenical works with the theology they are built upon taking a less pronounced position. That said, the ecumenical theology presented in Bonhoeffer's "Peace Sermon" nevertheless retains all four components of his concept of discipleship as its theological undergirding. Indeed, this particular text is beneficial to the current discussion not only to further demonstrate that Bonhoeffer's ecumenism is an ecumenism of discipleship, but the text is also beneficial as an example of how Bonhoeffer's ecumenical theology of discipleship could potentially be implemented. The crux of the address is found in these words:

> The ecumenical Church [concerns itself] with the commandments of God, and regardless of consequences it transmits these commandments to the world. . . . Peace on earth is not a problem, but a commandment given at Christ's coming. There are two ways of reacting to this command from God: the unconditional, blind obedience of action, or the hypocritical question of the Serpent: "Yea, hath God said . . .?" This question is the mortal enemy of obedience. . . . No, God did not say all that. What He has said is that there shall be peace among men—that we shall obey Him without further question. . . . There shall be peace because of the Church of Christ. . . . And the brothers who make up this Church are bound together, through the commandment of the one Lord Christ. . . . Once again, how will peace come? . . . The individual Christian cannot do it. . . . The individual church, too, can witness and suffer—oh, if it only would!—but it also is suffocated by the power of hate. Only the one great Ecumenical Council of the Holy Church of Christ over all the world can speak out so that the world, though it gnash its teeth, will have to hear.[80]

Bonhoeffer's approach to the issue of peace in his "Peace Sermon" is consistent with—and structured by—his concept of discipleship. The Christological orientation is observable in his claim that peace is a commandment from Christ.[81] Here, Bonhoeffer uses more language of "God" than "Christ," but he clarifies what he means when he identifies the commandment as "the commandment of the one Lord Christ."[82] In response to the command is "the unconditional, blind obedience of action," which evinces the component of a concrete command and simple obedience.[83] And this ecumenical action is all grounded within an ecclesiology, as Bonhoeffer begins by calling the ecumenical movement, "the ecumenical Church," speaking about the members being "bound together," and in his claim that—in the specific situation

---

[80] DBWE 13:307–309.
[81] DBWE 13:307.
[82] DBWE 13:309.
[83] DBWE 13:307.

facing the ecumenical movement in 1934—being heard requires for the church to proclaim Christ's commands on a global scale through the ecumenical movement.[84] As such, in this quotation, three of the components of Bonhoeffer's concept of discipleship are structuring the ecumenical theology he is presenting.

The final component of Bonhoeffer's concept of discipleship is found in his "Peace Sermon" as he brings his address to a close. After exhorting the World Alliance to give voice to the command for peace, he asks what they are waiting for before they make this command and asks, "Do we want to become involved in this guilt as never before?"[85] This question raises several significant points. First, the question implies that not proclaiming the command makes the church complicit in the guilt. In other words, it is possible for the church to be in sin. Second, ending the question with the words "as never before" implies that—at least to some degree—the church has been culpable of sin in the past.[86] For the most part, Bonhoeffer's certainty that peace was Christ's command for that time kept him from elaborating on repentance in this address. Instead, he was more interested that the church not become complicit in the sin of war and also culpable of disobeying the command of Christ. Thus, even though repentance is not brought up here, the same emphasis remains: Bonhoeffer maintains the reality of ecclesial sin and the possibility of future sin and urges obedience to the command in the concrete act of proclamation against war and in the name of peace.

In these ways, the theological content of the "Peace Sermon"—like the lecture in Ciernehorske Kupele and the "Address in Gland"—is demonstrably structured by the same components which structure Bonhoeffer's concept of discipleship. Bonhoeffer concludes that peace was the command given by Christ, which inheres a Christological orientation.[87] His conclusion to proclaim peace as Christ's command for that day is presented as an act of obedience, evincing an emphasis upon concrete command and obedience.[88] He argues that the command went out to the church as a whole to be proclaimed by the ecumenical movement as church, inhering an ecclesiological tenor to ecumenical action.[89] And he argued all of the above with full admission that the church has been guilty of sins, can commit more sins, and always stands in need of forgiveness.[90] Therefore, the ecumenical theology presented in this address is identical to Bonhoeffer's concept of discipleship, sharing the

---

[84] DBWE 13:307–309.
[85] DBWE 13:309.
[86] DBWE 13:309
[87] DBWE 13:308.
[88] DBWE 13:308.
[89] DBWE 13:307.
[90] DBWE 13:309.

concept's four fundamental components. Thus, along with the Ciernehorske Kupele lecture and his "Address in Gland," Bonhoeffer's concept of discipleship must be seen as the operative theological content of the ecumenism presented in his "Peace Sermon."

Discipleship in "The Confessing Church and the Ecumenical Movement"—1935

Although Bonhoeffer was pleased with the results of the Fano Conference,[91] he nevertheless found himself having to make the same ecumenical arguments the following year. By this time, the Confessing Church was no longer communing with the Reich Church in any form. As such, when Bonhoeffer was invited to speak at a conference in Denmark in 1935 at which there would be members of the Reich Church, he promptly declined.[92] Bonhoeffer's refusal to participate did not, however, keep him from articulating his thoughts on the ecumenical movement and its relation to the church struggle in Germany. Bonhoeffer submitted this essay to *Evangelische Theologie*, and it appeared in the August edition.[93] The essay went mostly unnoticed at the time[94] but stands as an important text for the study of Bonhoeffer's ecumenical theology. Clements has referred to the essay as "the great *summa* of Bonhoeffer's contribution to ecumenical thought."[95]

In the essay itself, Bonhoeffer argues that—having encountered one another—the ecumenical movement and the Confessing Church pose questions to one another.[96] The Confessing Church poses the question to the ecumenical movement as to whether or not the ecumenical movement is church;[97] the question posed to the Confessing Church is whether or not the Confessing Church is too exclusive and therefore actually in need of repentance and rebuke itself.[98] As was the case with the "Peace Sermon," this essay is focused sharply on the practicability of its content regarding a

---

[91] DBWE 14:396.
   Bethge and Clements have both covered the Fano Conference, its historical context, its resolutions, and Bonhoeffer's involvement in—and opinion of—it in rigorous detail. Bethge, *Dietrich Bonhoeffer: A Biography,* 372–392; Clements, *Dietrich Bonhoeffer's Ecumenical Quest,* 127–148.
[92] DBWE 14:393–394.
   For Bonhoeffer's correspondence with Hodgson, see DBWE 14: 68–69; 71–73; 76–80. Clements also details this correspondence. Clements, *Dietrich Bonhoeffer's Ecumenical Quest,* 165–166.
[93] DBWE 14:393.
[94] DBWE 14:394.
[95] Clements, *Dietrich Bonhoeffer's Ecumenical Quest,* 168.
   Clements provides a thorough account of the historical events and biographical events surrounding the essay in *Dietrich Bonhoeffer's Ecumenical Quest,* 165–174.
[96] DBWE 14:397.
[97] DBWE 14:399.
[98] DBWE 14:407–408.

specific situation (that of the ecumenical movement's status as church and its view of the church struggle, and of the Confessing Church and its approach to ecumenism and view of the Reich Church). That said, the main thrust of Bonhoeffer's argument maintains each of the four fundamental components of Bonhoeffer's concept of discipleship as the fundamental components funding the ecumenical theology he presents.

The Christological orientation of the ecumenical action Bonhoeffer posits in this essay is seen in his presentation of a "church capable of living only through Christ."[99] As for the concrete command and simple obedience, Bonhoeffer writes, "Historical speculation ends at God's commandments," and lauds the actions taken in Fano as "responsible obedience to God's commandment."[100] The component of command and obedience is perhaps most strongly evident in Bonhoeffer's concluding statement:

> [W]hether the witness of such a council will fall on receptive ears—that depends
> on our own obedience to the question now posed to us and on how God chooses
> to use our obedience. It is not an ideal that has been set up but a commandment
> and a promise—it is not high-handed implementation of one's own goals that is
> required but obedience. The question has been posed.[101]

The ecclesiological nature of discipleship is evident in Bonhoeffer's claim that "the Confessing Church participates in the ecumenical work *as church*," and his insistence throughout that the ecumenical movement as a whole do the same.[102] Finally, the component of acknowledging the church's history of sin and continued potential to sin, and the need for forgiveness is apparent in Bonhoeffer's statements identifying the Confessing Church as "one of daily penitence," "a church that confesses its own guilt in the discord of Christendom and that at every moment remains wholly dependent on the gift of God's grace," and a church that "is open to hear those others who might call it to penitence."[103]

In these ways, the components of Bonhoeffer's concept of discipleship are once again seen to be the rudimentary components of his ecumenical theology. He begins with a Christological orientation, stating that the church only lives through Christ. The action of ecumenical work he posits is obedience to God's commands, which is the action of discipleship. He bases this activity in an ecclesiology, proclaiming that the Confessing Church participates "as

---

[99] DBWE 14:411.
[100] DBWE 14:403
[101] DBWE 14:412.
[102] DBWE 14:399.
[103] DBWE 14:411.

church."[104] And Bonhoeffer maintains the capability and culpability for the Confessing Church to sin in his insistence that the first confession must be a confession of sin. As such, it is clear that the ecumenical theology Bonhoeffer has in mind in this essay mirrors the concept of discipleship he would later articulate in *Discipleship*. It can correctly be concluded, then, that the ecumenical theology being presented is an ecumenism of discipleship, in which discipleship is the operative theological content.

As this discussion has shown, this conclusion is not only true of the theology present in "The Confessing Church and the Ecumenical Movement" but is likewise true of each of Bonhoeffer's ecumenical works. The consistency of Bonhoeffer's presentation of this ecumenical theology validates the claim that discipleship is the operative theological content of Bonhoeffer's ecumenical theology. It should, therefore, be surmised that Bonhoeffer's ecumenical theology can aptly be described as an ecumenism of discipleship.

CONCLUSION

The preceding discussion has elucidated the key components of Bonhoeffer's concept of discipleship and highlighted those components as the rudiments of his ecumenical theology in each of his ecumenical works. Thus, even though Bonhoeffer never refers to his own ecumenical theology as an ecumenism of discipleship—or even uses the word "discipleship" a single time—it should be deduced that Bonhoeffer's ecumenical theology is structured by his concept of discipleship. Taken altogether, the findings in these texts illustrate a consistency in Bonhoeffer's ecumenical thought so deeply rooted, sustained, and ubiquitous as to render the proposition of a Bonhoefferian ecumenism of discipleship irrefutable. Now that Bonhoeffer's concept of discipleship has been established and proven to be the operative theological content of his ecumenical works, the book can move to its climax—providing a constructive systematic account of Bonhoeffer's ecumenism of discipleship. The final chapter explores precisely what an ecumenical vision founded upon Bonhoeffer's concept of discipleship yields.

---

[104] DBWE 14:399.

Chapter 5

Bonhoeffer's Ecumenism
of Discipleship

Bonhoeffer himself never wrote a full, systematic treatment of his ecumenical theology. The closest he came to doing so was his 1932 lecture in Ciernehorske Kupele. That said, his ecumenical works provide enough theological content to construct his ecumenical theology. From his Ciernehorske Kupele lecture, we learn that his ecumenical theology is grounded in his account of the church as *Christus Praesens*.[1] For this reason, the first three chapters of this book drew out that account of ecclesiology and the understandings of unity and visibility that come with it, and chapter 4 identified discipleship as the role of human work in Bonhoeffer's ecumenical theology. All told, Bonhoeffer's ecumenical theology is grounded in an ecumenical self-understanding as church, and the content of active ecumenical work for the human agent is discipleship. This is Bonhoeffer's ecumenical theology. It remains to be seen, however, what such an ecumenical theology yields when implemented.

Any attempt to construct Bonhoeffer's ecumenical theology is faced with a conundrum. By making discipleship the operative theological content of his ecumenical vision, Bonhoeffer ensures that his ecumenism cannot be systematized. If the sole focus of ecumenical work is obedience to the command of Christ, and Christ is free to command as Christ wills, then there is a contingent character—an elastic character—to the implementation of this ecumenical theology. Bonhoeffer explicitly states that the commandments of Christ are not general principles but are instead concrete and contingent in their specificity.[2] Such contingency results in a protean ecumenism, defying systematization or reduction to a formula or program. A systematic

---

[1] DBWE 11:358–359.
[2] DBWE 11:359–360.

constructive account of Bonhoeffer's ecumenical theology must, therefore, take a different approach.

If a constructive account of an ecumenism of discipleship cannot be systematized, the question must be asked: What *can* be said of Bonhoeffer's ecumenism of discipleship? How can an ecumenical theology that cannot be systematized be explicated? Although this ecumenism of discipleship cannot be systematized, there are, nevertheless, seven distinctive features that will always be present in the implementation of this ecumenical vision. Unpacking each of these seven distinctive features brings Bonhoeffer's ecumenical vision fully into view. Once these features have been established, it is possible to state the sum of Bonhoeffer's ecumenism of discipleship. What emerges is an ecumenical vision of a church that is governed by Christ, following after Christ in active, obedient discipleship; a church of disciples bound to one another in the person of Christ, and a church which is oriented *for* the world rather than *from* it; a church that is truly catholic—actively and concretely ecumenical from the global scale of the universal church, all the way down to the one to one discipleship of everyday faith; a church which is versatile in its expression, and accountable to one another under the command of Christ.

THE SEVEN DISTINCTIVE FEATURES OF
BONHOEFFER'S ECUMENISM OF DISCIPLESHIP

There are seven distinctive features of Bonhoeffer's ecumenism of discipleship: (1) Christological governance; (2) a goal of doing and proclaiming Christ's commands; (3) an internal ordering of ecumenical relationships within the church; (4) an external ordering of ecumenical relationships to (and for) the world; (5) ecumenism on a global and local scale; (6) versatility; and (7) accountability. These features are not distinctive in the sense that they are present exclusively in this ecumenical vision, but rather in the sense that each will *always* be present in the application of Bonhoeffer's ecumenical vision in spite of that vision's protean nature. As such, these features provide something like a general shape to this ecumenical vision and reveal the implications of its application.

The Christological Governance of Bonhoeffer's
Ecumenism of Discipleship

The first distinctive feature of Bonhoeffer's ecumenism of discipleship is its account of the governance of ecumenism. Bonhoeffer is consistent throughout his ecumenical thought regarding Christ's headship over ecumenism.[3] If the ecumenical movement understands itself as the church as *Christus Praesens*, then Christ's headship over ecumenism is fundamental to what ecumenism is. Moreover, if discipleship is the work of ecumenism and Christ is the authority over discipleship, then Christ's governance of ecumenism is made practical. To claim that Christ rules over and governs the activity of his church is significant in its own right.[4] The significance of this understanding of ecumenical governance for ecumenical discourse is that it moves ecumenical practice and discourse to be expansively inclusive—including more than simply the interactions of denominations—and preserves the theological heritages of the denominations.

Bonhoeffer articulates Christ's governance of ecumenism in his lecture in Ciernehorske Kupele, writing:

> Now one must first ask the question: *under which authority does the church speak, when it proclaims this claim of Christ on the world?* Under the only authority in which the church is in a position to speak, in the authority of the Christ who is present and living in it. The church is the presence of Christ on

---

[3] DBWE 11:358–359; DBWE 11:379–380; DBWE 13:308; DBWE 14:411.

Although Christ is universally embraced in some form as the head of his body (the church), ecumenical visions tend to place more emphasis on human agency than does Bonhoeffer by affording the systematized structuring of governance a significantly higher degree of priority than does Bonhoeffer. For instance, the authors of the Toronto Statement write, "The member churches of the Council believe that conversation, cooperation and common witness of the churches must be based on the common recognition that Christ is the Divine Head of the Body." TS: IV.1. The difference is that Bonhoeffer's emphasis upon Christ's *presence* within and constituting the church yields an ecumenical theology in which Christ's headship over the church more directly affects ecumenical practice in the orientation of the disciple to Christ.

Another example is the hierarchical, polity-driven understanding of church governance of the Roman Catholic Church, in which Christ is seen as the ruler of the church, but authority then runs from the top to the bottom via the church's hierarchical structure, starting with the Pope, running through the cardinals, the bishops, the priests, down to the laity. *Lumen Gentium,* 14; III–IV.

The WCC structures itself under its central committee (Constitution, 2). That committee, however, possesses only so much power as the constituent member churches lend it as "each church retains the constitutional right to ratify or to reject the utterances or actions of the Council" (TS: III.1). This approach to governance, thus, does not identify church with political structure as the Roman Catholic account does, and allows the member churches to maintain their own tradition regarding their own governance. This governmental structure also provides the WCC the ability to act or issue proclamations. These actions and proclamations, however, come with the caveat that any of them may or may not be accepted or rejected by any number of the WCC's member churches, resulting in an inconsistent voice (TS III.1).

[4] For a concise but engaging account of church authority unrelated to that of Bonhoeffer, see Jean-rond, Werner G. "Community and Authority: The Nature and Implications of the Authority of Christian Community" In *On the Living the Church: Essays on the Christian Community,* edited by Colin E Gunton and Daniel W Hardy, 81–110. Edinburgh: T&T Clark, 1989.

earth; the church is *Christus Praesens*. This alone gives its word authority. The word of the church is the word of the present Christ.[5]

By identifying the ecumenical movement as church—specifically, as church understood as *Christus Praesens*—Bonhoeffer immediately establishes Christ as the ruler of the ecumenical church and its actions.[6] The church as the person of Christ (the new humanity which Christ creates, rules over, and is) means that the church and its actions are *directly* governed by the living God.[7] A gut reaction against such a bold statement of Christ's direct governance over church action is reasonable, given the seemingly endless atrocities that are wrongly attributed to the "will of God." The final feature of Bonhoeffer's ecumenism of discipleship—accountability—helps to strike back against this fear. While it is important to recognize the abuses that have been done in God's name, it is even more important to proclaim the reality of Christ, who is living, active, and imminently near to his creation.

This approach to ecumenical governance has considerable impact upon ecumenical practice. One implication of the Christological governance of ecumenism is an expansion of the ecumenical cast. When the ecumenical movement is viewed *a priori* as church, denominational lines are no longer the primary location of ecumenical discourse and practice. Traditional approaches to discourse within organized ecumenical bodies tend to begin with discussion between denominations. In these instances, the denominations as a whole are seen as ecumenical actors because it is as denominations that churches enter as member churches into such organizations.[8] There is nothing

---

[5] DBWE 11:359.

   An instance of Christ's governance of ecumenism in Bonhoeffer's wider corpus is found in his "Lectures on Christology." Bonhoeffer's articulation of Christ creating, being, and ruling over the church as new creation applies also to ecumenical governance because Bonhoeffer identifies the ecumenical movement itself as church—as *Christus Praesens*. If ecumenism is church—is *Christus Praesens*—then its governance matches that of the church—Christ. DBWE 12:315.

[6] Bonhoeffer's treatment of church boundaries in his 1936 essay further exhibits what he intends in the Christological governance of ecumenism. There, he argues that the church as the present Christ only becomes concerned with its boundaries when that person of Christ encounters that which it is not. This, along with Bonhoeffer's concept of confession and his ecumenical approach to the Church Struggle in Germany are discussed in this chapter. DBWE 14:660.

[7] The National Council of the Church of Christ in the USA (NCC) addressed the issue of ecumenical authority in its 2010 document, "The Authority of the Church in the World." The authors affirm an authority that is intrinsic to the church by virtue of its communion with God. The authors further affirm that it is God's authority that the church proclaims. The author's write, "The Church's authority is rooted in its identify as the People of God, the Body of Christ, the New Creation of the Holy Spirit . . . if the Church is to speak and act with authority, it must first and foremost be the Church . . . only the Church can be the Church. Its authority is wrapped up in the integrity of being what it is." In this document, the NCC expresses a similar account of the authority of the church as does Bonhoeffer, but refuses to express ecumenism in ecclesial terms. http://www.nccusa.org/pdfs/authorityofthechurch.pdf, 2010.

[8] The WCC is one example of this.

inherently wrong with denominations being seen as ecumenical actors, and these organizations have been—and need to continue to be—vibrant parts of the ecumenical movement. The only thing problematic with this approach is that it results in most ecumenical discussions happening along denominational lines, meaning that a lot (but certainly not all) of ecumenical work boils down to discussion of doctrinal difference between denominations, and a lot (but not all) of ecumenical work takes place between denominations as actors. While such ecumenical work will inevitably take place as Christ calls his church to follow after him together, this specific work and cast do not encompass all (or even most) of the ecumenical work that can be expected when ecumenical work subsists in obedience to Christ.[9]

Bonhoeffer's approach is readily amenable to a more varied account of ecumenical actors. His own engagement with the ecumenical movement on behalf of the Confessing Church shows that denominations still act as individual actors, but Bonhoeffer's starting point of the ecumenical movement being church does not *necessarily* begin discourse along denominational lines. Instead of beginning with a sense of disunity, there is already a presupposition of unity. This unity, coupled with the focus on hearing and doing the commands of Christ, more readily engenders a more variegated cast of ecumenical actors.[10]

Another implication of Bonhoeffer's account of ecumenical governance is that it preserves the theological heritages of the churches involved. When the WCC clarified its self-understanding in the Toronto Statement in 1950, the authors wrote, "The WCC is not and must never become a super-church" and "cannot and should not be based on any one particular conception of church."[11] The primary purpose of such statements is to declare that the WCC will not be a single overpowering denomination, overriding the great variety of theological heritages present across the wide array of denominations throughout the world. These statements are a promise that membership within the WCC does not dissolve theological heritage. This is an important promise to have in place. By making this promise, the WCC has created a space within which a great variety of denominations can encounter one another and discuss and pursue the ongoing works of God in the world.

---

[9] An international dialogue between the Anglican Communion and the Roman Catholic Church yielded several agreed upon statements, the most noteworthy of which attended to the topic of authority. Even so, these statements do not envision authority in the same terms as Bonhoeffer. Authority is thought of in terms of polity. *The Gift of Authority: An Agreed Statement by the Second Anglican-Roman Catholic International Commission.* New York: Church Publishing Incorporated, 1999.

[10] This variegated cast of ecumenical actors is clarified in greater detail in the section addressing the global and local needs of communcommunion.

[11] TS: III.1; III.3.

That said, Bonhoeffer's ecumenical vision also does not promote what the WCC has labeled a "super-church"—even in his claim that ecumenical work emerges from a particular conception of church. The concern behind a "super-church" for the WCC is rooted in an understanding of the church in institutional terms. To claim that the WCC is not a super-church is to claim that it will not force a single polity and set of doctrines upon its members. But Bonhoeffer's account of church as *Christus Praesens* is not built upon institutional terms but upon the revelatory person of Christ. The Christological governance of the ecumenical movement as church does not create a uniform "super-church," but rather it envisions a united and variegated ecumenical church which follows after Christ in the world. As such, the theological heritages of various denominations are preserved in Bonhoeffer's ecumenical theology.[12]

None of this is to say that Bonhoeffer is a latitudinarian, or that doctrine and theology are inconsequential for him. Bonhoeffer himself maintained a distinctively Lutheran perspective, as evinced in his training of pastors for the Confessing Church at Finkenwalde. Moreover, he included Lutheran accounts of church offices in his university lectures on the visible church.[13] Bonhoeffer does not throw out polity but rather situates it peripherally to the church's primary being as the revelatory person of Christ. As such, the ecumenical movement, when viewed as church, does not subsist in a particular institutional structure but instead in the revelatory person of Christ. In terms of governance, Bonhoeffer's ecumenism of discipleship is concerned only with hearing and doing the commands issued from the church's authority—Christ.[14]

Doing and Proclaiming Christ's Commands: The Goal of Bonhoeffer's Ecumenism of Discipleship

To say that the goal of ecumenical work is to hear and do Christ's commands in the world is a rather large claim. And yet, this book has repeatedly posited the obedient doing of Christ's commands as the sole focus of Bonhoeffer's ecumenical theology. While the discernment of the command and the component of obedience to the command have already been addressed elsewhere,

---

[12] Clements writes: "The questions Bonhoeffer asked still await a full response today, for they engage with a major issue which the infant WCC had face within two years of its inauguration in 1948, which has repeatedly (and divisively) raised its head at intervals down to the present and still shows no sign of resolution given the assumed terms of the debate. This issue is the theological status of the WCC and, indeed, all ecumenical bodies at whatever level. Do they have ecclesial status? If so, of what kind?" Clements, *Dietrich Bonhoeffer's Ecumenical Quest*. 286.

[13] DBWE 14:462–471.

[14] DBWE 11:358–359.

this section focuses strictly on what is at stake in making obedience the goal of ecumenical action when put into practice.[15] This feature has weighty implications not only for what it says about ecumenical action but also what it *negates* as goals of ecumenism.

In his lecture in Ciernehorske Kupele, Bonhoeffer states,

> The church as the one church-community of the Lord Jesus Christ, who is the Lord of the world, has the task of speaking his word to the entire world . . . the task of the church [is] that of making the claim of Christ audible to the entire world.[16]

Again, by identifying the ecumenical movement as church, this task is also the task of ecumenism. Bonhoeffer illustrates this feature in his ecumenical works in his approach to the command of international peace for his day. Bonhoeffer advocates for international peace as the command of Christ rather than as a static, universal good; that command finds concretion because

---

[15] In contrast, the authors of the *Princeton Proposal* promote institutional, structural unity between the denominations as the goal of ecumenism, stating, "One must be able to see that the church, in its ordinary life and practice, is one community reconciled in Christ." *Princeton Proposal,* 43; see also 26.

The Constitution of the WCC states the Council's primary purpose as follows: "To call one another to visible unity in one faith and in one Eucharistic fellowship, expressed in worship and common life in Christ, through witness and service to the world, and to advance towards that unity in order that the world may believe." Here, the WCC promotes calling one another to visible unity in various ways as its objective. Constitution, 1.

Bonhoeffer's stance differs from that of the *Princeton Proposal* by the fact that his ecumenical thought does not promote visible institutional unity as its goal. Although the WCC's stance is not institutionally determined like that of the *Princeton Proposal* (which is, incidentally, the catalyst for the writing of the *Princeton Proposal*), the WCC nevertheless discusses visible unity as the goal of its work. That said, there remains an affinity between Bonhoeffer and the WCC in an end that includes witness and service to the world; the difference is that Bonhoeffer gets there by way of his concept of discipleship, while the WCC is—at times—more prescriptive along the lines of principles such as justice and peace. WCC, Commission on Faith and Order. "'Come and See': A Theological Invitation to the Pilgrimage of Justice and Peace." Forthcoming.

Brant Himes wrote an article promoting Bonhoeffer's concept of discipleship as a resource for theological education. Himes rightly identifies the interconnectedness of discipleship, ecclesiology, Christology, and revelation for Bonhoeffer, and even attends briefly to his concept of personhood. That said, Himes emphasizes the relation of these theological concepts to discipleship rather than discipleship's orientation to Christ. As a result, the disciple's relation to and for those outside the church is rightly emphasized, but the fact that such a relation is a result of a Christological orientation, and Christ's presence in the church as the foundation of the church is not addressed. Himes, Brant. "Discipleship as Theological Praxis: Dietrich Bonhoeffer as a Resource for Educational Ministry." *Christian Education Journal* 8, no. 2 (Fall 2011): 263–277.

[16] DBWE 11:358–359.

Suzanne de Dietrich has argued similarly, writing, "The church is the place where God's will is now to be revealed, where the life of Christ is to be manifested in word and deed. . . . It is to the immediate disciples, and through them to the whole church as a body, that Christ speaks these words which fill us with awe. The responsibility of representing him and speaking in his name lies on the fellowship of the believers." de Dietrich, Suzanne. *The Witnessing Community: The Biblical Record of God's Purpose.* Philadelphia: Westminster Press, 1958, 165–180.

Bonhoeffer is declaring international peace as the command regarding a particular war, in a particular place, at a particular time. In discussing how the church (the ecumenical movement being understood as a part of which) can make this command, Bonhoeffer writes:

> What can the church say about international peace as God's commandment? That is the question. First of all: like everyone who speaks God's commandment, it may be suspected of being Enthusiastic and of proclaiming dreams, that is, of speaking out of the flesh and not out of the spirit. It also cannot "qualify" its word as God's commandment by anything, except through a continued, monotone, sober pointing to this commandment. It will try in vain to refute the irritation of pacifist humanitarianism, where the commandment of peace itself has not already been understood as God's commandment. The church must know this and must renounce every attempt at a justification of the commandment of God. It conveys the commandment but nothing more.[17]

Bonhoeffer shows that the focus of ecumenical work is always on hearing and doing the command of Christ. Simply being the command of Christ is all the justification the church needs for doing the command.[18] For Bonhoeffer, it is the only basis of ecumenical action. In his articulation of the command for international peace for his day, Bonhoeffer displays practically what is intended in this feature of his ecumenism. The ecumenical movement seeks to hear and do the commands of Christ, commands which are practical, finding concrete expression in specific actions in specific contexts.[19] The weight of this claim cannot be overstated. According to Bonhoeffer, the ecumenical church is able to *actually do* the commands of Christ in the world. Not only *can* it do so, it *must* do so in obedience to Christ.

That said, Bonhoeffer's identification of this goal of ecumenical work does more than signal what ecumenical work consists of in his ecumenical theology. The goal of ecumenical work as doing the command also *negates* other possible goals of ecumenism. Maintaining obedience to Christ as the sole goal of ecumenism means that the goal of ecumenism is neither creating church unity nor manifesting visible unity. Additionally, the focus on obedience to Christ signifies the dismissal of conciliarism as the *focus* of ecumenism.

To clarify, there are generally two options for what is meant when speaking of "councils" as they relate to ecumenical discourse. Councils and

---

[17] DBWE 11:364–365.
[18] DBWE 11:364–365.
[19] This feature of Bonhoeffer's ecumenism of discipleship is particularly prevalent in *Discipleship*. The discussion of the key components of Bonhoeffer's concept of discipleship in chapter 4 attended to this material.

conciliarism in the first sense refer to the councils of the early church, which were focused primarily on addressing issues of orthodoxy and heresy in order to maintain uniform doctrine. At times, Protestant ecumenism has had a similar approach, though the enterprise has tended to be more concerned with investigating what denominations have in common than codifying a strict and complete account of doctrine which all churches must accept.[20] According to Michael Kinnamon—former general secretary of the National Council of the Churches of Christ in the USA (NCC)—councils of churches in the contemporary sense refers to "voluntary associations of separated churches within a given area—local, national, regional, and global," such as the WCC and NCC, which "are among the ecumenical movement's most widespread and widely recognized expressions."[21] Kinnamon, like many other ecumenists, is quick to point out that the relationship of such groupings of churches runs deeper than a mere organization; instead, such groups are frequently understood in terms such as "fellowship," as is the case with the WCC. Both of these meanings fit what the chapter intends by arguing that Bonhoeffer's emphasis on the command dismisses conciliarism as a focus of ecumenical work.[22] This is not to diminish or make little of these councils (in the former or latter sense) but rather to situate these downstream from obedient discipleship.[23] For Bonhoeffer, doctrinal uniformity is not given so highly prized a position.

To be sure, Bonhoeffer does not *disregard* theology or doctrine in his ecumenism of discipleship. From his first encounter with the ecumenical movement, Bonhoeffer was concerned with what he perceived as a lack of theology—specifically a theology of the church.[24] Indeed, his famous opening lines in Ciernehorske Kupele that "there is still no theology of the ecumenical movement" highlight a lack of theology of the ecumenical movement, and his intention is for the lecture to be, "an attempt to outline clearly some of the basic theological questions that particularly relate to the work of our World Alliance and to situate them theologically."[25] What he suggests immediately after calling for a theology of the ecumenical movement diverges from an

---

[20] In documents such as "Baptism, Eucharist, and Ministry," doctrinal agreement is not forced upon member churches of the WCC, but the convergences of thought between member churches are viewed as significant for the visible unity of the church and ecumenical work on the whole. BEM, v–vi.

[21] Kinnamon, Michael. *Can a Renewal Movement be Renewed? Questions for the Future of Ecumenism.* Grand Rapids: William B. Eerdmans Publishing Company, 2014, 10.

[22] For more on the councils of churches like the WCC and NCC, see Hayward, Victor. "A Survey of National Christian Councils," *International Review of Mission* 60 (1971): 512–521.

[23] For more on conciliarism and the ecumenical movement, see Kessler, Diane and Michael Kinnamon. *Councils of Churches and the Ecumenical Vision.* Geneva: WCC, 2000.

[24] DBWE 11:165–169.
Clemens, Dietrich Bonhoeffer's Ecumenical Quest, 33–38.

[25] DBWE 11:356–359.

account of complete doctrinal uniformity. Bonhoeffer states that ecumenical work emerges from an account of "[t]he church as the one church-community of the Lord Jesus Christ"—understanding the church as *Christus Praesens*—that "has the task of speaking [Christ's] word to the entire world."[26] Thus, the theology Bonhoeffer posits is his theology of discipleship as the ethical action and theological content of ecumenism.

Even so, in the closing paragraph of the lecture, Bonhoeffer again laments the lack of a theology, saying,

> When [the World Alliance member churches] say Christ or gospel, each of them means something very different. At present this is our most pressing problem in ecumenical work. We can speak only as the church that proclaims the truth out of the gospel.[27]

This statement suggests a desire for a form of doctrinal agreement. He concludes, however, that in spite of the church's "ruptured knowledge of the truth," "[the church] nevertheless must speak under God's commandment . . . on the basis of forgiveness alone."[28] In other words, the sole focus on discipleship remains despite the lack of doctrinal uniformity.[29]

These concluding thoughts reveal an important distinction for Bonhoeffer's ecumenical theology. It is true that discipleship is the only focus of ecumenism. That said, Bonhoeffer does not throw out conciliarism (here referring to the ordering and work of councils of churches in the sense of fellowships such as the WCC and NCC) but instead identifies its place in ecumenism.[30] Conciliarism is not the defining form of the practical content of ecumenism; neither is doctrinal uniformity the theological content of ecumenism.[31] Discipleship is the *only* focus of ecumenism; discipleship is the ethical action and theological content of ecumenism. Discourse regarding doctrine and the formation of organized ecumenical bodies such as the WCC and NCC will likely arise as a result of discipleship as Christ calls together the members of

---

[26] DBWE 11:358–359.

[27] DBWE 11:369.

[28] DBWE 11:369.

[29] In addition to providing a synopsis of ecumenical theology of the 1970s, a piece by M. M. Thomas also articulates the sentiment that different people mean different things by the same word. Thomas, M M. "Search for Wholeness and Unity." In *Towards a Theology of Contemporary Ecumenism,* 255–265. Geneva: WCC, 1978.

[30] For an early understanding of how councils were thought of in the WCC, see Temple, William. "Explanatory Memorandum on the Constitution of the World Council of Churches, 1938." In *The Genesis and Formation of the World Council of Churches,* edited by W.A. Visser't Hooft, 107–110. Geneva: WCC, 1982.

[31] In contrast, see "The Ecclesiological Significance of Councils of Churches." In *Growing Consensus: Church Dialogues in the United States, 1962 1991,* edited by Joseph A Burgess and Jeffrey Gros. New York: Paulist Press, 1995, 602–613.

his body, but doctrinal uniformity and the organizing of such fellowships are not the *telos* of ecumenism.

This move to situate doctrinal agreement downstream from the focal point of discipleship to Christ is prototypical for how Bonhoeffer attends to many of the issues at stake in an ecumenism of discipleship. He does not dismiss conciliarism but rather makes clear that it does not enter into the discussion of the primary focus of ecumenical work.[32] In doing so, Bonhoeffer reorients the ecumenical approach to theology. He prizes theology—but the theology he prizes is discipleship to Christ. The quest for common doctrine is, for Bonhoeffer, not the quest of ecumenism.[33] Discipleship to Christ—doing and proclaiming Christ's commands—alone is the goal.[34]

The Internal Ordering of Ecumenical Relations

The third distinctive feature of Bonhoeffer's ecumenism of discipleship is the internal ordering of ecumenical relations.[35] The previous section attended briefly to the treatment of polity in Bonhoeffer's ecumenism. Polity is not what the current section intends when referring to "internal ordering." Here, the phrase "internal ordering" refers to the ways in which ecumenical actors relate to one another within Bonhoeffer's account of ecumenical theology. The phrase itself is employed not only to illustrate that ecumenical actors relate to one another but to stress that those within the church are *inherently* ordered toward one another by virtue of Bonhoeffer's understanding of the church as *Christus Praesens.* Bonhoeffer understands those within the church as being bound together in Christ,[36] and that binding yields an inherent internal ordering of those within the church to one another. *Because Bonhoeffer conceives of the ecumenical movement as church, the internal ordering of the church is the internal ordering of Bonhoeffer's ecumenism.*

Material from Bonhoeffer's broader corpus is particularly needed in this section because the content of this feature of Bonhoeffer's ecumenism is largely presupposed in his ecumenical works. To be precise, because Bonhoeffer's ecumenical theology emerges from his account of the church as *Christus Praesens*, his understanding of the internal ordering of

---

[32] Lukas Vischer promotes councils not as manifestations of church communion but an anticipation of such communion. Vischer, Lukas. "Christian Councils: Instruments of Ecclesial Communion." *The Ecumenical Review* 24, no. 1 (1972): 79–87.

[33] See also "The Ecclesiological Significance of Councils of Churches," 599–600.

[34] DBWE 11:369.

[35] The language used here of "internal" and "external" ordering of the church mirrors Greggs' depiction of the church's internal and external dynamics in his *Dogmatic Ecclesiology.* Greggs, *Dogmatic Ecclesiology,* 00-11ff.

[36] DBWE 11:377.

ecumenism presupposes that same account.[37] Overall, the section posits that, for Bonhoeffer, ecumenism has the same internal ordering as the church: "being-with-each-other" and "being-for-each-other."

The "Address in Gland" is an example in which the internal ordering of relationships of those within the ecumenical movement (understood as the church) is expressed. This ordering comes to the fore in the following excerpt:

> We come together in order to hear Christ! . . . is it not precisely the sense of these meetings, that where we encounter a person who appears so totally strange and incomprehensible to us in his concerns and who still claims our attention, that there we hear the voice of Christ, in the voice of the brother, and that there we do not withdraw from this voice but rather take it completely seriously, hear it, and love the other precisely in his foreign nature? This is how Christ encounters us at such conferences, in that brethren encounter one another in all openness and truthfulness and need and ask to be heard by the others. Not as the community of those who know but rather as the community of those who are looking for the words of their Lord and look everywhere to see whether they might hear it . . . and so are we bound together. We encounter Christ in the brother . . . [T]he church imparts the message of a new humanity, of the holy fellowship in Christ . . . [The church is] the community of those who repent and carry their guilt of not hearing the commandments of God as they should, even though the kingdom of heaven is near.[38]

Bonhoeffer, in this quotation, provides insight into his understanding of ecumenical relations within the specific context of the conference at Gland. The conference itself is not the identifying form of ecumenical relations—it is only the setting. The form of ecumenical relations is identified as *encounter*.[39] This identification of encounter as the form of ecumenical relations is the critical center of this feature of Bonhoeffer's ecumenism.

Specifically, Bonhoeffer narrates this encounter as encountering Christ in each other and claims that those within the church are bound together as the new humanity. Bonhoeffer's understanding of the church as *Christus Praesens* is presupposed here, and it is the defining factor of ecumenical relations.

What does Bonhoeffer explicitly state in his ecumenical works concerning ecumenical relations? First, Bonhoeffer states that the goal of an ecumenical

---

[37] DBWE 11:358–359.
[38] DBWE 11:377–380.
[39] DBWE 11:377.

work is to "hear Christ."[40] Second, when those within the church encounter each other in the context of an ecumenical conference, they do so in a way that listens to each other.[41] Finally, those within the church encounter each other with the humble knowledge that their own stance may be in sin and require repentance of them.[42]

Taken in isolation, Bonhoeffer's ecumenical works do not capture the full magnitude of this feature of his ecumenism. Specifically, the internal ordering of ecumenical relations in his ecumenism is informed by his account of the church as *Christus Praesens*. When Bonhoeffer identifies ecumenical relations in terms of encountering the person of Christ in each other, his understanding of the church as *Christus Praesens* is presupposed. For Bonhoeffer, when one encounters any person, that one is called to responsibility;[43] when one encounters the person of Christ they are called to responsibility in a person forming way.[44] What is more, encountering the person of Christ means being called to repentance and discipleship to Christ;[45] in answering this call, one is created by Christ into the new humanity—the collective person of Christ—which Christ creates, is the head of, and *is* through his life, death, and resurrection. That new humanity is the church;[46] all of this means that to be created into the person of Christ inheres being in the church.[47]

Therefore, when Bonhoeffer identifies ecumenical relations in terms of encountering the person of Christ in each other, he intends an encounter of the church with *itself*. As such, ecumenical relations are defined in the same way as relations within the church. According to Bonhoeffer's ecumenism of

---

[40] DBWE 11:377.

This claim reiterates the second feature of Bonhoeffer's ecumenism: that hearing and doing Christ's commands is the goal of ecumenism.

[41] DBWE 11:377.

[42] DBWE 11:380.

Bonhoeffer demonstrates what is intended by this feature of his ecumenism in his 1935 essay "The Confessing Church and the Ecumenical Movement." This essay revolves around a specific instance of ecumenical relations: the relation of the Confessing Church and the ecumenical movement to one another. Bonhoeffer immediately classifies the ecumenical engagement as an encounter between the two groups. He then indicates that—in encountering the Confessing Church—the question put to the ecumenical movement is whether or not it is church. If the ecumenical movement is church, argues Bonhoeffer, then it must proclaim that the Reich Church is not church as the concrete command of Christ. The premise of this encounter requires that they are open to hearing each other so that they might hear the command of Christ in each other and proclaim it together. Finally, Bonhoeffer expresses that the first confession of the Confessing Church to the ecumenical movement is a confession of sin, acknowledging the Confessing Church's capability and culpability to sin. In all of these ways, Bonhoeffer shows in this essay precisely what he intended in his "Address in Gland." DBWE 14:397–407.

[43] DBWE 1:48.

[44] DBWE 1:54–56.

[45] DBWE 1:149–150.

[46] DBWE 1:149, 157.

[47] DBWE 1:127.

discipleship, then, all ecumenical activity between those within the church corresponds to the internal ordering of the church as *Christus Praesens*.[48]

By articulating ecumenical relations as encounters of the church with itself, Bonhoeffer applies the same internal ordering to ecumenism as he does to the church. Specifically, ecumenical actors interact and relate to one another along the lines of Bonhoeffer's articulation of "being-with-each-other" and "being-for-each-other." The "being-with-each-other" of ecumenism is the "being-with-each-other" of the church. Bonhoeffer expounds the "being-with-each-other" of the church thus:

> The church-community is so structured that wherever one of its members is, there too is the church-community in its power, which means in the power of Christ and the Holy Spirit . . . and in every situation and problem of life *the church-community is with this individual* . . . and wherever the church is, there the individual member is also. . . . Now where the church-community is, there is Christ.[49]

It is this same boundedness and unity that Bonhoeffer applies to ecumenical relations when he states that his audience in Gland is bound together in Christ.[50] Furthermore, this "being-with-each-other" of the church is what funds his stance in "The Confessing Church and the Ecumenical Movement." By questioning the ecumenical movement as to its ecclesial status, Bonhoeffer sets up the "being-with-each-other" of the church as a basic fact of ecumenism.[51]

This line of thinking persists in his 1936 work, "Essay and Discussion on Church Communion." Bonhoeffer argues that the boundaries of the church are only specified when the church encounters that which is not church.[52] In each text, it is this "being-with-each-other" of the church that Bonhoeffer is applying ecumenically. The 1935 essay questions the ecumenical movement regarding its ecclesial status because if the ecumenical movement is church, then the ecumenical movement and the Confessing Church are bound

---

[48] The authors of the *Princeton Proposal* write, "If Christians are to realize the unity for which Jesus prayed, they need structures, institutions and regular practices by which their communion in faith is expressed and formed. . . . How this Christian communion is to be given structural form is the concern of ecumenical activity in the strict sense." This approach to the internal ordering of the church is not what the section intends. When the section discusses the internal ordering of the church to itself, it is not doing so in institutional terms along denominational lines, or in terms of being ordered around a single church polity, or even having a shared structure. Instead, the internal ordering of the church to itself details the relation of the members of the church to each other—the members of the new humanity to itself. *Princeton Proposal,* 16.

[49] DBWE 1:178–182.

[50] DBWE 11:377.

[51] DBWE 14:398–399.

[52] DBWE 14:660.

together as church.[53] Likewise, Bonhoeffer's 1936 discussion of the boundaries of the church hinges upon ecclesial status.[54] Thus, it is demonstrable that Bonhoeffer's understanding of the "being-with-each-other" of the church applies to his account of ecumenical relations.

The same is true of his understanding of the "being-for-each-other" of the church. If ecumenism is based on Bonhoeffer's conception of the church as *Christus Praesens*, then those involved in ecumenism must relate to one another in the same form in which they do within the concept of the church as *Christus Praesens*. As the church encounters itself in ecumenical work, the members of the church relate to one another in the three ways that Bonhoeffer details in *Sanctorum Communio*: (1) "self-renouncing, active works for the neighbor," (2) "intercessory prayer," and (3) "the mutual forgiveness of sins."[55]

These three activities in which the members of the church act for each other do not throw out any other form of interaction for ecumenism such as theological discourse or councils. Rather, these activities highlight the fundamental ways in which members of the church act for each other. These are also the fundamental ways in which the members of the church are to act for each other *ecumenically*.

What are the implications of this internal ordering of ecumenical relations? Applying the internal ordering of the church to the internal ordering of ecumenical relations reiterates and reinforces several of the implications observed in the preceding features of Bonhoeffer's ecumenism of discipleship. First, this internal ordering of those within the church prioritizes hearing and doing the command of Christ together and for one another.[56] Second, the internal ordering of the church in ecumenical encounter implies church unity because ecumenical relations are encounters between the church and itself, understood as the revelatory person of Christ. Third, this internal ordering implies that ecumenical work is not defined exclusively along denominational lines but instead includes all the variegated relationships found within the church-community. Finally, while this internal ordering certainly does not dispose of conciliarism or doctrinal discourse, this internal ordering does attribute to them subsidiary status.

---

[53] DBWE 14:398–399.
[54] DBWE 14:656–661.
[55] DBWE 11:xxx.
[56] DBWE 11:377.

The External Ordering of Ecumenism to (and for) the World

While most ecumenical theologies maintain an external ordering of ecumenical relations to and for the world, it is nevertheless necessary to articulate Bonhoeffer's approach to this external relation, because this feature is integral to Bonhoeffer's ecumenism of discipleship. Bonhoeffer never envisioned a church that was cut off or separate from the world. The obedience of discipleship in doing and proclaiming the commands of Christ inevitably brings the disciple into contact with those outside of the church. Therefore, an ecumenism of discipleship also entails an external ordering toward the world.[57] As with the internal ordering of Bonhoeffer's ecumenism of discipleship, this external ordering is built upon his understanding of the ecumenical movement as *Christus Praesens*.[58] As such, the actions of ecumenism (the church) toward the world are defined in the same terms as the actions of discipleship—obedience in doing and proclaiming the commands of Christ.[59]

In his Ciernehorske Kupele lecture, Bonhoeffer indicates an external ordering of his ecumenical vision when he explicitly states that the church (which he has identified the World Alliance with) "has the task of speaking [Christ's] word to the entire world."[60] With this statement, Bonhoeffer not only acknowledges an external ordering of ecumenical action but also identifies the subject toward which that action is ordered—the world. In his "Address in Gland," Bonhoeffer expounds on the relation of ecumenical work to the world:

> The World Alliance is the community of those who want to hear the Lord as they anxiously cry to the Lord in the world on earth . . . [who] want to hear the call of Christ obediently in faith within it, and know that through this call they are responsible to the world. It is not the world-reforming dimension of activity in the church that has become weary of meditating on God's word, but rather it is the church, which knows about the sinfulness of the world and of Christianity,

---

[57] Garcia discusses the relation of the church to the world in Bonhoeffer's thought, arguing for a similarity with that of Calvin and the Reformed tradition. Garcia, *Recovering the Ecumenical Bonhoeffer*, 135–159.

[58] DBWE 11:358–359.

   Willem Visser't Hooft is another ecumenical voice who spoke of the importance of not only the vertical relation of the church to God but also the horizontal relation of the church to the world. Visser't Hooft, Willem. "The Mandate of the Ecumenical Movement." In *The Uppsala Report 1968: Official Report of the Fourth Assembly of the World Council of Churches, Uppsala July 4-20, 1968,* edited by Norman Goodall, 316–322. Geneva: World Council of Churches, 1968.

   Likewise, the conference in Lausanne in 1927 addressed the subject of the church's message to the world. "The Church's Message to the World—The Gospel." In *Faith and Order: Proceedings of the World Conference, Lausanne 1927,* edited by H.N. Bate, 461–463. London: SCM, 1927.

[59] DBWE 11:358–360.

[60] DBWE 11:358.

that awaits all the best from God and wants to be obedient to this God in the world.[61]

The external ordering of ecumenical action is *for* the world rather than *from* it. The form this action takes is discipleship to the command of Christ. Bonhoeffer makes this form evident as he narrates the church's action toward the world in terms of obediently doing Christ's command in and to a world that the call has made the church responsible to.[62]

Bonhoeffer demonstrates how the external ordering of ecumenical action takes the form of obedience to the command of Christ in his identification and explication of international peace as Christ's command for the world.[63] He rejects the notion of peace as a universal ideal that must be maintained.[64] Instead, he identifies peace as the proclamation of the church to the world on the basis of peace being the specific command of Christ for that day.[65] He emphasizes the specificity of the command of international peace for that particular time. As such, the church does not act for the world as a static monolith of universal truths, or as a pure cloister in isolation from the world, instead, the church acts toward—and for—the world by way of its obedience to the command of Christ. The external ordering of ecumenism to the world, therefore, takes the form of discipleship. As the disciples seek after Christ, they hear, do, and proclaim his commands to and for the world.[66]

Just as the internal ordering of ecumenical relations was determined as an encounter between the revelatory person of Christ in the church with itself, the external ordering of ecumenical relations—of the church to the world—is to be understood as an encounter between the revelatory person of Christ in the church and the person of Adam in the world.[67] This encounter—as is the case with any encounter with the person of Christ—calls the parties involved to responsibility. It is in this encounter that the church—the ecumenical church as *Christus Praesens*—finds its responsibility for the world. It is not an encounter of condemnation, but of invitation and responsibility, just as any encounter with Christ entails. The church is called to proclaim Christ

---

[61] DBWE 11:378.

[62] DBWE 11:378.

[63] DBWE 11:364–365.

[64] DBWE 11:364–366.

[65] DBWE 11:364.

[66] One example of this feature in Bonhoeffer's broader corpus is found in his *Ethics* essay, "On the Possibility of the Church's Message to the World." See particularly DBWE 6:356–357.

[67] Ulrich Schmiedel has also written about Bonhoeffer and his understanding of the church opening itself up to the other, noting the influence of Troelsch in Bonhoeffer's thought. Schmiedel, Ulrich "Opening the Church to the Other: Dietrich Bonhoeffer's Reception of Ernst Troeltsch." *International Journal for the Study of the Christian Church* 17, no. 3 (2017): 184–198.

and Christ's concrete commands to the world.[68] As such, the external ordering of the church to the world in Bonhoeffer's ecumenism of discipleship is
determined in terms of discipleship—in hearing and doing Christ's concrete
commands.[69] This external ordering of ecumenical relations to and for the
world is significant because it means that ecumenical work always has a
world-oriented dimension. Ecumenical work always involves an aspect of the
disciple both taking the command of Christ out into the world and hearing the
command of Christ in the other whom Christ loves.[70]

The Global and Local Scale of Bonhoeffer's Ecumenism of Discipleship

Discussion of the external ordering of ecumenism to the world begins to
hint at the scope of ecumenism in Bonhoeffer's thought. What is the scope
of Bonhoeffer's ecumenism of discipleship? Bonhoeffer's ecumenism has
a scope spanning from a global scale to a local scale, and everything in
between. Both of these lines of inquiry—the largest scale and the smallest
scale of ecumenism—carry meaningful implications for Bonhoeffer's ecumenism as a whole. At stake in the global scale of an ecumenism of discipleship is the claim that ecumenism *can do and proclaim Christ's commands
at a global level*, enabling the church to speak Christ's commands regarding
whatever international situation Christ would speak to; at stake in the one
to one scale of ecumenism is the claim that *everyone within the church is
actively ecumenical*. Taken altogether, the scope of Bonhoeffer's ecumenism
evinces the catholicity of his account.[71]

The material from Bonhoeffer's Ciernehorske Kupele lecture is once
again applicable for attending to the global scale of his ecumenical theology.
Immediately after identifying the ecumenical movement's task of proclaiming Christ's commands to the world, Bonhoeffer addresses the global scope
of ecumenism:

---

[68] DBWE 6:356–357.

[69] For more on Bonhoeffer's understanding of the world and the church's relation to it, see Feil,
Ernst. "Dietrich Bonhoeffer's Understanding of the World." In *A Bonhoeffer Legacy: Essays in
Understanding*, edited by A.J. Klassen, 237–255, Grand Rapids: Eerdmans, 1981.

[70] Marsh's work does a noteworthy job articulating how being in Christ transforms one's relatedness
to others in Bonhoeffer's works. Marsh, *Reclaiming Dietrich Bonhoeffer*.

[71] The WCC came close to expressing the form of church and catholicity present in Bonhoeffer's
ecumenical theology in Uppsala in 1968. The authors of "The Holy Spirit and the Catholicity of
the Church" express catholicity as a gift of God and given reality of the church, but simultaneously
describe the current status of the church as being called "on the way to a fully catholic mission and
ministry," which suggests that the catholicity of the church is still something that must be attained,
going so far as to describe a "quest for catholicity." "The Holy Spirit and the Catholicity of the
Church." In *The Uppsala Report 1968*, edited by Norman Goodall, 13–18. Geneva: WCC, 1968.

The range of the one church of Christ is the entire world. There are local boundaries for the proclamation of each individual church, but the *one* church has no
boundaries around it. The churches of the World Alliance have joined together
in order to express their claim, or rather the claim of our Lord, on the entire
world. They understand the task of the church as that of making the claim of
Christ audible to the entire world.[72]

Bonhoeffer highlights that ecumenism enables the church to act and proclaim on a global level in ways that individual congregations are incapable
of. Furthermore, Bonhoeffer's identification of the ecumenical movement as
church allows him to assert the global scale of ecumenism. In making this
assertion, Bonhoeffer is reclaiming the literal meaning of *oikumene* of "the
whole inhabited world," which here refers to both the church's place and the
delineation of its jurisdiction for proclaiming the command of Christ.

The way in which the global scale of ecumenism is shown in Bonhoeffer's
treatment of the command of peace further informs the magnitude this scope
has for his ecumenism:

The churches bound together in the World Alliance believe that they recognize
a very specific order as that commanded us by God today. The order of *international peace* is God's commandment for us today. Through this, a completely
concrete understanding of God's will for our time is expressed. . . . International
peace is not a reality of the gospel, not a piece of the kingdom of God, but rather
a commandment . . . Today's war destroys soul and body. Because there is no
way for us to understand war as God's order of preservation and therefore as
God's commandment, and because war needs to be idealized and idolatrized in
order to live, today's war, the next war, must be *condemned* by the church.[73]

Bonhoeffer's clarion call for peace as the command of Christ exemplifies precisely the global scale of his ecumenism. He calls for the church as a whole
to make a concrete proclamation against war. In doing so, Bonhoeffer depicts
how organizing ecumenical action under the command of Christ enables the
church to have a unified front without requiring doctrinal uniformity. When
Bonhoeffer declares this same command in his address in Fano, he laments
how individual Christians and individual congregations are unable to raise
their voices loud enough as to be heard by the world, and he concludes, "Only
the one great Ecumenical Council of the Holy Church of Christ over all the
world can speak out so that the world, though it gnash its teeth, will have to

---

72 DBWE 11:318–330,
73 DBWE 11:364–365.

hear."[74] Here again, Bonhoeffer asserts the global scale of his ecumenical vision and his belief that this form of ecumenical hearing and proclaiming of the command is one which could be heard by the world. The focus throughout remains firmly upon hearing and doing Christ's command in the world rather than seeking specific results.[75]

The scope of Bonhoeffer's ecumenism of discipleship is not limited only to global proclamations; his ecumenical vision has space for any scope. For instance, his approach to the Church Struggle in Germany displays that his ecumenism can operate on a smaller than global scale. Admittedly, the Church Struggle in Germany was still nationwide, and Bonhoeffer was trying to bring the ecumenical movement into the conversation as well, which would have expanded the situation to a more global scale.[76] All the same, the Confessing Church was addressing a specific group in a specific localized context. Although Bonhoeffer was calling for a concrete peace, the localized context of the Church Struggle added further specificity to the command of Christ being spoken by the Confessing Church to the Reich Church.[77]

Bonhoeffer is not unique in envisioning a global scope for ecumenism.[78] Regardless of the thinker or ecumenical body, the global church is an inevitable vision. What is significant about the global scope of Bonhoeffer's ecumenical vision is that, by defining ecumenical action in terms of obedient discipleship to Christ, it is possible for the church to have a unified voice giving practicably concrete commands on the largest scale while leaving space within itself for the many varied theological heritages held by the various denominations. What is more, when this global scope is applied to the internal ordering of this ecumenism of discipleship, *the church encounters itself on a global scale*; that global self-encounter of the church allows for the members of the church to be with and for each other on a global scale— bearing the burdens of one another, praying for one another, forgiving one

---

[74] DBWE 13:309.

[75] DBWE 11:364–365.

[76] DBWE 14:399.

[77] "On the Possibility of the Church's Message to the World," from *Ethics* enriches the discussion of the global scale of Bonhoeffer's ecumenism. The responsibility of the church for the world establishes a global scope of the church's interaction with the world consistent with Bonhoeffer's ecumenism. Furthermore, Bonhoeffer's statement, "[i]n calling individuals and nations to faith and obedience toward the revelation of God in Jesus Christ, the church at the same time defines a space within which this faith and this obedience is at least not made impossible," adds to this consistency as it verifies this scope is meant for proclaiming the command of Christ and calling for obedience to that command. DBWE 6:357–360.

[78] For instance, the authors of CUV write: "While the ecumenical movement has a worldwide scope . . . it points more specifically to the catholicity of the church, that is globally. In each place and in all places, the ecumenical movement is concerned with the true being and life of the church as an inclusive community." World Council of Churches Central Committee. "Common Understanding and Vision of the WCC." Geneva: WCC, 1997. 2.8.5.

another. The global self-awareness of the church provides a layer of account-ability in the proclamation of the command.

All of this said, the global scope of Bonhoeffer's ecumenism of disciple-ship is only one end of its scope. Indeed, the scope of this ecumenical vision extends from global all the way down to the local, in the obedience of everyday discipleship. The way in which this ecumenism of discipleship is able to define the discipleship of a single individual as ecumenical car-ries a different significance than was discussed with ecumenical action's global scale.

The critical point to be made is that *the obedient discipleship of any individual qualifies as ecumenical action under Bonhoeffer's ecumenism.* To be clear, the section does not attend simply to the ecumenicity of the actions of an individual participating in organized ecumenism (though such action would be included warranting such action was done in obedience to Christ). The section contends that *any* act of obedient discipleship is ecumenical.

Bonhoeffer never explicitly attends to the ecumenicity of the actions of an individual disciple in his ecumenical works. The section, therefore, starts by illumining the feature in Bonhoeffer's broader corpus, then highlighting the feature in Bonhoeffer's ecumenical theology, finally providing an original statement that fits Bonhoeffer's ecumenical works. What is at stake in the ecumenicity of daily discipleship is the *active participation in ecumenism by everyone within the church.* This active participation evinces the catholicity found in Bonhoeffer's ecumenism.

The basic question being asked is, how can the activity of an individual dis-ciple be defined as ecumenical? Or, how can an act by an individual be given a designation implying a community? To begin to answer, for Bonhoeffer, the individual disciple subsists within the church-community rather than the church-community subsisting in the individual disciple. Bonhoeffer attests to this claim in *Act and Being*:

> Thus revelation happens in the community of faith; it requires primarily a specific Christian sociology. There is a fundamental difference between think-ing of revelation individualistically and thinking of it as something related to community. All that we have examined so far in this study was individualisti-cally oriented. The transcendental attempt of pure actualism as well as that of ontology, which was to establish the continuity of the I, pointed to the individual human being and for that reason failed. In searching for "reality" it overlooked the fact that in reality human beings are never individuals only, not even those "addressed by the You." Human beings, rather, are always part of a commu-nity, in "Adam" or in "Christ"   Faith has, as its presupposition, being in the church. Faith invariably discovers itself already in the church; it is there already

when it becomes aware of its presupposition. To believe means much the same
as to find God, God's grace, the community of faith of Christ already present.[79]

For the purposes of the present discussion, there are two important claims
here. First, Bonhoeffer claims that humans are "always part of a community,
in 'Adam' or in 'Christ'"—never only individuals. Second, he claims that
faith (discipleship) never precedes one's being in the church. Put differently,
the individual disciple is attributable to the church-community rather than the
church-community being attributable to the individual disciple. There is no
individual disciple apart from the church.

When this idea that there is no individual disciple apart from the church is
paired with the internal ordering of the church as "being-with-each-other"—
how this ordering binds all of the members of the church together—it
becomes evident that any act of everyday discipleship is an ecumenical act.
The internal ordering of "being-with-each-other" entailed by the conception
of church as *Christus Praesens* determines that wherever one member of the
church is, the whole church is there too, and vice versa.[80] The individual disciple carries the church with them—the same church that is the basis of ecumenism. As a result, everyday discipleship can be described as ecumenical
because in the obedient act of the individual disciple, there the church is also.

Three serious questions must be put forward at this point: First, is organized ecumenical work rendered unnecessary if the everyday discipleship of
the individual disciple is ecumenical? No. Organized ecumenical work has
simply been re-narrated regarding its purpose. In following after Christ in
discipleship, the church *will* encounter itself and *will* be commanded to do
and proclaim Christ's commands together. Prioritizing obedience to Christ
over empirical form does not eliminate organized empirical ecumenical work,
rather, obedience to Christ serves as the basis for that organized work—a
basis which affords various organized expressions.[81]

The second and third questions can be asked together: in defining the
everyday discipleship of the individual disciple as ecumenical, has ecumenism become individualized, thus excluding the whole of the church? And, if
every act of discipleship is ecumenical, is nothing really ecumenical? Again,
the answer to both is no. Bonhoeffer's ecumenical vision encompasses the
whole of the church in a real way through discipleship. The individual act
of discipleship is ecumenical *only because it carries with it the whole of the*

---

[79] DBWE 2:113–117.
[80] DBWE 1:178–182.
[81] This is addressed in greater detail in the chapter's discussion of the versatility of Bonhoeffer's
ecumenical vision.

church. What is at stake in the local scope of an ecumenism of discipleship is *catholicity.*

The catholicity of Bonhoeffer's account is founded on the action of divine agency, as Christ creates and is the new humanity—the church.[82] But this catholicity is not merely an invisible spiritual reality bearing no impact on the concrete events of space and time. If it were, catholicity would be meaningless as a theological category. The catholicity of the church is only meaningful if it is concrete in spatio-temporality. Bonhoeffer accounts for the concreteness of the church's catholicity in his concept of discipleship. Because the individual act of discipleship carries with it the entirety of the church, the catholicity of the church is concrete in discipleship.[83] As such, identifying the everyday discipleship of the individual disciple as ecumenical does not individualize ecumenism but instead concretely *universalizes* ecumenism across the church as the individual disciple subsists in the church. Likewise, articulating every act of discipleship as ecumenical does not mean that nothing is ecumenical but instead articulates an ecumenical vision in which the ecumenicity of the church concretely involves all those within the church, thereby truly being "ecumenical."

Taken altogether, defining ecumenical action in terms of discipleship provides Bonhoeffer's ecumenical vision with a scope extending from the one-to-one interactions of everyday discipleship all the way up to the doing and proclaiming of Christ's commands from the church to the entire world.[84] At

---

[82] DBWE 12:314–315.

[83] Greggs depicts catholicity in a similar manner, discussing the priestliness of the church's catholicity: "Catholicity is one way of accounting for and dogmatically capturing the interrelation of the dynamic activity of the one God in the Spirit and the Son in the life of the church as the church participates actively through the Spirit's gracious event in the unique high priesthood of Christ. Catholicity is both a means of addressing the internal bounds of the life of the church . . . and a means of addressing the universality of the church in the world . . . In the first instance, therefore, catholicity is grounded in the objectivity of the perfect, complete high priesthood of Christ . . . Of course, there is then the question of how this singular, once-for-all, and complete priesthood of Christ and its foundational significance for catholicity relates to the experience of the extensity of creaturely space-time . . . The activity of the Spirit in ordering the individual to God and the community . . . and the community to God and the world is an expression of dynamic catholicity within the terminus of the divine economy in creation." In a similar way, the internal and external ordering of the church toward itself and the world in Bonhoeffer's thought evinces the catholicity of his ecumenical thought, as the discipleship of the church universal to Christ's commands carries the individual disciple and the discipleship of the individual disciple carries with it the discipleship of the church universal. Greggs, *Dogmatic Ecclesiology Vol. 1*, 428–431.

[84] DBWE 11:358–359.

The WCC expresses a global and local scope to their ecumenical vision as well. The authors of CUV state: "To be a member means participating in ministries that extend beyond the boundaries and possibilities of any single church and being ready to link one's own specific local context with the global reality and to allow that global reality to have an impact in one's local situation." Bonhoeffer and the WCC both present ecumenical visions that concretely have a global and local scope. It would be argued that the ministry of the WCC does not account for the practical involvement of everyone within the church in ecumenical work. Bonhoeffer's ecumenical theology could

stake in this scope is the involvement of all within the church in ecumenism, and the possibility of a unified voice of the church regarding Christ's commands in the world. As such, the scope of Bonhoeffer's ecumenism of discipleship also evinces the catholicity of the account—a catholicity grounded in the oneness of Christ and practically expressed in obedient discipleship.[85]

The Versatility of Bonhoeffer's Ecumenism of Discipleship

By predicating his ecumenical vision upon obedience to the commands of Christ, Bonhoeffer promotes a protean ecumenism. Ecumenical action defined in terms of discipleship provides ecumenism the freedom to be what the command of Christ demands it to be.[86] This versatility pervades every part of Bonhoeffer's ecumenism of discipleship. Each of the five distinctive features hitherto articulated demonstrates this versatility. Solely focusing on discipleship to Christ engenders an *elastic* ecumenism capable of taking a multitude of forms. This elasticity is due to the immovability of Christ's authority over the church and the freedom with which Christ commands, and ecumenism's obedience to Christ's commands.

The Versatility of the Christological Governance of Bonhoeffer's Ecumenism

Christ's status as Head of ecumenism is immovable. This immovability, however, creates flexibility regarding the organizing of ecumenical action and expression. The chapter's earlier explication of this feature established polity as a downstream issue for ecumenism in terms of governance. Polity is not cast away or rendered irrelevant but rather is subservient to the fact that Christ is the Head of the church. Polity is afforded versatility under Bonhoeffer's ecumenical vision, but this versatility is a qualified one.

The chapter has averred that defining ecumenical action in terms of discipleship gives ecumenism primarily an ecclesiological and catholic form rather than an organizational or institutional form. This ecclesiological form, however, does not signify that there is no organization of ecumenism. In *Discipleship*, Bonhoeffer writes, "The church-community is at liberty to

---

be a helpful resource for understanding the practical involvement of everyone within the church in the *ecumenicity* of the church, including and going beyond involvement in organized ecumenical work. CUV: 3.7.3.

[85] DBWE 11:358–359.

See also Greggs, Tom. "The Catholic Spirit of Protestantism: A Very Methodist Take on the Third Article, Visible Unity, and Ecumenism." *Pro Ecclesia* 26, no. 4 (Fall 2017): 353–372.

[86] By contrast, there are thinkers such as Robert Jenson, who appear to have a much more rigid conception of ecumenism, in their emphasis upon visible unity via doctrinal convergence and ecumenical structure. Jenson, *Unbaptized God*.

modify the form of its ordering according to its needs."[87] Here, he is writing about the ordering of the church—not specifically the ordering of ecumenism. That said, because Bonhoeffer understands the ecumenical movement as church as *Christus Praesens*, his understanding of the ordering of the ecumenical movement matches that of the church. Thus, it could likewise be said that the ecumenical movement "is at liberty to modify the form of its ordering according to its need."[88] The church's—and ecumenism's—need is dictated by the command of Christ, meaning that the ecumenical movement has the freedom to take the organizational form commanded by Christ for its day in order to suit the needs required by Christ's command.[89] What is significant is that the organization of ecumenical practice is not ecumenism's *form*, but rather a part of ecumenism's *function*.

Put differently, the form of ecumenism is ecclesiological—is *Christus Praesens*; the function of ecumenical action is discipleship. It is in doing Christ's command that ecumenism becomes organized. The versatility of ecumenical governance is the result of allocating the organizing of ecumenical action to the doing of the command. If ecumenical organizations form because the church is commanded to organize itself in that particular way, then the organization of ecumenical action is necessarily versatile. Bonhoeffer never understands the command of Christ in terms of universal principles, and the same is true of the organization of ecumenical action. The versatility is again found in the command.

The Versatility of Focusing on Hearing and Doing Christ's Command

The focus on hearing and doing Christ's command displays the versatility of Bonhoeffer's ecumenism of discipleship in the contingency of the command itself. Christ has the freedom to command anything he wills, which means that ecumenical action can take as many forms as can the command of Christ. The versatility of Bonhoeffer's ecumenism is evinced in the contingent nature of the command of Christ.[90]

Positing the command of Christ as the sole focus of ecumenical action establishes further versatility in the specificity of the command.[91] Bonhoeffer is adamant that Christ commands concretely in the "real situation" in which the church finds itself.[92] The specificity of the command, therefore, adds another layer of versatility to Bonhoeffer's ecumenism of discipleship

---

[87] DBWE 4:230.
[88] DBWE 4:230.
[89] Clements writes that Bonhoeffer "sits loose to particular ecumenical forms while utterly committed to their theological purpose." Clements, *Dietrich Bonhoeffer's Ecumenical Quest*. 300.
[90] DBWE 11:363–364.
[91] ПЛWГ 11 ПЈؘ Јϋϋ.
[92] DBWE 11:360.

because such specificity requires *elasticity* on the part of ecumenical action to be able to proclaim each unique, concrete command of Christ.

Both in the command's contingency upon Christ's commanding and in the specificity of each command, Bonhoeffer's ecumenism of discipleship is observably versatile. The specific command itself is inflexible and demands obedience.[93] In spite of this obedience, the focus of Bonhoeffer's ecumenism solely on the command of Christ engenders a versatility because of the freedom of Christ to command, and the specificity with which he commands.

The Versatility of the Internal Ordering of Ecumenical Relations

Again, the versatility of Bonhoeffer's ecumenism of discipleship has to do with the immovability of ecumenism's nature as *Christus Praesens* and the flexibility inherent to the obedience of discipleship. The relationship of Christians to one another within ecumenism is established in ecumenism's form as *Christus Praesens*. The relationship is therefore fixed; the specific actions of their relation are flexible.

When the person of Christ encounters itself in ecumenism, those within the church hear and obey the command of Christ they hear within one another.[94] Although Bonhoeffer outlines three actions of the church's being-for-each-other,[95] this being-for-each-other has the concrete specificity with which Christ always commands.[96] Christ commands a specific "self-renouncing active work for the neighbour"; he commands a specific intercessory prayer; he commands mutual forgiveness for specific sins.[97] The specificity of Christ's commanding yields a versatility in the different specific acts by which those within the ecumenical church relate to one another. The same is true of the external ordering of ecumenical relations in Bonhoeffer's ecumenism.

The Versatility of the External Ordering of Ecumenical Relations

Ecumenism is ordered toward the world through obedience to Christ's commands, making the external ordering of ecumenism similarly versatile. As was the case with the internal ordering of ecumenism, so too with the external ordering. The external ordering of ecumenism is evinced in Christ's capacity to command what he wills.

Bonhoeffer illustrates this versatility when discussing the particular command he posits for the ecumenical movement in his day.[98] This versatility

---

[93] DBWE 13:307.
[94] DBWE 11:377.
[95] DBWE 1:184.
[96] DBWE 11:359–360.
[97] DBWE 1:184.
[98] DBWE 11:364.

becomes more evident when Bonhoeffer writes: "The church thus dares to say, for instance: do not wage this war; be socialists today, this commandment as *God's* commandment . . .".[99] When Bonhoeffer gives these examples, he is not giving timeless commands but is rather giving examples of what a command *might* be. Thus, as the church—the ecumenical church—is oriented toward the world, the form of its actions is versatile due to its dependence upon the command of Christ.

The versatility of the external ordering of ecumenical relations in Bonhoeffer's ecumenism of discipleship means that ecumenical action can take a multitude of forms, given that the particular form, proclamation, or action is what is commanded by Christ.[100] Once again, therefore, the undivided focus Bonhoeffer gives to obedience to Christ's commands—discipleship—engenders an ecumenism that is adaptable to the contingencies of Christ's command in the concrete situation. In both its internal and external orderings, Bonhoeffer's ecumenism of discipleship is demonstrably versatile, capable of obedient action to Christ's specific command.

The Versatility of the Global and Local Scope of Bonhoeffer's Ecumenism of Discipleship

Finally, Bonhoeffer's ecumenism displays versatility in its scope. The scope of Bonhoeffer's ecumenism is tied strictly to his defining of ecumenical action in terms of discipleship. In addition to demonstrating the catholicity established in Bonhoeffer's ecumenism, defining ecumenical action in terms of discipleship also imbues his ecumenical vision with a great level of adaptability.

The structure of this versatility takes the same form as it has for each of the previous features of Bonhoeffer's ecumenism. In discipleship, the disciple focuses solely on the command of Christ. On the one hand, obedience to that command may call the disciple to one-to-one interactions of loving the neighbor in a concrete way; on the other hand, discipleship carries with it the whole of the church community, and thus, obedient discipleship may also call the church throughout the world to specific, concrete proclamations of the command of Christ. Moreover, because obedience to Christ can lead to one-to-one interactions, global interactions, and every level of interaction in between, the scope of Bonhoeffer's ecumenism of discipleship is adaptable around Christ's commands.

---

[99] DBWE 11:361.
[100] DBWE 11:361.

The Accountability Afforded by Bonhoeffer's Ecumenism of Discipleship

The final feature of Bonhoeffer's ecumenism of discipleship is accountability. This accountability is found in the inherently ecclesial nature of discipleship and the sinfulness and need for repentance of the disciple. In both of these components of discipleship, the members of the church are held accountable to one another in word and deed. The significance of the accountability of Bonhoeffer's ecumenism of discipleship is that it provides the answer for the concern of over-subjectivity that could be levied at an account of ecumenical action defined as hearing and doing the command of Christ.

In the Ciernehorske Kupele lecture, Bonhoeffer admits to the possibility that the church—in seeking to hear and proclaim Christ's commands—could actually proclaim something other than Christ's commands and therefore find themselves to be in sin.[101] This ability to proclaim wrongly highlights the need for accountability in Bonhoeffer's ecumenism of discipleship. Bonhoeffer's specific answer for proclaiming wrongly is repentance and Christ's forgiveness of sins, or, as Bonhoeffer puts it, "The church cannot command unless it itself stands in the belief in the forgiveness of sins and without directing all those whom it commands to emphasize this proclamation of the forgiveness of sins."[102] This approach to the potential sinfulness of the church's proclamation does not yet, however, provide an answer for how those within the church hold each other to account regarding the specific commands that the church is proclaiming.

One instance in which Bonhoeffer demonstrates the accountability found in his account of ecumenism is in his 1935 "Essay on the Confessing Church and the Ecumenical Movement." Bonhoeffer's explication of the stance of the Confessing Church regarding the Reich Church brings this understanding of accountability to the forefront, as he insists that the ecumenical movement take the same approach to the Reich Church.[103] Bonhoeffer's staunch refusal to identify the Reich Church as church stems from the accountability found in his understanding of the church. His rejection of the ecclesial status of the Reich Church was not a decision made in haste, but one in which the Reich Church had time and again been called to repent of its false proclamations and refused. Here, the problem was not primarily one of doctrinal uniformity, but of what it means to be church; Bonhoeffer's questioning of the ecumenical movement as to its ecclesial status does not seek ecclesial definition in terms of a set of uniform doctrines, but in terms of what being the church in

---

[101] DBWE 11:361.
[102] DBWE 11:361.
[103] DBWE 14:403–407.

the world means—hearing and doing the command of Christ.[104] In his essay, Bonhoeffer was not rejecting the ecclesial status of the ecumenical movement but questioning it as to its ecclesial status. He did so in order to find a common proclamation of Christ's command regarding the Reich Church. He also concluded that it was possible that the Confessing Church could be too exclusive, removing the possibility of ecumenism, and therefore itself needing to repent.[105]

Such an engagement evinces the accountability found in Bonhoeffer's ecumenism of discipleship. All of the church's proclamations rest on the doctrine of the forgiveness of sins—their first confession is "a confession of sin."[106] Furthermore, the proclamation is afforded some accountability because it is to be grounded in the church. Those within the church hold each other to account, so by situating the command within the church understood as *Christus Praesens*, Bonhoeffer's ecumenism of discipleship has a form of accountability.

This feature of Bonhoeffer's ecumenism of discipleship is present in his treatment of church discipline in *Discipleship*.[107] There, Bonhoeffer states,

> The aim of church discipline is not to create a community of those who are perfect. Its sole aim is to build up a community of those who truly live under God's forgiving mercy. . . . The proclamation of the word with regard to both keys remains the sole basis for exercising church discipline.[108]

Again, church discipline does not aim at creating uniform doctrine, but accountable discipleship. Bonhoeffer goes on to discuss a series of levels of church discipline—admonishment from the pastor to the individual church member, mutual admonishment of believers within the community, and separation from the community with the goal of leading to repentance and reconciliation.[109] This same form of accountability takes place ecumenically because of Bonhoeffer's understanding of ecumenism as church as *Christus Praesens*. Thus, even within ecumenism there is a need for mutual admonishment and repentance. It is not the case that every doctrinal difference signifies an encounter of the church with that which it is not.[110] Instead, the internal relationship of being-with-each-other and being-for-each-other includes

---

[104] DBWE 14:412.
[105] DBWE 14:409.
[106] DBWE 14:407.
[107] DBWE 4 270–274.
[108] DBWE 4:270.
[109] DBWE 4.271 272.
[110] DBWE 14:664.

space for admonition and repentance regarding the wrongful proclamation of Christ's command.[111]

This feature of Bonhoeffer's ecumenism of discipleship provides an answer to a significant concern that could be levied against it; the focus of Bonhoeffer's ecumenism of discipleship upon hearing and doing Christ's commands in the world results in an account that could be classified as an example of divine command theory—albeit an example nuanced in a particularized way; the concern regarding an ecumenism built upon an account of divine command theory is that such an account is too subjective—and therefore dangerous—due to the way in which such an account can sanctify *any* action one might claim to be the will of God.

Regarding Bonhoeffer's ecumenism of discipleship, the concern would be that discipleship—understood as hearing and doing the command of Christ—is too subjective. The concern that the account is too subjective is two-fold. First, there is the concern that an account so reliant on hearing and doing the command of Christ may result simply in a theology of consciousness in which the hearer is actually only hearing their own thoughts and wants and is presenting these as Christ's commands. Second, there is the concern that an ecumenism built on divine command theory could lead to abuse on the part of those within the empirical church using claims of Christ's commands to manipulate others to their own ends, or even that such subjectivity could lead to the promotion of religious fanaticism masquerading as Christ's commands.

Bonhoeffer's account of ecumenism has an answer to this concern about the subjectivity of discipleship. Bonhoeffer's ecumenism of discipleship defends against this type of subjectivity because of how his concept of discipleship is uniquely tethered to his account of ecclesiology. One of the components of Bonhoeffer's concept of discipleship is that it always carries ecclesiology with it. In *Discipleship*, Bonhoeffer writes, "[e]veryone enters discipleship alone, but no one remains alone in discipleship. Those who dare to become single individuals trusting in the word are given the gift of the church-community."[112] Bonhoeffer's account of the church as the new humanity created by Christ's vicarious representative action on behalf of

---

[111] CUV briefly touches upon accountability. The authors write, "By their mutual engagement in the Council the churches open themselves to be challenged by one another to deeper, more costly ecumenical commitment. This *mutual accountability* takes many forms: recognizing solidarity with each other, assisting each other in cases of need, refraining from actions incompatible with brotherly and sisterly relations, entering into spiritual relationships to learn from each other, consulting with each other 'to learn of the Lord Jesus Christ what witness he would have them bear to the world in his name' (Toronto)." Again, the difference between the WCC and Bonhoeffer is that Bonhoeffer understands the ecumenical movement as church rather than a fellowship of churches. Therefore, Bonhoeffer can speak of ecumenical accountability and ecclesial accountability in much the same way. CUV: 3.3.6.

[112] DBWE 4:99.

mankind means that discipleship always finds itself in the church. This ecclesial *a priori* builds in a level of accountability that already begins to provide protection against the possibility of discipleship being overly subjective.

That said, to claim that discipleship is inherently tied to the church-community is not enough of a safeguard against the possibility of discipleship being overly subjective. Bonhoeffer's particular articulation of the unique way in which the command is heard in the church, however, strengthens his position. Bonhoeffer identifies three ways in which Christ is present in the church: as Word, sacrament, and church-community, and it is in these three places that the command is heard.[113] Each of these three places to hear the command demand encounter with the church-community that discipleship has brought the disciple into. In this way, there is greater accountability for the command being heard and less subjectivity.

Even so, Bonhoeffer is insistent that the church is capable and culpable of sin.[114] Therefore, even this layer of accountability is not enough to entirely turn away the claim of the command being overly subjective or defend against the possibility of abuse in the guise of Christ's command. Bonhoeffer's ecumenism of discipleship, however, provides a final layer of accountability.

Bonhoeffer's ecumenism of discipleship maintains a consistent awareness of ecclesial sinfulness, which it undergirds with the doctrine of the forgiveness of sins.[115] Specifically, Bonhoeffer writes in his 1932 Ciernehorske Kupele lecture, "The proclamation of the commandment is founded in the proclamation of the forgiveness of sins."[116] Furthermore, in his 1935 essay, "The Confessing Church and the Ecumenical Movement," Bonhoeffer writes, "[t]he Confessing Church is the church that lives not from its purity but from its impurity—the church of sinners, the church of penitence."[117] In each of these instances, Bonhoeffer highlights the sinfulness of the church and the church's need for repentance. These claims serve not only to acknowledge the sinfulness of the church, but they also serve as a warning of the possibility of someone knowingly proclaiming something other than the command of Christ under the guise of a command of Christ. Thus, in addition to being a source of grace for the church when it finds its proclamation to *incidentally* be something other than Christ's command, Bonhoeffer's acknowledgment of the church's impurity also raises awareness of the possibility of someone *knowingly* abusing the command.

---

[113] DBWE 4:202.
[114] DBWE 4:217.
[115] DBWE 11:361–362.
[116] DBWE 11:361.
[117] DBWE 14:411.

In these ways—being tethered in a particular way to the church-community and with a strong account of ecclesial sinfulness and need for repentance—has Bonhoeffer's ecumenism of discipleship completely dispelled the possibility of Christ's commands being abused? No. Unfortunately, the continued sinfulness of the church will always mean the possibility of abuse. In spite of this conclusion, Bonhoeffer's safeguards are substantial enough that this concern does not threaten the viability of Bonhoeffer's ecumenism of discipleship.

CASE STUDY: AN INSTANCE OF BONHOEFFER'S ECUMENICAL THEOLOGY IN PRACTICE

This book would be remiss if it did not touch on one particular historical event. Bonhoeffer's ecumenical approach to the church struggle between the Confessing Church and Reich Church provides an example of an instance in which Bonhoeffer put his ecumenical theology into practice. The theological content of Bonhoeffer's 1936 essay "On the Question of Church Communion" establishes his approach to the Reich Church. In order to fully grasp this theological content, it is helpful to briefly address the historical context surrounding it.[118]

The occasion of this essay followed a correspondence between Bonhoeffer and Leonard Hodgson (secretary of the Faith and Order Movement) in which Bonhoeffer declined an invitation to attend an ecumenical conference at which representatives of the Reich Church would also be present. Hodgson's position—and that of Faith and Order—was that they could not exclude any group which "accepts our Lord Jesus Christ as God and Savior."[119] Bonhoeffer's position—and that of the Confessing Church—was that the Reich Church was not church, and that their claim of acceptance of Christ's Lordship was empty. Bonhoeffer wrote, "Obedience to the only heavenly Lord Jesus Christ continues to be . . . subordinated to obedience towards worldly masters and powers. The Reich Church thereby continues to betray the only Lord Jesus Christ."[120] The following year, Bonhoeffer wrote "On the Question of Church Communion," in which he expands upon his stance against communing with the Reich Church by addressing the boundaries of the church, the meaning of confession, and situating this discussion in the context of the church struggle in Germany.[121]

---

[118] For more on this essay, see Duchrow, Ulrich. "The Confessing Church and the Ecumenical Movement." *The Ecumenical Review* 33, no. 3 (July 1981): 212–231.

[119] DBWE 14:68–69.

[120] DBWE 14:71–73.

[121] Peter W. L. Walker has also addressed Bonhoeffer and the topic of church communion. Walker, Peter W L. "Bonhoeffer and the Basis of Union." *Uniting Church Studies* 13, no. 1 (March 2007): 1–17.

Taken at face value, Bonhoeffer's stance against the Reich Church may appear antithetical to the ecumenical theology presented thus far and antithetical to the ecumenical enterprise writ large. Indeed, one church body rejecting another on the basis that the other is not church is the epitome of what is *not* desired in ordinary ecumenical discourse. But the church struggle in Germany was not an ordinary event. And Bonhoeffer's 1936 essay was not the start of that event. No, to begin with Bonhoeffer's refusal to ecumenically engage with the Reich Church is to begin the story *in media res.*[122] The Confessing Church itself was founded in response to the infiltration of the church by the German Christians (a group of fanatical Nazi protestants) and the implementation of Nazi ideologies such as the Aryan paragraph (which defrocked clergy of Jewish heritage and those married to non-Aryans). By 1936, the Nazi regime had arrested hundreds of Confessing Church pastors, applied harsh financial restrictions upon the Confessing Church, and forced Confessing Church seminaries underground (as was the case with the Finkenwalde seminary at which Bonhoeffer taught).[123] The Reich Church cooperated and supported these actions. The Reich Church was an ecclesiastical institution that had been co-opted by the state and used to promote state agendas, including but not limited to racist and anti-Semitic stances and activity. For these reasons, the ecumenical relationship (or lack thereof) between the Reich Church and Confessing Church into which Bonhoeffer inserted this essay was anything but an ordinary instance of ecumenical discourse. This was not an instance of a simple doctrinal disagreement. This was an instance of an ecclesiastical institution cooperating in the perpetuation of heinous acts and allowing the state to dictate the church. As such, though Hodgson's stance was certainly a reasonable one, it should be stated that Bonhoeffer's stance was likewise reasonable.

In light of this setting, a close examination of the *theological content* of Bonhoeffer's 1936 essay provides a case study of an instance in which Bonhoeffer implemented his ecumenical theology. Such a case study is helpful as an example of one way this theological vision was implemented in a specific situation.

Bonhoeffer's opening move in this essay is to establish a stance on church boundaries. He argues that the Reformation Church was concerned to determine what the church is, but not to define its boundaries.[124] Put differently, the church is not concerned with determining from the outset what specifically is

---

[122] For more on the historical context surrounding this essay, see Bethge, *Dietrich Bonhoeffer: A Biography*, 517–526.

[123] For a small sample of the persecution felt by the Confessing Church as it relates to Bonhoeffer's life and the events leading up to this 1936 Essay specifically, see Bethge, *Dietrich Bonhoeffer: A Biography*, 493–517.

[124] DBWE 14:656.

not church; instead, the church is only concerned with being and proclaiming what it is—*Christus Praesens*, where Christ is "efficaciously present."[125] The church only asks the question of its boundaries when it *encounters* that which it is not.[126] It is worth quoting Bonhoeffer at length on this subject:

> It is not the church that sets boundaries excluding people. It is the world that arbitrarily sets these boundaries to exclude itself from the church by not hearing and not believing. . . . Hence the determination of its boundaries will always be different. Because no theoretical knowledge is available for determining that scope, that is, because such knowledge must always be acquired anew, there are also no theoretical norms according to which membership in the church might be determined. . . .This view introduces a *living decision* into the Reformation's understanding of the church. Just where the boundaries of the church are to be found is thus always determined only in the *encounter* between the church and unbelief and is thus an act of *decision* on the part of the church. . . . Its most characteristic decision must be to recognize and to confirm as such any boundary that the world sets for it. It must itself decide whether and where its call *encounters* ultimate limits. Hence the question of church communion can only be answered in the authoritative *decision* of the church itself.[127]

This quotation is the crux of Bonhoeffer's argument in this essay. In these words, Bonhoeffer states that the church does not set its own boundaries but rather identifies its boundaries through an encounter with that which is not church;[128] as such, the church's boundaries are always a matter of *encounter* and *decision* rather than *a priori* dogmatic statements.[129] By identifying the church's boundary as a matter of encounter and decision, Bonhoeffer sets up his argument against the Reich Church. In the Reich Church, Bonhoeffer argues, the church encounters its boundary, and must therefore *confess* that boundary.[130]

Significant, here, is Bonhoeffer's concept of confession. For Bonhoeffer, the confession of the Confessing Church is not an *a priori* formulation of the church's boundaries but is instead a lived decision of the church identifying a boundary set for it through an encounter with something that is not church—in this instance, the Reich Church.[131] He describes confession in just this way, writing:

---

[125] DBWE 14:657–658.
[126] DBWE 14:660.
[127] DBWE 14:660–661, Italics added.
[128] DBWE 14:660–661.
[129] DBWE 14:660–661.
[130] DBWE 14:668.
[131] DBWE 14:664.

The confession is not a compilation of dogmatic statements from which all subsequent conclusions are drawn. Otherwise . . . any disagreement regarding any single doctrinal point would of necessity become schismatic. . . . The confession is the church's decision concerning its own boundaries on the basis of theological considerations. It is not a presentation of the entirety of doctrine but rather the decision that the church makes based on the entirety of doctrine to take up the battle at a specific place. In the confession, theology is implemented in a contemporary situation through a decision the church itself makes.[132]

The language that Bonhoeffer uses in describing confession in terms of a "decision" and identifying church boundaries through "encounter" reveals that the ecclesiological basis of Bonhoeffer's stance against the Reich Church is also ultimately Christological.

Chapter 1 described personhood as a crucial building block for Bonhoeffer's account of ecclesiology. It was established that Bonhoeffer understands personhood individually and collectively and that he understands the church as a person—specifically the revelatory person of Christ. Furthermore, in Bonhoeffer's thinking, personhood arises from an *encounter* with an other—an encounter that calls those involved to responsibility.[133] In *Sanctorum Communio*, Bonhoeffer locates personhood in "the moment of being addressed," when "the person enters into a state of *responsibility*, or, in other words, of *decision*."[134] Moreover, chapter 1 drew out Bonhoeffer's understanding of the collective person of Christ built on Christ's action on behalf of humanity, by which he both creates and is the new humanity—the collective person of Christ—which is present on earth today in the church.

Bonhoeffer's stance against the Reich Church—specifically, that in encountering the Reich Church, the church has encountered a boundary which it must confess—is completely consistent with his ecclesiology. As previously stated, Bonhoeffer's concept of confession begins with the church encountering that which the church is not;[135] the church does not determine its own boundaries from the start but rather the church's boundaries are "always determined only in the *encounter*" with that which the church is not.[136] In the same way, Bonhoeffer's concept of personhood (as it relates to the collective person of Christ) begins with encounter—an encounter with the transformative person of Christ.[137] In the case of the church encountering a boundary, the church's responsibility is a confession—which Bonhoeffer refers to as

---

[132] DBWE 14:664.
[133] DBWE 1:48.
[134] DBWE 1:48.
[135] DBWE 14:660–661.
[136] DBWE 14:660–661, William Andrew
[137] DBWE 1:48.

a "living *decision*"—that the church has, indeed, encountered a boundary, thereby proclaiming that boundary concretely.[138] Likewise, Bonhoeffer identifies personhood emerging when "the person enters into a state of *responsibility*, or, in other words, of *decision*."[139] Put otherwise, Bonhoeffer constructs his stance against the Reich Church in precisely the same manner as he constructs his understanding of the church as the person of Christ. A person enters the collective person of Christ through an *encounter* with the person of Christ, which calls the one encountered to a *decision* of *responsibility*; in the same way, Bonhoeffer narrates his stance against the Reich Church as an *encounter* between the church (the collective person of Christ) and that which is not church—an encounter which calls for a *decision* on the part of both parties involved. When placing these statements side by side, it is clear that Bonhoeffer's stance against communing with the Reich Church is consistent with his understanding of church as the revelatory person of Christ. Both are constructed along the ideas of encounter and decision.

In encountering its boundary, the church—the revelatory person of Christ—encounters the person of Adam, and the first responsibility such an encounter places upon those within the church is to profess that such a boundary has been encountered.[140] In proclaiming this boundary, the church is not making a permanent judgment against the world but actually continues "to proclaim the unrestricted call of salvation" to those outside the church.[141] Just as the individual person is called to responsibility when encountering the person of Christ, so too the world is called to responsibility when it encounters the person of Christ in the church. Thus, the identification of the boundary in the confession is not ultimately an excluding act on the part of the church but is instead an act that provides space for an encounter with the transformative person of Christ.[142] It is ultimately an act which invites inclusion as Christ's words "follow me" encounter the person of Adam in the world.

This understanding of confession determines that the stance of Bonhoeffer and the Confessing Church in refusing to ecumenically engage with the Reich Church was not a matter of the Reich Church not fitting into an *a priori* dogmatic formula; instead, it was a Christological statement that the encounter between the Confessing Church and the Reich Church was a concrete encounter between the person of Christ and the person of Adam. Such an encounter demands that the person of Christ identify the boundary which has

---

[138] DBWE 14:660–661, Italics added.
[139] DBWE 1:48, Italics added.
[140] DBWE 14:660–661.
[141] DBWE 14:664.
[142] For more on Bonhoeffer and responsibility, see Penamora, Aldrin M. Aldrin M. "Ethics of Responsibility: Christ-Centered Personal and Social Ethics for Church and Society," *Journal of Asian Evangelical Theology* 19, no. 1 (March 2015): 91–107.

been set for it and proclaim Christ's command in word and deed to the person of Adam. This is the essence of what Bonhoeffer continually envisioned as the core of ecumenical theology: to boldly proclaim the commands of Christ to the world and to proclaim those commands as the church which is Christ's presence in the world. As such, Bonhoeffer's refusal to commune with the Reich Church is an informative instance of Bonhoeffer putting his ecumenical theology into practice. Bonhoeffer bases his theology in his account of the church as *Christus Praesens* and then asserts the necessity of the church to do and proclaim Christ's commands—discipleship.

Bonhoeffer's ecumenical approach to the Reich Church does not dissolve ecumenical discourse but instead provides a concrete example of putting his ecumenical theology into practice. That said, this is just one example of how this ecumenical theology could be implemented in a particular situation. The protean nature of Bonhoeffer's ecumenical theology enables it to take whatever form the command of Christ dictates. Now that the features of Bonhoeffer's ecumenical theology have been elucidated along with an example of Bonhoeffer's own implementation of this theology, what can be said of this ecumenical theology as a whole?

SYNTHESIS OF BONHOEFFER'S ECUMENISM OF DISCIPLESHIP

In shortest terms, Bonhoeffer's ecumenical theology is an account of the church and what it means to exist therein. The church is a person, not an institution. The church is the revelatory person of Christ, created and sustained through the work of the triune God; the activity of the human agents within this revelatory person is discipleship—hearing and doing Christ's commands. The triune God creates the church in and through the person of Christ and creates space within God's own working for human agents to actively work in discipleship. This is Bonhoeffer's ecumenism of discipleship.

The church is *Christus Praesens*—the revelatory person of Christ—through the vicarious representative action of Christ to create and rule over the collective person of Christ through his life, death, and resurrection. Christ encounters human beings and opens them up both to God and to others, at which time those human beings discover themselves already to be within the collective person of Christ—the church. This transformational encounter with Christ determines human relationships both with God and with each other as human beings seek to hear and do the commands of Christ as they encounter them. The result is an understanding of a church that exists through the work of God and which is actively related both to God and the world through the concrete discipleship of those within it.

It is clear that this theology enumerates an active ecclesiology, but what makes it an *ecumenical* theology?

The ecumenicity of this theology is found, first of all, in the fact that it accounts for the church as a whole. Bonhoeffer is not concerned with detailing one particular denomination or the church in one area, but with the whole church. As such, the theology presented is ecumenical by definition.

And the ecumenicity of this theology goes beyond the fact that it encompasses the whole church. Bonhoeffer employed this theology in the arena of organized ecumenism. It is evident, therefore, that he meant to articulate not only an account of the church which was ecumenical by definition of including the whole church but one which was also practicably deployable as ecumenical work itself. In other words, the theology is ecumenical both in definition and practical intent.

What can be said of this ecumenical theology beyond that it is built on an account of the church as the person of Christ and has discipleship as its operative theological content?

It can be said that this ecumenical theology carries with it an account of church unity. Specifically, by identifying the church as the collective person of Christ, Bonhoeffer indicates an inherent unity of the church. The person of Christ is one, and therefore so is the church. And this unity is not a mystical mystery, but a concrete reality through the active discipleship of the church to Christ.

This active discipleship adds an understanding of church visibility to this ecumenical theology. Whereas many other accounts of ecumenical theology are deeply concerned with creating or manifesting visible unity, Bonhoeffer sees church visibility as a matter of course through the discipleship of the church. For Bonhoeffer, the church lacks the capacity to assess its own visibility. Indeed, the attempt at such assessment results in a loss of visibility. Instead, Bonhoeffer argues that the disciples should look only to the one they follow—Christ—and that in actively following Christ, the church will inevitably become visible both to Christ and those outside the church.

This emphasis on actively hearing and doing the command of Christ as the practical content of ecumenism places this account of ecumenical theology in an apparent conundrum. Discipleship is not a formula, a universal principle, or a checklist of do's and don'ts. Discipleship is actively following after Christ, obeying Christ's commands. If this is the operative content of Bonhoeffer's ecumenical theology, it follows that this ecumenical theology cannot be systematized. Even so, there are seven features of this ecumenical theology which will always be present in its deployment. These features, therefore, provide something of a shape to this ecumenical theology.

The first feature is Christ's governance over the church. As has been stated, Christ creates, rules over, and is the church. Moreover, the emphasis upon hearing and doing Christ's commands places Christ in a real position of authority over the church. The second feature is that very emphasis upon hearing and doing Christ's commands. These two features are the core of this ecumenical theology—an understanding of the church as the person of Christ, which is ruled by Christ, the operative theological content of which is discipleship.

The third and fourth features are that this understanding of the church and its activity in the world determines the relationships both of those within the church toward each other, and of the church to (and for) the world. As the collective person of Christ, those within the church are bound to each other, and as they encounter each other their relationships are characterized in what Bonhoeffer describes as "being-with-each-other" and "being-for-each-other." And, as the collective person of Christ encounters the collective person of Adam in the world, the church discovers its relationship to and for the world. As with any encounter with Christ on the individual level, the encounter of the collective person of Christ with the collective person of Adam in the world is both a call to discipleship and a call to be opened up both to God and neighbor. It is a liberating encounter. It is an invitational encounter. And, as with all encounters with Christ, it is an encounter with the command of Christ. The role of the church is to hear and proclaim Christ's commands to and for the world as the person of Christ.

In describing the third and fourth features, the fifth reveals itself—this ecumenical theology maintains a local and global scale. As the collective person of Christ, the church is able to hear and do Christ's commands on a global scale, which is what Bonhoeffer intended in his exhortations that the ecumenical movement proclaim peace as the command of Christ in the ramp up to World War II. But this ecumenical theology is not only global in scale. It also contains the local scale of everyday discipleship and everything in between. Discipleship is not only individual, but communal—it is active participation in the collective person of Christ. Therefore, the individual act of discipleship carries within it the whole of the church. As such, the act of discipleship universalizes ecumenism across the church, demonstrating the concrete catholicity of the church in the practical involvement of everyone in the church in ecumenism.

Versatility is the sixth feature of Bonhoeffer's ecumenism of discipleship. The emphasis placed upon hearing and doing the command of Christ evinces a versatility—an elasticity—to this ecumenical theology. To be solely focused on discipleship to Christ means that this ecumenical theology can take innumerable forms, so long as that form is what is commanded by Christ. This versatility pervades all of the previous features of this ecumenical theology due to the emphasis on hearing and doing Christ's commands.

The final feature of Bonhoeffer's ecumenism of discipleship is account-ability. By anchoring his ecumenism in a concept of the church, Bonhoeffer provides his ecumenical vision with accountability. The command of Christ is found in the church where Christ is present as Word, sacrament, and church-community;[143] grounding the command ecclesially in this way promotes accountability for the command. Additionally, because the disciple subsists in the church, there is always a relatedness of discipleship in which those within the church hold each other to account in their being-with-each-other and being-for-each-other.[144] This accountability includes the need to repent and seek the forgiveness of sins when the church finds its proclamations to be anything other than the command of Christ.[145] As such, accountability is a strong feature of Bonhoeffer's ecumenism of discipleship in spite of the continued culpability and capability of the disciple to sin.

What is Bonhoeffer's ecumenism of discipleship? Put simply, Bonhoeffer's ecumenism of discipleship can be described as concretely following after Christ together as the church. Bonhoeffer's ecumenical theology is not a sys-tem or formula; it is not an organizational structure to apply to an ecumenical body. Instead, it is a theology with a particular self-understanding of church as the body of Christ, and those within it as active followers of Christ. This is Bonhoeffer's ambitious vision for the ecumenical movement: to be church and do Christ's commands in the world.

CONCLUSION

This chapter has brought Bonhoeffer's ecumenical theology fully into view. To be ecumenical is to be a disciple of Christ. And the reverse is likewise true: to be a disciple is to be ecumenical. There is no following after Christ that does not include the church, and there is no church without the *whole* church. The church is the person of Christ, and it can, therefore, only be one. The creation and sustenance of this ecumenical church and its unity is the work of the Triune God. The action left to those within the church—the action of ecumenism itself—is obedient discipleship to Christ.

---

[143] DBWE 4:202.
[144] DBWE 1:178–182.
[145] DBWE 11:361.

Conclusion

This book has provided a systematic constructive account of Dietrich Bonhoeffer's ecumenical theology. Undergirding this book has been the conviction that this ecumenical theology makes a valuable contribution to ongoing efforts to reflect on the nature and work of the ecumenical movement. To this point, the focus has simply been on developing this ecumenical theology. Now, in drawing the book to a close, this chapter places Bonhoeffer's ecumenical theology in conversation with some of the contemporary landscape of ecumenism. What can Bonhoeffer's ecumenical theology contribute to the discourse surrounding the declining interest in traditional ecumenism? How does this theology relate to current ecumenical approaches? What can this theology offer in the context of a global Christianity in which the center of Christianity is shifting away from the West?

BONHOEFFER AND THE DECLINING
INTEREST IN TRADITIONAL ECUMENISM

In recent decades, many within the ecumenical movement have been self-aware of a crisis facing the movement in the twenty-first century. Essentially, a number of factors (the decline of mainline denominations, the rise of Pentecostal and non-denominational churches, globalization, secularization, the southward shift of the center of Christianity globally, etc.) have led to a decline in interest in traditional ecumenism, and declining engagement with the ecumenical movement.[1] Added to these factors is the internal struggle

---

[1] Works that have addressed this situation include Clemens, *Ecumenical Dynamic: Living in More than One Place at Once*; Raiser, *Ecumenism in Transition: A Paradigm Shift in the Ecumenical*

within denominations over divisive issues such as human sexuality, resulting in denominations drawing inward into themselves and a struggle for funding for traditionally organized ecumenical bodies. Former general secretary of the NCC, Michael Kinnamon, has approached this topic, noting

> over the past generation, councils of churches have lost vitality or shut down altogether, not only in the United States but around the world. Nearly every council I have observed struggles to obtain adequate funding, with the result that concern for survival takes precedence over innovative thinking.[2]

The aim of this chapter is to investigate what Bonhoeffer's ecumenism of discipleship can contribute to the conversation around these challenges facing the ecumenical movement today and suggest that Bonhoeffer's ecumenical theology possesses insights for the organized ecumenical movement going forward.[3]

The first word that must be said is that the ecumenical church is a reality, and it is not going away. Although the traditional forms of ecumenical discourse and practice are facing challenges, the church that is the person of Christ is—and can only be—one. This ecumenical church that is the church as the person of Christ exists as a work of the triune God, and it is not so feeble that it could be undone by the deterioration of institutional forms. This is the starting point for Bonhoeffer's contribution to the current state of the

---

Movement?; Kinnamon, *Can a Renewal Movement be Renewed?*; Avis, *Reshaping Ecumenical Theology*; Pottmeyer, "The Reception Process: The Challenge at the Threshold of a New Phase of the Ecumenical Movement"; World Council of Churches Program on Ecumenical Theological Education. "Ecumenical Formation in Theological Education: Ten Key Convictions"; Kasper, "May They All Be One: But How? A Vision of Christian Unity for the Next Generation"; O'Gara, "Ecumenical Dialogue: The Next Generation"; Kasper, *That They May All Be One: The Call to Unity Today.*

[2] Kinnamon, *Can a Renewal Movement be Renewed?* 125.

[3] This book is not naïve enough to posit that Bonhoeffer's ecumenism of discipleship is the *only* solution—or even that there *is* only a single solution—to the issues facing the ecumenical movement in the twenty-first century. Rather, the book merely suggests that Bonhoeffer's ecumenical theology has much to offer the current situation.

   A number of experienced ecumenists have identified the issues facing the ecumenical movement and have offered solutions of their own. Extended study of Bonhoeffer's ecumenism of discipleship in this direction would engage these voices. Works representing such voices include Kobia, Sam. "Report of the General Secretary, Ninth Assembly of the World Council of Churches, 2006." In *God, in Your Grace: Official Report of the Ninth Assembly of the World Council of Churches,* edited by Luis, N. Rivera-Pagan, 138–151. Geneva: WCC, 2007; Tamez, Elsa. "Breaking Down Walls in Our Globalized Society: A Relevant Ecumenism." *Ecumenical Trends* 38, no. 7 (2009): 1–7; Tveit, Olav Fykse. "Renewed Mission of the WCC in the Search for Christian Unity." In *That They All May Be One: Selected Sermons, Speeches, and Articles,* 100–105. Geneva: WCC, 2011; Kinnamon, Michael. "New Contours of Ecumenism in the 21st Century." *Ecumenical Review* 66, no. 1 (March 2014). 10–24; Rausch, Thomas P. "A New Ecumenism?: Christian Unity in a Global Church." *Theological Studies* 78, no. 3 (September 2017): 596–613.

ecumenical movement: the ecumenical church is a reality, it is one, and it is not going away, regardless of what happens to its institutional forms.

Keith Clements has argued that "Bonhoeffer will ever be a challenge to the ecumenical movement, or at any rate he will be well ahead of it for as long as we can see at present."[4] His basis for this statement is Bonhoeffer's insistence that the ecumenical movement be church. While Clements is certainly right in his assessment that Bonhoeffer remains ahead of the ecumenical movement regarding its ecclesial self-understanding, it is nevertheless also true that Bonhoeffer's ecumenical theology is not so far ahead that there is nothing of it that can be implemented now. Indeed, it would be naïve to suggest that none of what has been done ecumenically for the past century has been done in obedient discipleship (though the assessment of such accomplishments remains ever beyond our grasp). Furthermore, Bonhoeffer's ecumenical theology can serve as a helpful voice for the organized ecumenical movement as it navigates the challenges of the present time.

But what specifically does Bonhoeffer's ecumenical theology offer regarding the challenges facing the ecumenical movement? Before this is addressed, it is helpful to briefly consider how the declining state of the organized ecumenical movement has been diagnosed by one of the movement's thinkers. Michael Kinnamon, in his book, *Can a Renewal Movement Be Renewed? Questions for the Future of Ecumenism*, identifies four weaknesses in the ecumenical movement and suggests two remedies.

The four weaknesses Kinnamon identifies are a decline in commitment among church leaders to the goal of Christian unity, division within denominations, a growing ideological split between ecumenists as to whether ecumenical work should be more concerned with doctrinal convergence or issues of justice, and the "Diminishment of key instruments of the ecumenical movement, including councils of churches."[5] The two remedies he supplies are (1) "Renewed emphasis on spiritual ecumenism," by which he encourages intercession and an emphasis on the fact that "God is the Chief Actor in this movement" and (2) "Renewed interest and commitment among the laity."[6] Put otherwise, Kinnamon emphasizes a need for prayer for one another and for the church as a whole, a remembrance that it is God who is the head of the ecumenical movement, and renewed ecumenical interest in the laity as responses to the current state of the ecumenical movement.

Kinnamon's assessment of the current state of the ecumenical movement is helpful for considering what contribution Bonhoeffer's thought can make. Bonhoeffer's ecumenical theology does not provide a solution for the first

---

[4] Clements, *Dietrich Bonhoeffer's Ecumenical Quest*, 289–290.
[5] Kinnamon, *Can a Renewal Movement be Renewed?* 147–152.
[6] Kinnamon, *Can a Renewal Movement be Renewed?* 152–155.

two weaknesses Kinnamon points out. It does not provide a miracle cure either for revitalizing disappointed or uninterested church leaders or for helping to resolve divisive issues within each denomination. What Bonhoeffer's ecumenism of discipleship *does* do regarding these two weaknesses is to provide a challenge and a hope. To ground ecumenical work in discipleship challenges disappointed church leaders within ecumenical discourse not to look for "results" but instead to focus on obedience to Christ; this same ecumenism of discipleship ought to give disappointed church leaders within the ecumenical movement hope that not only is there ecumenical work to be done but that it can *actually be done* when understood as obedient discipleship to Christ. The unity of the church Bonhoeffer posits in the person of Christ presents a challenge to denominations who find themselves facing internal division to value their institutional unity as an echo of that unity which defines the reality of the church (although this echo is nothing constitutive of the church itself—which is created and sustained in the work of divine agency); moreover, an ecumenism of discipleship presents these institutional churches with a hope that obedient discipleship does not require uniformity of opinion but obedience to Christ.

Bonhoeffer's ecumenical theology has somewhat more to offer the other two weaknesses Kinnamon identifies, and also promotes and bolsters his two suggested remedies. It is not a secret in ecumenical circles that there have long been two schools of thought regarding ecumenical work (this is an over-generalization, but the point remains). On the one hand, there are those (typically understood to be in line with Faith and Order) who emphasize the need for the many institutional churches in the world to be visibly united by way of recognizing the church in one another and the convergence of doctrinal thought. Kinnamon notes that for this group, "confessing Christ together, sharing the eucharist, recognizing the baptisms and ordinations performed in other parts of the body, and having a structure that allows, when needed, for common decision making" is the "highest ecumenical priority and the basis for authentic Christian witness."[7] Within this school of thought is the idea that there is something significant in the ability of the institutional churches to acknowledge the ministry each one performs and to articulate together their common beliefs.

The other school of thought (typically understood to be in line with Life and Works) emphasizes works of justice and peace as the way in which the ecumenicity of the church is expressed. Kinnamon writes that constituents of this school of thought "would argue that the fundamental

---

[7] Kinnamon, *Can a Renewal Movement be Renewed?*, 151.

divide in human community is between rich and poor, oppressor and oppressed; and that the basic division in the church has to do with how Christians respond to and participate in these divisions in the world," and "focus not on agreed statements of faith or common structures, but on a shared willingness to act together in response to human need."[8] Kinnamon is of the mind that the ecumenical movement is weakened not by emphasizing either of these schools of thought, "but by those who split the agenda, playing one off against the other."[9]

Alongside Kinnamon, Bonhoeffer's ecumenism of discipleship reveals this split for the false dichotomy that it is. When presented with these two options, the answer is simultaneously neither and both. For Bonhoeffer, the starting point and emphasis of ecumenical work is neither doctrinal statements and structures evincing unity, nor is it activity for justice and peace. The starting point and sole emphasis of ecumenical work, for Bonhoeffer, is discipleship to Christ. To start with doctrinal convergence and institutional structures would be to wrongly identify that in which the unity of the church subsists (which is the work of the triune God rather than institutional or doctrinal uniformity) and, therefore, also to wrongly identify doctrinal statements and institutional structures with the work required for that unity. Likewise, to emphasize justice and responding to human need would be to turn justice into a universal principle outside of the command of Christ, thereby focusing not on Christ, but a perceived universal principle. As such, neither of these are adequate viewpoints of ecumenical work for Bonhoeffer.

Starting with an understanding of the church as *Christus Praesens* within which the sole work of the human agent is discipleship reveals that these two schools of thought are two sides of the same coin, although neither of them is the focus of ecumenical work. While discipleship to Christ is the sole focus of Bonhoeffer's ecumenical theology, such discipleship will inevitably mean that the churches encounter one another and seek Christ together. As has been argued elsewhere, Bonhoeffer does not throw away conciliarism but rather locates it downstream from discipleship. Conciliar work, and work toward recognizing the church between the institutional churches, therefore, is

---

[8] Ibid., 151.
[9] Ibid., 151.
   Catholicos of Cilicia—former moderator of the WCC's Central Committee—has identified this problem with different names. He sees what he calls an "institutional ecumenism" and a "people's ecumenism" and he argues that the two are not actually competitive with or opposed to one another, but that the two belong together. Catholicos of Cilicia. "Ecumenism in the Process of Transformation." In *Ecumenism in the 21ˢᵗ Century: Report of the Consultation Convened by the World Council of Churches*, 38–45. Geneva: WCC, 2005.

derivative of discipleship. As disciples of Christ encounter one another in the world, the church as the person of Christ encounters itself and hears Christ's commands in each other. When this happens, the church is internally ordered with and for each other. Such internal ordering is likely to produce some form of conciliarism. As such, the work of producing doctrinal statements and forming structures in which this work can take place is not in and of itself the core of ecumenical work. Rather, ecumenical work subsists in discipleship to Christ, whose command comes to us in encountering each other.

Bonhoeffer's sole focus upon discipleship likewise means that ecumenical work does not subsist in acts of justice. And yet the orientation of the church for the world in proclaiming Christ's commands in word and deed will inevitably lead the church to act for those in the margins. Discipleship is always action. It is always concretely following Christ's concrete commands. As such, the pursuit of justice is not in and of itself the content of ecumenical work. Rather, ecumenical work subsists in discipleship to Christ, whose command comes to those within the church through the encounter with an other, an encounter which calls forth the responsibility of active and obedient discipleship. In this way, Bonhoeffer's ecumenical theology holds together conciliar work and work for justice, while subordinating them to discipleship to Christ.

Bonhoeffer's ecumenism of discipleship also holds insights for the ongoing diminishment of ecumenical instruments, such as councils of churches. While it is true that, for Bonhoeffer, the ecumenical church (which is to say the church writ large) does not subsist in its institutional forms, this does not mean that institutional forms of ecumenism and organized ecumenical bodies should not exist. It must be pointed out that Bonhoeffer's ecumenical works were given in the setting of the World Alliance. As such, even with Bonhoeffer's exhortation that the ecumenical movement be more than an association of Christians, he was able to make such exhortations by utilizing the apparatus of the World Alliance. It can safely be said, then, that the way forward is not to dismantle all that has come before. Although the importance of conciliarism and councils of churches are subsidiary to discipleship in Bonhoeffer's thinking, they are not useless or meaningless.

To dismantle, discredit, or diminish the many accomplishments of the ecumenical movement of the past century would be an insult to the great ecumenical leaders of the past and a disservice to the ecumenical movement going forward. The hard work of ecumenists over the last century has played an integral role in leading the organized ecumenical movement through significant early strides—opening communications between the denominations on a global scale and beginning to address ills of the past, healing ages of division.

Bonhoeffer's understanding of the ecumenicity of the church as the reve- latory person of Christ means that the church is inherently ecumenical as the person of Christ rather than as an institution. Even so, the institutional forms of ecumenism ought not be cast aside. The institutional forms of church exist because Christ has chosen to be present in the church as Word, sacrament, and church-community. A similar account ought to be given for the institutional structures of the ecumenical movement. The apparatuses of the ecumenical movement are places in which the person of Christ can encounter itself, hear Christ's commands in one another as Christ is present as church-community, and proclaim those commands in word and deed. Even in this way, ecumenical discipleship does not subsist in institutional forms, but rather those institutional forms are helpful as a place where the person of Christ can encounter itself and hear Christ's commands as Christ is present as church-community. To throw away the structures of international ecumenism that have been developed would be to waste an instrument for discipleship. To be beholden to those structures would be to prioritize them over against the contingent commanding of Christ.

That said, Bonhoeffer's insistence upon discipleship has two weighty implications for approaching the diminishing institutional forms of ecumen- ism. First, Bonhoeffer's concept of discipleship means that the ecumenical movement needs to be willing to adapt its forms according to the commands of Christ. The institutional forms of the ecumenical movement exist, for Bonhoeffer, not for the sake of a particular institutional form but for the sake of obedience to Christ. Such an understanding means that the institutional forms of the ecumenical movement need to be willing to adapt according to Christ's command as the movement moves into its future.

The focus of Bonhoeffer's ecumenical theology upon discipleship also means that the success of the ecumenical movement is not correlative to its financial strength. The assessment of the ecumenical movement, like the assessment of the visible church, is beyond our grasp. The sobering news this stance brings is that discipleship does not guarantee financial flourishing. Indeed, it may mean financial weakness. But the church has been ecumenical from the moment of its creation and will continue to be so in feast or famine. The ecumenical church is not called to economic riches but to faithfulness and obedience—which possess riches of a different kind. Regardless of its financial status, the goal of the ecumenical movement as it moves forward ought not be survival, but discipleship.

Finally, Bonhoeffer's ecumenical theology promotes and bolsters the two remedies Kinnamon suggests. First, the internal ordering of ecumeni- cal relationships of being with and for each other in the church promotes intercession on behalf of one another and the type of spiritual ecumenism

Kinnamon posits. Moreover, Bonhoeffer's ecumenical theology emerges from an understanding of the church which maintains and emphasizes the creation, unity, and sustenance of the church in the work of God, demonstrating congeniality with Kinnamon's reminder that "God is the Chief Actor in this movement."[10] Second, Bonhoeffer's ecumenical theology promotes renewed lay engagement with ecumenical work. As has been seen, Bonhoeffer's ecumenical theology universalizes ecumenical work across the entire breadth of the church by positing discipleship as ecumenical. This stance does not guarantee that laypeople will take a stronger position in organized ecumenical work. As Kinnamon suggests, there is work to be done in regards to increasing lay involvement in organized ecumenical work. Even so, recognizing *the ecumenicity of all acts of discipleship* is a radical claim regarding the concrete and ecumenical catholicity of the church.

Implementing Bonhoeffer's ecumenical vision does not ensure that the traditional forms of ecumenism will be revitalized. It does not ensure any sort of success accessible to our assessment. What it does ensure is that the church can, should, and does follow after Christ together today.

BONHOEFFER AND THE WCC'S
PILGRIMAGE OF JUSTICE AND PEACE

At each meeting of the General Assembly every eight years, the WCC chooses a theme that the council will focus its work around until the next meeting. The current theme is a "pilgrimage of justice and peace."[11] The Faith and Order Commission produced a document on this theme entitled *Come and See: A Theological Invitation to the Pilgrimage of Justice and Peace.* As the title suggests, the document provides an invitation to explore ecumenical theology and life together as churches through the lens of pilgrimage, built upon Christ's invitation to his soon-to-be disciples to "come and see" where he was staying and directed toward justice and peace.

This theme is an exciting and promising development for the work of the WCC. The authors of *Come and See* identify a deliberate effort by the WCC to emphasize moving and acting together as the core goal of the theme of pilgrimage of justice and peace, rather than simply staying together—that is, the emphasis is not solely on agreed-upon statements, but on what it means

---

[10] Kinnamon, *Can a Renewal Movement be Renewed?* 152–155.
[11] *"Come and See."*
     For more on the WCC's approach to peace and justice, see WCC material related to JPIC, such as "Ten Affirmations on Justice, Peace, and the Integrity of Creation" and "JPIC and the Church as Moral Community."

to live and work side by side as churches.[12] This theme represents a big step in the direction of Bonhoeffer's ecumenical theology, though differences remain. Placing *Come and See* in conversation with Bonhoeffer's ecumenical theology highlights the strides the WCC has made while also illumining several limitations and challenges facing the theme of pilgrimage of justice and peace.

The similarities between *Come and See* and Bonhoeffer's ecumenical theology are immediately evident. By focusing the theology as a response to Christ's invitation to "come and see," the document already bears striking resemblance to Bonhoeffer's approach of following single-mindedly after Christ in discipleship. And the similarities do not end here. The theology of *Come and See* is based in Christ's invitation to "come and see"—the response to which the authors identify as pilgrimage—and promotes specific stances on a just and sustainable world and peace in interreligious relationships.[13] In this way, the document resembles the structure of Bonhoeffer's own ecumenical works—a theological foundation in the church as the person of Christ, practiced in obediently following after Christ in discipleship and concluding with specific commands for the church in his day (usually, that command happens to be peace).

Furthermore, the authors define pilgrimage as "transformative journeys that are ultimately directed at the reign of God" and conclude the document with the claim that the pilgrimage of justice and peace invites churches to be open to the ways in which the Holy Spirit answers the church's prayer: "Thy will be done."[14] This direction toward God's will and God's reign resemble the centrality of God's will in Bonhoeffer's ecumenical theology in its singular focus upon doing the commands of Christ. As such, the theme of pilgrimage of justice and peace has much in common with Bonhoeffer's ecumenical theology and represents a step being taken by the WCC in the direction of Bonhoeffer's thought.

These similarities between *Come and See* and Bonhoeffer's ecumenical theology provide excitement and hope regarding the ongoing work of the WCC. This new theme of a pilgrimage of justice and peace holds great potential for rich work together in the world as the churches respond to Christ's invitation to "come and see." That said, differences do remain between the pilgrimage of justice and peace and Bonhoeffer's ecumenism of discipleship, and these differences bring some limitations and challenges facing the theme of pilgrimage of justice and peace into view.

---

[12] *Come and See*, 9.
[13] *Come and See*, 11.
[14] *Come and See*, 9; 27.

The primary difference between the pilgrimage of justice and peace and Bonhoeffer's ecumenism of discipleship is the difference that has existed from the moment Bonhoeffer first voiced his ecumenical thoughts. Bonhoeffer always insists that the ecumenical movement self-identify as church; the WCC has been equally insistent that it not self-identify as church but as a "fellowship of churches."[15] When the WCC clarified its stances in the Toronto Statement in 1950—two years after the WCC's formation—the writers stated, "The WCC is not and must never become a super-church" and "cannot and should not be based on any one particular conception of the church."[16]

This distinction arises from differing presuppositions of what self-identifying as church would entail ecumenically. As has been demonstrated, when Bonhoeffer speaks of the ecumenical movement as a church, he understands church to be *Christus Prasesens*. This understanding of church recognizes the church as a creation of God, realized in the person of Christ, and actualized by the Holy Spirit.[17] For Bonhoeffer, the church is the presence of the revelatory person of Christ in the world today, which is visible through discipleship, and which is inherently one, as Christ is one.

The WCC, on the other hand, identifies itself as a "fellowship of churches"[18] that "is not and must never become a super-church."[19] In CUV ("Common Understanding and Vision of the WCC"), the WCC acknowledges that "the churches in this fellowship themselves maintain different conceptions of the church."[20] These twin claims (that the WCC is not a super-church, and that the member churches of the WCC "maintain different conceptions of the church")[21] reveal a presupposition on the part of the WCC about what identifying as church would require. Although the Toronto Statement includes language about Christ being the head[22] of the one "true Church,"[23] and the statement that "the Church of Christ is one,"[24] the foundational documents of the WCC nevertheless make clear the presupposition that self-identifying as church would mean that the WCC would necessitate a polity-driven institutional understanding of the church—an understanding which would likely require strict doctrinal uniformity by the member churches.

---

[15] Constitution, 1.
[16] TS: III.1; III.3
[17] DBWE 14:438–446.
[18] Constitution, 1.
[19] TS: III.1.
[20] CUV: 3.2.
[21] CUV: 3.2.
[22] TS: IV.1.
[23] TS: IV.5.
[24] TS: IV.2

The WCC's stance is rather reasonable when one considers the thought process behind it. The authors of the Toronto Statement write,

[The WCC] is not the world church. It is not the Una Sancta of which the Creeds speak . . . if the Council should in any way violate its own constitutional principle, that it cannot legislate or act for its member churches, it would cease to maintain the support of its membership,[25]

and further, "no church need fear that by entering into the World Council it is in danger of denying its heritage."[26] In other words, the WCC maintains its stance against self-identifying as church in order to create a space where various denominations can encounter each other and work together without worrying that in doing so they will lose their theological heritage. It is a noble stance, and it has served the WCC well, as it has been successful in creating precisely that sort of space.

Even so, this unwillingness to self-identify as church is not only the principal source of distinction between the pilgrimage of justice and peace and Bonhoeffer's ecumenism of discipleship, but it is also the principal cause of the theme's limitations. In spite of the numerous similarities between Bonhoeffer's ecumenical theology and the theology within *Come and See*, the differences are notable.

The first limitation of the theme of pilgrimage of justice and peace is the support in scripture and the Christian tradition of the use of pilgrimage as an ecumenical category. The authors of *Come and See* provide examples of such support. One problem with this is that the scriptural examples used either do not explicitly identify as pilgrimage or do not promote what the WCC is promoting in its utilization of this category. For instance, the authors use Jesus' self-identification as "the way, the truth, and the life" as a scriptural precedent for pilgrimage with an emphasis placed on Jesus as the way and an identification of the way with pilgrimage. But this passage is not about pilgrimage. The passage is from John 14, and in John 14 and 15, Jesus self-identifies as the way, the truth, and the life at the beginning of a conversation over what being a *disciple of Christ* requires, culminating in claims such as "If you love me, you will keep my commandments" and "if you keep my commandments, you will abide in my love." In other words, the passage in question is more appropriate support for discipleship as an ecumenical category than pilgrimage. Moreover, Christ's invitation to "come and see"—the titular verse and central anchor of the theology in *Come and See*—is not an invitation to pilgrimage but explicitly an invitation to *discipleship*. As such, one

---

[25] TS: III.1

[26] TS: IV.8.

limitation of the pilgrimage of justice and peace is that pilgrimage does not have a strong scriptural basis as an ecumenical category. In fact, the primary scriptural examples provided actually lend stronger support to discipleship as an ecumenical category than they do to pilgrimage.

The same is true of the examples given of pilgrimage in the Christian tradition. The authors of *Come and See* admit that pilgrimage "has sometimes been corrupted and turned into an occasion for consumerism, acquisitiveness, injustice, or even violence" and that "pilgrimage to distance places can be an elite practice, accessible only to those with the financial and physical means to undertake it."[27] In other words, the authors themselves admit that pilgrimage is a category freighted with baggage and negative connotations. In light of the thin basis for pilgrimage in scripture and tradition, the term itself becomes limited as an ecumenical category.

This limitation regarding the thin basis for pilgrimage in scripture and tradition leads to a further limitation: a lack of clarity regarding the goals of the pilgrimage of justice and peace. Again, the difference between discipleship and pilgrimage as the response to Christ's invitation to "come and see" is significant here, since the practical content of the response to that invitation is the practical content of the ecumenical theology being forwarded. Bonhoeffer's concept of discipleship carries with it a singular focus upon hearing and doing the command of Christ.[28] What keeps the concept of discipleship from being abstract or ambiguous as an ecumenical category is its reliance on a strong account of revelation in which the command of Christ must always be heard anew, and in which Christ is understood to command specifically and concretely.[29] Put otherwise, discipleship depends upon Christ's free and contingent commanding, thereby positing an absolutely specific and practicable ecumenical vision with a clear goal—obedience to Christ—in spite of an inability to systematize or formulate such a vision.

The concept of pilgrimage is afforded no such luxury because it does not necessitate this form of concrete command and obedience. Without it, the practical content of an ecumenism of pilgrimage remains vague and ambiguous; because of this ambiguity, the authors are forced to conjure up the universalized goals of justice and peace, and from there the goals only multiply to accommodate all the various tasks that confront such an ecumenism (such as creating visible unity, healing creation, affirming human dignity, and even more goals the authors of *Come and See* attribute to pilgrimage), all of which become the work and goal of the human agent in ecumenism under this

---

[27] *Come and See,* 15.
[28] DBWE 4:288.
[29] DBWE 11:359–360.

conception of a pilgrimage of justice and peace.[30] Bonhoeffer's ecumenism of discipleship maintains a singular, clear goal of following after Christ. A pilgrimage of justice and peace presents an ever-growing list of goals without the same Christological basis for pursuing them.

All of these limitations ultimately boil down to the WCC's unwillingness to self-identify as church. Bonhoeffer's concept of discipleship appears to accomplish all that the WCC is hoping to accomplish in its use of pilgrimage. Moreover, discipleship has a stronger foundation in scripture and tradition. Discipleship even maintains the emphasis on moving together because discipleship requires a communal *following after* Christ. But the WCC is unable to posit Bonhoeffer's concept of discipleship as its guiding ecumenical category while maintaining its stance against self-identifying as church. As has been demonstrated, Bonhoeffer's concept of discipleship necessitates his understanding of church.

What remains to be stated is that Bonhoeffer's ecumenism of discipleship neither results in a "super-church," nor does it dissolve the theological heritages of denominations as the WCC fears would be the result of self-identifying as church. Bonhoeffer's ecumenical theology envisions the church as the present person of Christ, bound with and for each other through Christ's activity on humanity's behalf. Participating in this church entails following after Christ in obedient discipleship. This is not an institutional, polity-driven "super-church." It is an understanding of the church as a person and the activity of those within it as obedient discipleship as they follow after Christ together—moving together, as the WCC would have it.

Put otherwise, Bonhoeffer's ecumenical theology offers the chance to overcome the hurdle of the ecumenical movement's ecclesiological self-understanding—a hurdle that has been present from the earliest days of the contemporary ecumenical movement. The WCC's stance against self-identifying as church has been reasonable and has served its purpose well. Now that the space has been created for the denominations to encounter each other in the WCC, it must be asked whether the time has come for the WCC to reconsider what it means to self-identify as church, especially if doing so does not result in a "super-church" or the dissolution of theological heritages. If that time has indeed come, Bonhoeffer's ecumenism of discipleship provides a rich resource for this reconsideration—particularly in light of the striking similarities between it and the theological theme the WCC is already pursuing. Bonhoeffer's ecumenical theology offers a path toward understanding the ecumenical movement as church as the person of Christ, and the actions of ecumenical work as discipleship.

---

[30] *Come and See*, 9–27.

BONHOEFFER'S ECUMENICAL THEOLOGY AND THE
SHIFT OF THE GLOBAL CENTER OF CHRISTIANITY

It has been well documented that the center of global Christianity is shifting southeast. The days of Christendom and Western Christianity being the center of the church and the only locale whose voice gets to be heard in theology are nearing their end (indeed, their end is already here). Mainline denominations are declining in the West and, in general, non-denominational churches and Pentecostal churches are the sites of numerical church growth in the West. And, the sites of the greatest numerical growth globally are across the global south. As global Christianity shifts, so too must ecumenical discourse. Much of the ecumenical discourse of the past century has been driven by Western thinkers and Western ideology. Even a document as recent as "The Church: Towards a Common Vision" (TCV) in 2013 has drawn criticism for being too Western in its vision of the church.[31] Although Bonhoeffer is a Western thinker, his ecumenical theology provides a resource for moving into the global ecumenical future.

The chief offering of Bonhoeffer's ecumenism of discipleship to the global ecumenical future is its emphasis on the church as the present person of Christ and upon discipleship as the focus of ecumenical work. Admittedly, Bonhoeffer's understanding of Christ's presence as Word and sacrament is very Lutheran and Western. Even so, his approach to Christ's presence as community has tremendous potential for ecumenical discourse. Bonhoeffer's account of a church that is bound with and for each other in Christ as the person of Christ envisions a diverse and ecumenical church in which the person of Christ that is the church can encounter one another globally and hear Christ's command in one another. This approach does not depend upon uniformity regarding an account of baptism or Eucharist. Instead, it requires those within the church to *see* each other, to be broken open from themselves to be bound with and for each other, to act for each other in concrete discipleship as the command of Christ is encountered in one another.

As the center of the church shifts, the need is not for non-Western or non-mainline churches to simply assimilate Western theology. The need is for a church that understands itself as the person of Christ and lives out its discipleship together in the world. Bonhoeffer's ecumenical theology provides the necessary resources for envisioning such a church.

Another facet of Bonhoeffer's ecumenical theology that lends itself to global ecumenism is its simplicity. Despite the complexity of the theology that this book has presented, at its core, Bonhoeffer's ecumenical theology

---

[31] Rausch, Thomas. "A New Ecumenism? Christian Unity in a Global Church." *The Reformation Centenary: Ecumenism Today* 78. no. 3 (2017): 596–613.

simply asks the question he asked in *Discipleship*, "What does [Jesus] want from us today?"[32] The basic idea is that the church is the person of Christ and that those within the church are called to continually ask what Jesus wants from them and to be obedient when Christ responds. This fairly simple ecumenical theology—the church as the revelatory person of Christ, concretely active in the world through its discipleship to Christ—is an approach that is generous and expansive in scope. The simplicity of the approach and its emphasis on discipleship make this an ecumenical vision that is open and viable for the many diverse viewpoints of the church throughout the world. And yet, this simplicity should not be mistaken for shallowness. If the church is the person of Christ, then those who are in the church are in Christ. And in Christ are the full depths of God.

This chapter is not the place for an exhaustive account of what Bonhoeffer's ecumenism of discipleship offers global ecumenism. And, indeed, much of what this theology offers global ecumenism can only be discovered in practice as the church encounters the command of Christ through encountering itself globally and responds in obedient discipleship. Ultimately, the fullness of what this ecumenical vision can offer can only be discovered in the fullness of the God that is encountered in Jesus Christ as the church seeks ever to follow after Christ together in discipleship.

Bonhoeffer's ecumenism of discipleship has ongoing significance for the ecumenical movement. As traditional ecumenism faces the crisis of decline, and as Christianity shifts to the global south, an ecumenical theology of discipleship provides resources for living and acting together in the world. Perhaps the most significant insight of Bonhoeffer's ecumenical theology is that the center of all ecumenical action can be found in the very question Bonhoeffer asked in *Discipleship*: "What does [Jesus] want from us today?"[33]

---

[32] DBWE 4:37.

[33] DBWE 4:37.

Bibliography

Aveling, Harry G. "Dietrich Bonhoeffer's Christology." *Colloquium* 16, no. 1 (October 1983): 23–30.

Avis, Paul. *Reshaping Ecumenical Theology.* London: T&T Clark International, 2010.

Barker, Gaylon. *The Cross of Reality: Luther's Theologia Crucis and Bonhoeffer's Christology.* Minneapolis, MN: Fortress Press, 2015.

Barnett, Victoria. "Dietrich Bonhoeffer's Ecumenical Vision." *The Christian Century* 112, no. 14 (April 26, 1995): 454–457.

———. "The Ecumenical and Interfaith Landscape in Bonhoeffer's Times." *The Ecumenical Review* 67, no. 2 (July 2015): 302–307.

Bethge, Eberhard. *Dietrich Bonhoeffer: A Biography.* Minneapolis: Fortress Press, 2000.

Bonhoeffer, Dietrich. *Act and Being: Transcendental Philosophy and Ontology in Systematic Theology.* Dietrich Bonhoeffer Works, Volume 2. Edited by Wayne Whitson Floyd, Jr. Translated by H. Martin Rumscheidt. Minneapolis: Fortress Press, 1996.

———. *Barcelona, Berlin, New York: 1928–1931.* Dietrich Bonhoeffer Works, Volume 10. Edited by Clifford J. Green. Translated by Douglass W. Stott. Minneapolis: Fortress Press, 2008.

———. *Berlin: 1932–1933.* Dietrich Bonhoeffer Works, Volume 12. Edited by Larry L. Rasmussen. Translated by Isabel Best and David Higgins. Minneapolis: Fortress Press, 2009.

———. *Conspiracy and Imprisonment: 1940–1945.* Dietrich Bonhoeffer Works, Volume 16. Edited by Mark S. Brocker. Translated by Lisa E. Dahill. Minneapolis: Fortress Press, 2006.

———. *Creation and Fall.* Dietrich Bonhoeffer Works, Volume 3. Edited by John W. de Gruchy. Translated by Douglas Stephen Bax. Minneapolis: Fortress Press, 1997.

————. *Discipleship.* Dietrich Bonhoeffer Works, Volume 4. Translated by Barbara Green and Reinhard Krauss. Minneapolis: Fortress Press, 2001.

————. *Ecumenical, Academic, and Pastoral Work: 1931–1932.* Dietrich Bonhoeffer Works, Volume 11. Edited by Victoria J. Barnett, Mark S. Brocker, and Michael B. Lukens. Translated by Anne Schmidt-Lange, Isabel Best, Nicolas Humphrey, and Marion Pauck. Minneapolis: Fortress Press, 2012.

————. *Ethics.* Dietrich Bonhoeffer Works, Volume 6. Edited by Clifford J. Green. Translated by Reinhard Krauss, Charles C. West, and Douglas W. Stott. Minneapolis: Fortress Press, 2005.

————. *Fiction From Tegel Prison.* Dietrich Bonhoeffer Works, Volume 7. Edited by Clifford J. Green. Translated by Nancy Lukens. Minneapolis: Fortress Press, 1999.

————. *Letters and Papers From Prison.* Dietrich Bonhoeffer Works, Volume 8. Edited by John W. de Gruchy. Translated by Isabel Best, Lisa E. Dahill, Reinhard Krauss, and Nancy Lukens. Minneapolis: Fortress Press, 2009.

————. *Life Together: The Prayerbook of the Bible.* Dietrich Bonhoeffer Works, Volume 5. Edited by Geffrey B. Kelly. Translated by Daniel W. Bloesch and James H. Burtness. Minneapolis: Fortress Press, 1996.

————. *London: 1933–1935.* Dietrich Bonhoeffer Works, Volume 13. Edited by Keith Clements. Translated by Isabel Best. Minneapolis: Fortress Press, 2007.

————. *Sanctorum Communio: A Theological Study of the Sociology of the Church.* Dietrich Bonhoeffer Works, Volume 1. Edited by Clifford J. Green. Translated by Reinhard Krauss and Nancy Lukens. Minneapolis: Fortress Press, 1998.

————. *Theological Education at Finkenwalde: 1935–1937.* Dietrich Bonhoeffer Works, Volume 14. Edited by H. Gaylon Barker and Mark S. Brocker. Translated by Douglas W. Stott. Minneapolis: Fortress Press, 2013.

————. *Theological Education Underground: 1937–1940.* Dietrich Bonhoeffer Works, Volume 15. Edited by Victoria J. Barnett. Translated by Victoria J. Barnett, Claudia D. Bergmann, Peter Frick, and Scott A. Moore. Minneapolis: Fortress Press, 2012.

————. *The Young Bonhoeffer: 1918–1927.* Dietrich Bonhoeffer Works, Volume 9. Edited by Paul Duane Mathey, Clifford J. Green, and Marshall D. Johnson. Translated by Mary C. Nebelsick and Douglas W. Stott. Minneapolis: Fortress Press, 2003.

Bonino, Jose Miguez. "A Latin American Attempt to Locate the Question of Unity." In *What Kind of Unity? Faith and Order Paper No. 69*, 51–60. Geneva: WCC, 1973.

Brock, Brian. *Singing the Ethos of God: On the Place of Christian Ethics in Scripture.* Grand Rapids: Eerdmans, 2007.

Busch Nielsen, Kirsten. "Community Turned Inside Out: Dietrich Bonhoeffer's Concept of the Church and Humanity Reconsidered." In *Being Human, Becoming Human: Dietrich Bonhoeffer and Social Thought,* edited by Jens Zimmermann and Brian Gregor, 91–101. Cambridge: James Clarke & Co., 2010.

Castro, Emilio. "The Unity of the Church." In *A Passion for Unity: Essays on Ecumenical Hopes and Challenges,* edited by Emilio Castro, 1–13. Geneva: WCC Publications, 1992.

Catholicos of Cilicia. "Ecumenism in the Process of Transformation." In *Ecumenism in the 21st Century: Report of the Consultation Convened by the World Council of Churches*, 38–45. Geneva: WCC, 2005.

Clements, Keith. "Community in the Ethics of Dietrich Bonhoeffer." *Studies in Christian Ethics* 10, no. 1 (April 1997): 16–31.

———. *Dietrich Bonhoeffer's Ecumenical Quest*. Geneva: World Council of Church Publications, 2015.

———. *Ecumenical Dynamic: Living in More than One Place at Once*. Geneva: WCC Publications, 2013.

Dahill, Lisa E. "Con-Formation With Jesus Christ: Bonhoeffer, Social Location, and Embodiment." In *Being Human, Becoming Human: Dietrich Bonhoeffer and Social Thought*, edited by Jens Zimmermann and Brian Gregor, 176–190. Cambridge: James Clarke & Co., 2010.

———. "Probing the Will of God: Bonhoeffer and Discernment." *Dialog* 41, no. 1 (Spr 2002): 42–49.

Daley, Brian E. "Rebuilding the Structure of Love: The Quest for Visible Unity Among the Churches." In *The Ecumenical Future*, edited by Carl E. Braaten and Robert W. Jenson, 73–105. Grand Rapids: Eerdmans, 2004.

de Dietrich, Suzanne. *The Witnessing Community: The Biblical Record of God's Purpose*. Philadelphia: Westminster Press, 1958.

De Gruchy, John. "Dietrich Bonhoeffer as Christian Humanist." In *Being Human, Becoming Human: Dietrich Bonhoeffer and Social Thought*, edited by Jens Zimmermann and Brian Gregor, 3–24. Cambridge: James Clarke & Co., 2010.

DeJonge, Michael P. *Bonhoeffer on Resistance: The Word Against the Wheel*. Oxford: Oxford University Press, 2018.

———. *Bonhoeffer's Reception of Luther*. Oxford: Oxford University Press, 2017.

———. *Bonhoeffer's Theological Formation: Berlin, Barth, and Protestant Theology*. Oxford: Oxford University Press, 2012.

Dodson, Christopher. "The God Who is Given: Bonhoeffer's Sacramental Theology and His Critique of Religion." PhD Dissertation, University of Aberdeen, 2016.

Duchrow, Ulrich. *Conflict Over the Ecumenical Movement: Confessing Christ Today in the Universal Church*. Translated by David Lewis (Geneva: WCC, 1981); idem, "The Confessing Church and the Ecumenical Movement." *Ecumenical Review* 33 (1981): 212–231.

Feil, Ernst. "Dietrich Bonhoeffer's Understanding of the World." In *A Bonhoeffer Legacy: Essays in Understanding*, edited by A. J. Klassen, 237–255. Grand Rapids: Eerdmans, 1981.

———. *The Theology of Dietrich Bonhoeffer*. Minneapolis: Fortress Press, 1985.

Fergus, Donald Murdoch. "Lebensraum: Just What is This 'Habitat' or 'Living Space' That Dietrich Bonhoeffer Claimed for the Church?" *Scottish Journal of Theology* 67, no. 1 (2014): 70–84.

———. "'To Do What is Good is to Take the Form of Jesus Christ:' Dietrich Bonhoeffer's Approach to a Dynamic Ethic." *The Bonhoeffer Legacy* 3, no. 1 (2015): 51–68.

Fiddes, Paul S. *Participating in God: A Pastoral Doctrine of the Trinity.* London: Darton, Longman & Todd; Westminster John Knox, 2000.

Floyd, Wayne. "Encounter With an Other: Immanuel Kant and G.W.F. Hegel in the Theology of Dietrich Bonhoeffer." In *Bonhoeffer's Intellectual Formation*, edited by Peter Frick, 83–119. Tubingen: Mohr Siebeck, 2008.

Fortin, Jean-Pierre. "The Church as Confessing Community: Dietrich Bonhoeffer's Theology of Forgiveness and Reconciliation." *Touchstone* 34, no. 3 (October 2016): 14–24.

Frick, Peter. "Bonhoeffer's Theology and Economic Humanism: An Exploration in Interdisciplinary Sociality." In *Being Human, Becoming Human: Dietrich Bonhoeffer and Social Thought*, edited by Jens Zimmermann and Brian Gregor, 49–70. Cambridge: James Clarke & Co., 2010.

Garcia, Javier A. *Recovering the Ecumenical Bonhoeffer: Thinking After the Tradition.* Lanham: Lexington Books/Fortress Academic, 2019.

Germanos of Thyateira. "The Call to Unity." In *Faith and Order: Proceedings of the World Conference, Lausanne 1927*, edited by H. N. Bate, 18–23. London: SCM, 1927.

Green, Clifford J. *Bonhoeffer: A Theology of Sociality.* Cambridge: Cambridge University Press; Eerdmans, 1999.

———. "Human Sociality and Christian Community." In *The Cambridge Companion to Dietrich Bonhoeffer*, edited by John W. De Gruchy, 113–133. Cambridge: Cambridge University Press, 1999.

———. "Sociality, Discipleship, and Worldly Theology in Bonhoeffer's Christian Humanism." In *Being Human, Becoming Human: Dietrich Bonhoeffer and Social Thought*, edited by Jens Zimmermann and Brian Gregor, 71–90. Cambridge: James Clarke & Co., 2010.

———. "Trinity and Christology in Bonhoeffer and Barth." *Union Seminary Quarterly Review* 60, no. 1–2 (2006): 1–22.

Greggs, Tom. "Bearing Sin in the Church: The Ecclesial Hamartiology of Bonhoeffer." In *Christ, Church and World: New Studies in Bonhoeffer's Theology and Ethics*, edited by Michael Mawson and Philip G. Ziegler, 77–100. London, UK: Bloomsbury T&T Clark, 2016.

———. *Dogmatic Ecclesiology, Volume 1: The Priestly Catholicity of the Church.* Grand Rapids: Baker Academic, 2019.

———. "Ecclesial Priestly Mediation in the Theology of Dietrich Bonhoeffer." *Theology Today* 71, no. 1 (April 2014): 81–91.

———. "Proportion and Topography in Ecclesiology: A Working Paper on the Dogmatic Location of the Doctrine of the Church." In *Theological Theology: Essays in Honour of John Webster*, edited by R. David Nelson and Darren Sarisky, 89–106. London, UK: Bloomsbury T&T Clark, 2015.

———. "The Catholic Spirit of Protestantism: A Very Methodist Take on the Third Article, Visible Unity, and Ecumenism." *Pro Ecclesia* 26, no. 4 (Fall 2017): 353–372.

———. *Theology Against Religion: Constructive Dialogues With Bonhoeffer and Barth.* London: T & T Clark International, 2011.

Gregor, Brian. "Following-After and Becoming Human: A Study of Bonhoeffer and Kierkegaard." In *Being Human, Becoming Human: Dietrich Bonhoeffer and Social Thought*, edited by Jens Zimmermann and Brian Gregor, 152–175. Cambridge: James Clarke & Co., 2010.

Gunton, Colin E. "The Church on Earth: The Roots of Community." In *On Being the Church: Essays on the Christian Community*, edited by Colin E. Gunton and Daniel W. Hardy, 48–81. Edinburgh: T&T Clark, 1989.

Harasta, Eva. "Adam in Christ? The Place of Sin in Christ-Reality." In *Christ, Church and World: New Studies in Bonhoeffer's Theology and Ethics*, edited by Michael Mawson and Philip G. Ziegler, 61–76. London, UK: Bloomsbury T&T Clark, 2016.

———. "One Body: Dietrich Bonhoeffer on the Church's Existence as Sinner and Saint at Once." *Union Seminary Quarterly Review* 62, nos. 3–4 (2010): 17–34.

———. "The Responsibility of Doctrine: Bonhoeffer's Ecclesiological Hermeneutics of Dogmatic Theology." *Theology Today* 71, no. 1 (April 2014): 14–27.

Harmon, Steven R. *Ecumenism Means You, Too: Ordinary Christians and the Quest for Christian Unity*. Eugene, OR: Cascade Books, 2010.

Harvard, Joseph S. "The Continuing Cost of Discipleship." *Journal for Preachers* 7, no. 4 (Pentecost 1984): 2–7.

Harvey, Barry. "The Narrow Path: Sociality, Ecclesiology, and the Polyphony of Life in the Thought of Dietrich Bonhoeffer." In *Being Human, Becoming Human: Dietrich Bonhoeffer and Social Thought*, edited by Jens Zimmermann and Brian Gregor, 102–126. Cambridge: James Clarke & Co., 2010.

Hauerwas, Stanley. *Performing the Faith: Bonhoeffer and the Practice of Nonviolence*. Grand Rapids: Brazos Press; SPCK, 2004.

Hayward, Victor. "A Survey of National Christian Councils." *International Review of Mission* 60 (1971): 512–521.

Hefner, Philip J. "The Church." In *Christian Dogmatics: Volume 2*, edited by Carl E. Braaten and Robert W. Jenson, 183–253. Philadelphia: Fortress Press, 1984.

Himes, Brant. "Discipleship as Theological Praxis: Dietrich Bonhoeffer as a Resource for Educational Ministry." *Christian Education Journal* 8, no. 2 (Fall 2011): 263–277.

Holmes, Christopher R. J. "Beyond Bonhoeffer in Loyalty to Bonhoeffer: Reconsidering Bonhoeffer's Christological Aversion to Theological Metaphysics." In *Christ, Church and World: New Studies in Bonhoeffer's Theology and Ethics*, edited by Michael Mawson and Philip G. Ziegler, 29–44. London, UK: Bloomsbury T&T Clark, 2016.

Hooton, Peter. "Community and Christology in the Theology of Dietrich Bonhoeffer." *St Mark's Review* 233 (October 2015): 26–41.

Jeanrond, Werner G. "Community and Authority: The Nature and Implications of the Authority of Christian Community." In *On Being the Church: Essays on the Christian Community*, edited by Colin E. Gunton and Daniel W. Hardy, 81–110. Edinburgh: T&T Clark, 1989.

Jenson, Robert W. *Unbaptized God: The Basic Flaw in Ecumenical Theology.* Minneapolis: Fortress Press, 1992.

Kasper, Walter. "May They All Be One: But How? A Vision of Christian Unity for the Next Generation." *Ecumenical Trends* 40 (2011): 1–15.

Kasper, Walter Cardinal. "May They All Be One: But How? A Vision of Christian Unity for the Next Generation." *Ecumenical Trends* 40 (2011): 1–15.

———. *That They May All Be One: The Call to Unity Today.* New York: Burns & Oates, 2004.

Kelly, Geffrey B. "Revelation in Christ: A Study of Bonhoeffer's Theology of Revelation." *Ephemerides Theologicae Lovanienses* 50, no. 1 (May 1974): 39–74.

Kelly, Geffrey B., and F. Burton Nelson. "Dietrich Bonhoeffer's Theological Interpretation of Scripture for the Church." *Ex Auditu* 17 (2001): 1–30.

Kessler, Diane, and Michael Kinnamon. *Councils of Churches and the Ecumenical Vision.* Geneva: WCC, 2000.

Kinnamon, Michael. *Can a Renewal Movement be Renewed? Questions for the Future of Ecumenism.* Grand Rapids: Eerdmans, 2014.

———. "New Contours of Ecumenism in the 21st Century." *Ecumenical Review* 66, no. 1 (March 2014): 16–24.

Knight, M. J. "Christ Existing in Ordinary: Dietrich Bonhoeffer and Sanctification." *International Journal of Systematic Theology* 16, no. 4 (October 2014): 414–435.

Kobia, Sam. "Report of the General Secretary, Ninth Assembly of the World Council of Churches, 2006." In *God, in Your Grace: Official Report of the Ninth Assembly of the World Council of Churches*, edited by Luis N. Rivera-Pagan, 138–151. Geneva: WCC, 2007.

Leahy, Breandan. "'Christ Existing as Church-Community': Dietrich Bonhoeffer's Notion of Church." *Irish Theological Quarterly* 73, nos. 1–2 (2008): 32–59.

Lindbeck, George A. *The Nature of Doctrine: Religion and Theology in a Postliberal Age.* Louisville: Westminster John Knox Press, 1984.

Luther, Martin. *Luther Works, Volume 39: Church and Ministry I.* Edited by Eric E. Gritsch. Philadelphia: Fortress Press, 1970.

Marsh, Charles. "Human Community and Divine Presence: Dietrich Bonhoeffer: Dietrich Bonhoeffer's Theological Critique of Hegel." *Scottish Journal of Theology* 45, no. 4 (1992): 427–448.

Mawson, Michael G. *Christ Existing as Community: Bonhoeffer's Ecclesiology.* Oxford: Oxford University Press, 2018.

———. "Creatures Before God: Bonhoeffer, Disability and Theological Anthropology." In *Christ, Church and World: New Studies in Bonhoeffer's Theology and Ethics*, edited by Michael Mawson and Philip G. Ziegler, 119–140. London, UK: Bloomsbury T&T Clark, 2016.

———. "Suffering Christ's Call: Discipleship and the Cross." *The Bonhoeffer Legacy* 3, no. 2 (2015): 1–18.

———. "The Politics of Jesus and the Ethics of Christ: Why the Differences Between Yoder and Bonhoeffer Matter." In *The Freedom of a Christian Ethicist: The Future of a Reformation Legacy*, edited by Brian Brock and Michael Mawson, 127–143. London: T&T Clark, 2016.

———. "The Spirit and the Community: Pneumatology and Ecclesiology in Jenson, Hutter and Bonhoeffer." *International Journal of Systematic Theology* 15, no. 4 (October 2013): 453–468.

McBride, Jennifer M. "Christ Existing as Concrete Community Today." *Theology Today* 71, no. 1 (April 2014): 92–105.

———. *The Church for the World: A Theology of Public Witness.* Oxford: Oxford University Press, 2012.

———. "Thinking Within the Movement of Bonhoeffer's Theology: Towards a Christological Reinterpretation of Repentance." In *Religion, Religionlessness and Contemporary Western Culture: Explorations in Dietrich Bonhoeffer's Theology*, edited by Stephen Plant and Ralf K. Wustenberg, 91–109. New York: Peter Lang, 2008.

McClendon, James. *Systematic Theology: Ethics*, Vol. 1. Nashville: Abingdon Press, 2002.

McGarry, Joseph. "Christ Among a Band of People: Dietrich Bonhoeffer and Formation in Christ." PhD Dissertation, University of Aberdeen, 2013.

———. "Con-Formed to Christ: Dietrich Bonhoeffer and Christian Formation." *Journal of Spiritual Formation & Soul Care* 5, no. 2 (Fall 2012): 226–242.

———. "Formed While Following: Dietrich Bonhoeffer's Asymmetrical View of Agency in Christian Formation." *Theology Today* 71, no. 1 (April 2014): 106–120.

Meyer, Harding. *That They May All Be One: Perceptions and Models of Ecumenicity.* Translated by William G. Rusch. Grand Rapids: Eerdmans, 1999.

Moses, John A. "Dietrich Bonhoeffer's Concept of the 'True' Church." *St Mark's Review* 169 (Aut 1997): 16–22.

———. "Dietrich Bonhoeffer's Prioritization of Church Unity (*Oekumene*)." *Journal or Religious History* 24, no. 2 (June 2000): 196–212.

Nation, Mark, Anthony G. Siegrist, and Daniel P. Umbel. *Bonhoeffer the Assassin?: Challenging the Myth, Recovering His Call to Peacemaking.* Grand Rapids: Baker Academic, 2013.

Nessan, Craig L. "What If the Church Really is the Body of Christ?" *Dialog* 51, no. 1 (Spre 2012): 43–52.

Neumann, Katja. "The Authority of Discipleship: An Approach to Dietrich Bonhoeffer's Commentary on the Sermon on the Mount." *Vision (Winnipeg, Man.)* 13, no. 2 (Fall 2012): 78–86.

Nissen, Ulrik Becker. "Responding to Human Reality: Responsibility and Responsiveness in Bonhoeffer's Ethics." In *Being Human, Becoming Human: Dietrich Bonhoeffer and Social Thought*, edited by Jens Zimmermann and Brian Gregor, 191–214. Cambridge: James Clarke & Co., 2010.

Northcott, Michael S. "'Who am I?': Human Identity and the Spiritual Disciplines in the Witness of Dietrich Bonhoeffer." In *Who Am I?: Bonhoeffer's Theology Through His Poetry*, edited by Bernd Wannenwetsch, 12–29. London: Bloomsbury, 2009.

O'Gara, Margaret. "Ecumenical Dialogue: The Next Generation." *CTSA Proceedings* 63 (2008): 91–103.

Owens, L. Roger. "Preaching as Participation: Dietrich Bonhoeffer's Christology of Preaching." *Currents in Theology and Mission* 36, no. 1 (February 2009): 47–54.

Pangritz, Andreas. "Who is Christ for Us Today?" In *The Cambridge Companion to Dietrich Bonhoeffer*, edited by John De Gruchy, 134–153. Cambridge: Cambridge University Press, 1999.

Pannenberg, Wolfhart. *Systematic Theology, Volume 3*. Grand Rapids: Eerdmans, 2009.

Peck, William Jay. "Proposal Concerning Bonhoeffer's Concept of the Person." *Anglican Theological Review* 50, no. 4 (1968): 311–329.

Penamora, Aldrin M. "Ethics of Responsibility: Christ-Centered Personal and Social Ethics for Church and Society." *Journal of Asian Evangelical Theology* 19, no. 1 (March 2015): 91–107.

Phillips, John. *Christ for Us in the Theology of Dietrich Bonhoeffer*. New York: Harper and Row, 1967.

Plant, Stephen J. *Taking Stock of Bonhoeffer: Studies in Biblical Interpretation and Ethics*. Surrey: Ashgate Publishing Limited, 2014.

Pottmeyer, Hermann J. "The Reception Process: The Challenge at the Threshold of a New Phase of the Ecumenical Movement." In *Ecumenism: Present Realities and Future Prospects*, edited by Lawrence S. Cunningham, 149–169. Notre Dame, IN: University of Notre Dame Press, 1998.

Radner, Ephraim. *A Brutal Unity: The Spiritual Politics of the Christian Church*. Waco: Baylor University Press, 2012.

Rahner, Karl. *Bishops: Their Status and Function*. Compass Books 5. London: Burns & Oates, 1964.

Raiser, Konrad. "Bonhoeffer and the Ecumenical Movement." In *Bonhoeffer for a New Day: Theology in a Time of Transition*, edited by John de Gruchy. Grand Rapids: Eerdmans, 1997.

———. *Ecumenism in Transition: A Paradigm Shift in the Ecumenical Movement?* Geneva: WCC Publications, 1991.

Rausch, Thomas P. "A New Ecumenism?: Christian Unity in a Global Church." *Theological Studies* 78, no. 3 (September 2017): 596–613.

Rochelle, Jay C. "Bonhoeffer: Community, Authority, and Spirituality." *Currents in Theology and Mission* 21, no. 2 (April 1994): 117–122.

Root, Andrew. *Bonhoeffer as a Youth Worker: A Theological Vision for Discipleship and Life Together*. Grand Rapids: Baker Academic, 2015.

Root, Michael. "Essential Unity and Lived Communion: The Interrelation of the Unity We Have and the Unity We Seek." In *The Ecumenical Future*, edited by Carl E. Braaten and Robert W. Jenson, 106–125. Grand Rapids: Eerdmans, 2004.

Schlingensiepen, Ferdinand. *Dietrich Bonhoeffer 1906–1945: Martyr, Thinker, Man of Resistance*. Translated by Isabel Best. London: T&T Clark, 2010.

Schmiedel, Ulrich. "Opening the Church to the Other: Dietrich Bonhoeffer's Reception of Ernst Troeltsh." *International Journal for the Study of the Christian Church* 17, no. 3 (2017): 184–198.

Schneider, Laurel C. "'The Call Was Not Meant for You Alone:' Dietrich Bonhoeffer on Discerning the Call." *Chicago Theological Seminary Register* 94, nos. 2–3 (Sum 2007): 17–22.

Sundermeier, Theo. "Der Kirchenbegriff von Dietrich Bonhoeffer – Eine missiologische Perspektive. Mission und Religion in der Theologie Bonhoeffers." *Interkulturelle Theologie. Zeitschrift fur Missionswissenschaft* (no. 4/2016) *Dietrich Bonhoefferzu Mission und Okumene*: 331–350.

Tafilowski, Ryan. "A Reappraisal of the Orders of Creation." *Lutheran Quarterly* 31, no. 3 (Fall 2017): 288–309.

Tamez, Elsa. "Breaking Down Walls in Our Globalized Society: A Relevant Ecumenism." *Ecumenical Trends* 38, no. 7 (2009): 1–7.

Tang, Andres S. K. "Confucianism and Bonhoeffer on Individualism and Community: From the Perspective of the Way of Humanization." *ChingFeng* 1, no. 1 (Spr 2000): 97–103.

———. "The Ecclesiology of Dietrich Bonhoeffer: Reflections on *Sanctorum Communio*." *Hill Road* 7, no. 2 (December 2004): 71–80.

Tanner, Mary. "On Being Church." *The Ecumenical Review* 53, no. 1 (2001): 64–71.

Temple, William. "Explanatory Memorandum on the Constitution of the World Council of Churches, 1938." In *The Genesis and Formation of the World Council of Churches*, edited by W. A. Visser't Hooft, 107–110. Geneva: WCC, 1982.

Thomas, M. M. "Search for Wholeness and Unity." In *Towards a Theology of Contemporary Ecumenism*, 255–265. Geneva: WCC, 1978.

Tietz, Christiane. "Bonhoeffer on the Ontological Structure of the Church." In *Ontology and Ethics: Bonhoeffer and Contemporary Scholarship*, edited by Adam C. Clark and Michael Mawson, 32–46. Eugene, OR: Pickwick Publications, 2013.

———. "The Mysteries of Knowledge, Sin, and Shame." In *Mysteries in the Theology of Dietrich Bonhoeffer: A Copenhagen Bonhoeffer Symposium*, edited by Kirsten Busch Nielsen, Ulrik Nissen, and Christiane Tietz, 27–48. Gottingen: Vandenhoeck & Ruprecht, 2007.

———. "The Role of Jesus Christ for Christian Theology." In *Christ, Church and World: New Studies in Bonhoeffer's Theology and Ethics*, edited by Michael Mawson and Philip G. Ziegler, 9–28. London, UK: Bloomsbury T&T Clark, 2016.

Tveit, Olav Fykse. "Renewed Mission of the WCC in the Search for Christian Unity." In *That They All May Be One: Selected Sermons, Speeches, and Articles*, 100–105. Geneva: WCC, 2011.

VandenBerg, Mary. "Bonhoeffer's Discipleship: Theology for the Purpose of Christian Formation." *Calvin Theological Journal* 44, no. 2 (November 2009): 333–349.

Van der Ziel, Albert. "Following Jesus: The Continuing Challenge of Dietrich Bonhoeffer." *Reformed Journal* 27, no. 11 (November 1977): 22–25.

Vischer, Lukas. "Christian Councils: Instruments of Ecclesial Communion." *The Ecumenical Review* 24, no. 1 (1972): 79–87.

Visser't Hooft, Willem. "The Mandate of the Ecumenical Movement." In *The Uppsala Report 1968: Official Report of the Fourth Assembly of the World Council of Churches, Uppsala July 4–20, 1968*, edited by Norman Goodall, 316–322. Geneva: World Council of Churches, 1968.

———. *The Pressure of Our Common Calling*. Garden City, NY: Doubleday, 1959.

Visser't Hooft, W. A. "Dietrich Bonhoeffer and the Self-Understanding of the Ecumenical Movement." *Ecumenical Review* 28 (1976): 198–203.

Volf, Miroslav. *Exclusion and Embrace: A Theological Exploration of Identity, Otherness, and Reconciliation.* Nashville: Abingdon Press, 1996.

Walker, Peter W. L. "Bonhoeffer and the Basis of Union." *Uniting Church Studies* 13, no. 1 (March 2007): 1–17.

Webster, John. "Communion with Christ: Mortification and Vivification." In *Sanctified by Grace: A Theology of the Christian Life*, edited by Kent Eilers and Kyle Strobel. London: Bloomsbury, 2014.

———. "'In the Society of God': Some Principles of Ecclesiology." In *Perspectives on Ecclesiology and Ethnography*, edited by Pete Ward, 200–222. Cambridge, UK: William B. Eerdmans Publishing Company, 2012.

Wilkes, Nicola J. "Private Confession of Sin in the Theology of Dietrich Bonhoeffer." *Tyndale Bulletin* 66, no. 2 (2015): 317–320.

Yoder, John Howard. "The Christological Presuppositions of Discipleship." In *Being Human, Becoming Human: Dietrich Bonhoeffer and Social Thought*, edited by Jens Zimmermann and Brian Gregor, 127–151. Cambridge: James Clarke & Co., 2010.

———. *The Politics of Jesus: VicitAgnusNoster.* Grand Rapids: Eerdmans, 1972.

Zerner, Ruth. "Bonhoeffer on Discipleship and Community." *Lutheran Forum* 30, no. 2 (May 1996): 35–38.

Ziegler, Philip G. "Christ for us Today: Promeity in the Christologies of Bonhoeffer and Kierkegaard." *International Journal of Systematic Theology* 15, no. 1 (January 2013): 25–41.

———. "'Completely Within God's Doing:' Soteriology as Meta-Ethics in the Theology of Dietrich Bonhoeffer." In *Christ, Church and World: New Studies in Bonhoeffer's Theology and Ethics*, edited by Michael Mawson and Philip G. Ziegler, 101–118. London, UK: Bloomsbury T&T Clark, 2016.

———. "Dietrich Bonhoeffer: Theologian of the Word." In *Bonhoeffer, Christ, and Culture*, edited by Keith L. Johnson and Timothy Larsen, 17–37. Nottingham: InterVarsity Press, 2013.

———. "Graciously Commanded: Dietrich Bonhoeffer and Karl Barth on the Decalogue." *Scottish Journal of Theology* 71, no. 2 (2018): 127–141.

———. *Militant Grace: The Apocalyptic Turn and the Future of Christian Theology.* Grand Rapids: Baker Academic, 2018; especially 187–200.

———. "The Humanity of Divinity." *Union Seminary Quarterly Review* 65, no. 1–2 (2015): 171–180.

Zimmermann, Jens. "Being Human Becoming Human: Dietrich Bonhoeffer's Christological Humanism." In *Being Human, Becoming Human: Dietrich Bonhoeffer and Social Thought*, edited by Jens Zimmermann and Brian Gregor, 25–48. Cambridge: James Clarke & Co., 2010.

———. "Dietrich Bonhoeffer and Martin Heidegger: Two Different Visions of Humanity." In *Bonhoeffer and Continental Thought: Cruciform Philosophy*, edited by Brian Gregor and Jens Zimmermann, 102–133. Bloomington, IN: Indiana University Press, 2009.

Sources with Unspecified Authorship in Chronological Order

"Baptism, Eucharist, and Ministry (Faith and Order Paper no. 111, the 'Lima Text')." World Council of Churches. https://www.oikoumene.org/en/resources /documents/commissions/faith-and-order/i-unity-the-church-and-its-mission /baptism-eucharist-and-ministry-faith-and-order-paper-no-111-the-lima-text (February 20, 2019).

"Called to Be One Church." In *God, in Your Grace: Official Report of the Ninth Assembly of the World Council of Churches*, 255–261. Geneva: WCC, 2006.

"Come and See: A Theological Invitation to the Pilgrimage of Justice and Peace. Faith and Order Paper 224." World Council of Churches. https://www.ncca.org.au/ all-documents/504-2019-wcc-faith-order-come-and-see/file (July 24, 2021).

"Constitution and Rules of the World Council of Churches." As Amended by the Central Committee of the WCC in Geneva, Switzerland, 2018. http://www.nccusa .org/pdfs/authorityofthechurch.pdf, 2010. http://www.oikoumene.org/en/resources /documents/assembly/2013-buas/adopted-documents-statements/unity-statement, 2013.

In One Body Through the Cross: The Princeton Proposal for Christian Unity. Edited by Carl E. Braaten and Robert W. Jenson. Grand Rapids: Eerdmans, 2003.

Marks of the Body of Christ. Edited by Carl Braaten and Robert W. Jenson. Grand Rapids: Eerdmans, 1999.

"The Church's Message to the World – The Gospel." In *Faith and Order: Proceedings of the World Conference, Lausanne 1927*, edited by H. N. Bate, 461–463. London: SCM, 1927.

"The Church: Towards a Common Vision." World Council of Churches. https://www .oikoumene.org/en/resources/publications/the-church-towards-a-common-vision (February 20, 2019).

"The Ecclesiological Significance of Councils of Churches." In *Growing Consensus: Church Dialogues in the United States, 1962–1991*, edited by Joseph A. Burgess and Jeffrey Gros, 602–613. New York: Paulist Press, 1995.

"The Holy Spirit and the Catholicity of the Church." In *The Uppsala Report 1968*, edited by Norman Goodall, 13–18. Geneva: WCC, 1968.

The New Delhi Report: The Third Assembly of the World Council of Churches, 1961. Edited by W. A. Visser't Hooft. London: SCM, 1962.

"The Unity of the Church as *koinonia*: Gift and Calling." In *Documentary History of Faith and Order 1968–1993*, edited by Gunther Gassmann, 3–5. Geneva: WCC, 1993.

"Theological and Historical Background of the WCC Basis." World Council of Churches. https://www.oikoumene.org/en/resources/documents/other/theological -and-historical-background-of-the-wcc-basis (February 20, 2019).

"Towards Unity in Tension." In *Documentary History of Faith and Order 1968– 1993*, edited by Gunther Gassmann, *Faith and Order Paper No. 159*, 144–147. Geneva: WCC, 1993.

Vatican Council. *Dogmatic Constitution on the Church: Lumen Gentium, Solemnly Promulgated by His Holiness, Pope Paul VI on November 21, 1964*, Boston: St. Paul Editions, 1965.

"What Unity Requires." In *Breaking Barriers, Nairobi 1975: Official Report, Fifth Assembly, World Council of Churches*, edited by David M. Paton, 59–64. Geneva: WCC, 1976.

World Council of Churches Central Committee. *Common Understanding and Vision of the WCC*. Geneva: WCC, 1997.

World Council of Churches Central Committee. *The Church, the Churches, and the World Council of Churches*. Geneva: WCC, 1950.

World Council of Churches, Commission on Faith and Order. "Baptism, Eucharist and Ministry." Faith and Order Paper No. 111. Geneva: WCC Publications, 1982.

World Council of Churches, Commission on Faith and Order. "The Church: Towards a Common Vision." Faith and Order Paper No. 214. Geneva: WCC Publications, 2013.

World Council of Churches Program on Ecumenical Theological Education. "Ecumenical Formation in Theological Education: Ten Key Convictions." *Ministerial Formation* 110 (April 2008): 82–88.

Index

About the Author

Cole Jodon (PhD, University of Aberdeen) teaches theology at Houston Graduate School of Theology. This is his first book.

Lightning Source UK Ltd.
Milton Keynes UK
UKHW041402060622
404001UK00004B/30